CROWOOD METALWORKING GUIDES

CASTING FOR THE HOME WORKSHOP

HENRY TINDELL AND DAVE COOPER

CROWOOD METALWORKING GUIDES

CASTING FOR THE HOME WORKSHOP

HENRY TINDELL AND DAVE COOPER

THE CROWOOD PRESS

First published in 2018 by
The Crowood Press Ltd
Ramsbury, Marlborough
Wiltshire SN8 2HR

www.crowood.com

© The Crowood Press 2018

All rights reserved. No part of this publication may be reproduced or transmitted in any form or by any means, electronic or mechanical, including photocopy, recording, or any information storage and retrieval system, without permission in writing from the publishers.

British Library Cataloguing-in-Publication Data
A catalogue record for this book is available from the British Library.

ISBN 978 1 78500 353 0

Dedication
To Richard, Laura and Henry;
Alistair and Lucy;
in memory of Susan;
and Jenny

Safety is of the utmost importance in every aspect of metalworking. The practical workshop procedures and the tools and equipment used in metalworking are potentially dangerous. Tools should be used in strict accordance with the manufacturer's recommended procedures and current health and safety regulations. The author and publisher cannot accept responsibility for any accident or injury caused by following the advice given in this book.

Typeset by Derek Doyle & Associates, Shaw Heath
Printed and bound in India by Parksons Graphics

Contents

	Acknowledgements	6
	Preface	7
	Introduction – The History of Casting	9
1	Fundamentals of the Casting Process	19
2	Setting up a Home Workshop Foundry	35
3	Methods of Casting	50
4	Design for Castings	75
5	Materials for Castings	94
6	Post-Casting Processes	123
7	Case Studies, Processes and Projects	139
	Appendix I Safety Aspects	161
	Appendix II Useful Data	163
	Appendix III Glossary	165
	Bibliography	168
	Suppliers	169
	Postscript	171
	Index	172

Acknowledgements

Firstly, thanks are due to all at The Crowood Press, including our editors without whom this book would never have begun and certainly never been completed. And Joanne Hulse for again turning a scrawled and scrambled script into an orderly typed submission. We acknowledge the many friends and colleagues not mentioned who have freely contributed their knowledge and thoughts on casting topics. Peter Whitehead of the Whitehead Foundry for his casting wisdom and freedom to explore and photograph his works; Chas King and colleagues at Nortest for their expertise and assistance with NDT over the years; Ross Nolan and colleagues at Exova for help and guidance in a modern Materials Test House; Stephen Foster of Engineering and Foundry Supplies, Colne, for valuable advice and help with casting supplies; Ben Hale of the Cast Metals Association for the cast iron micrographs, supplied from the Thomas Dudley Foundry, Dudley, W.Midlands; Les Hall, master patternmaker for recalling a fascinating life in industry and home workshop; The Whitechapel Bell Foundry for insights into a remarkable casting history; Matthew McGillicuddy of PI Castings, Altringham, for illustrations of their precision investment castings; Manchester University, Joule and John Rylands libraries for their extensive resources and help; Peter Gilmartin of Gilwoods Fabricators for for the encouragement (DC); and colleagues and friends at Hick Hargreaves and Edwards, Bolton (HAT).

Finally, we are indebted to Professor John Campbell for his invaluable advice, general comments, and first-hand knowledge of the Liberty Bell examination – as well as his fundamental theory of bifilms – proving, in the twenty-first century, as important for sound castings as the discovery, in the twentieth century, of dislocations was for plasticity in metals.

Despite this substantial support, the resulting contents, and possibly not uncontroversial opinions, remain those of the authors. In the continually developing technology of casting, it is merely to be hoped that this is satisfactory at the present, until superseded by the inevitable developments of the future – or to mis-quote the old aphorism, 'where there's life, there's casting. . . .'

Preface

'What have the Romans ever done for us. . . ?' was the plaintive cry from the famous Monty Python film. So amusing, as the Romans' contribution to a wild Britain were legion – no roads were built for 1,000 years after their departure in 400AD – perhaps we could adapt this rather adroit approach to posit, 'What have Castings ever done for us. . . ?'

For castings have become so familiar in our modern world as to have been rendered invisible. This is particularly unfortunate as the once omnipresent local ferrous (iron), or non-ferrous, foundry is rapidly becoming an endangered species in the developed West where, apparently, the virtual world has displaced the need for actually *manufacturing things*, other than the primary purpose of simply juggling binary digits off into the ether. . . .

But are metal castings really so ubiquitous? Perhaps we need to remind ourselves of their existence and a little of how our modern world is dependent upon, and has been fashioned by, 'Castings'. A few random examples:

- Tiny dental implants, from investment castings
- Exotic jewellery, in precious metals
- Replacement hip joints, in cobalt-chromium alloys
- High-value camera bodies, in magnesium alloys
- Lightweight bicycle frame parts, in aluminium alloys
- Car engine parts; crankshafts in ductile cast iron, carburettor bodies in zinc alloy, high pressure die castings
- Front-end jet engine turbine blades, single crystal casts of nickel base alloys
- Machine tools, from the watchmaker's bench-top lathe, to massive vertical boring machines, in grey cast iron – providing machines to make machines, to make machines, to make parts. . . .

The list is nigh on inexhaustibly long, indeed a more sensible approach could be to compile a list of areas of human activity *not* dependent upon castings.

Even from this brief list, it is apparent that castings are employed where it is vital to use a precisely chosen alloy, often viable only through the casting route. Also from this list is the hint of the many and varied processes that have been developed to produce castings, from the basic sand casting – described in some detail for the aspirant amateur foundry worker in the home workshop – to the near net shape techniques such as investment (or lost-wax) casting.

The introduction explores the historical perspective, for no other manufacturing process can compete with an ancestry of some 5,000 years – with the oldest surviving manufacturing business in the UK, the Whitechapel Bell Foundry, established in 1570AD. And yet we are only just, in the last few decades, coming to terms with a sound theoretical basis for understanding some fundamentals of the casting process, from bifilm theory, see Bibliography, *Campbell, (2011)*.

Chapter 1 'Fundamentals of the Casting Process' sets this within the well-established theoretical background of the complete process, from melting, pouring and casting; with a closer look at the liquid flows through the gating system, into the solidification and cooling of the final cast product. How and why defects are inherent in virtually all castings is found in Chapter 1, and their elimination pursued. Practical aspects of subsequent defect correction and testing is included in Chapter 6, 'Post-Casting Process'.

Chapter 3, 'Methods of Casting', Chapter 4, 'Design of Castings', and Chapter 5, 'Materials for Casting', provide a sense of how castings are manufactured. This is preceded by Chapter 2, 'Setting Up a Home Workshop Foundry', which considers its practicalities, limitations, and prospects – for this is an undertaking not to be underestimated.

This rather mechanistic outline should not obscure the truly dramatic

Photo 1 Whitechapel Bell Foundry, front entrance, Whitechapel Road, London E1.

Photo 2 Bell Foundry, goods inwards, Plumbers Row, London E1.

nature of the whole casting process. For it is great creative work, involving huge elemental forces as the original molten charge is raised to super-heated temperature – white hot – ready for pouring from the crucible. This liquid can have fluidity akin to that of water (for cast irons) and is tipped into the mould in-gate, sending a violent stream of onrushing fluid into the casting mould cavity. Within seconds the mould is filled, flowing up the risers as solidification erupts through the casting from mould wall inwards, as vast numbers of tiny tree-like, dendritic, crystals form and crash around in the microscopic trauma of alloy formation. The solidified metal's cooling phase can be hardly less dramatic as the temperature races down and different structures are wrought, until finally set at the near-ambient temperature of microstructural completion.

And this is just the metallurgical aspect of the business, albeit responsible for the strength and toughness of the casting – to the naked eye only the gross features of this process are apparent, as surface finish and, hopefully, lack of surface faults such as laps, tears, cavities, porosity, shrinkage and distortion.

When some grasp of these complexities of metal casting is attained, it should hardly be surprising that it is such a challenging business – but what could be more rewarding, notwithstanding the myriad obstacles, than the creation of a fine and everlasting casting?

HAT and DC
Cheadle Hulme
November 2016

Postscript: On 2 December 2016, the Whitechapel Bell Foundry announced – as reported by the Economist magazine in its 'Obituary' published on Christmas Eve 2016 – that it too would be joining the ranks of the world's great foundries in the sky.

Introduction – The History of Casting

Detail of the earliest cast objects is, at best, rather imprecise but evidence of the pre-historical world is growing steadily. What is certain, however, is that casting was preceded by the Wertime Pyrotechnology period, where around 10,000 years ago fire was being exploited by primitive humans for heat-treating stone, one of the earliest materials utilized by man. Expertise with handling fire was useful in the manipulations of stone such as by carving; then the development of plaster from burning of lime; then to the firing of clay for the development of pottery.

The earliest metal objects were produced from native copper, as found in copper ore deposits, by wrought methods such as hammering with stone tools. This was sufficient to produce simple cutting tools and decorative artefacts made by beating to profile, possibly (but as yet unproven) with the use of fire-annealing to alleviate the effects of work hardening. This activity is associated with the Neolithic period, when ceramic work (production of pottery) become widespread, pre-dating the origins of metal casting (see Table 1).

The Chalcolithic Period is the name given to the time when metals were developed in a more technological manner, essentially the start of the casting era, with its continuous thread to the present day. At 5000–3000BC, it immediately proceeds the Bronze Age (3000–1500BC). These are not precise periods of history but merely serve as a shorthand guide, with extensive overlap and mismatch across the world of metallurgical progress.

Although claims have been made for various early cast objects, such as the fine bronze anklets from lost-wax castings of 4500BC from Southeast Asia, it seems that the earliest sure evidence relates to the remarkable finds of the Nahal Mishmar Treasure, from a cave in the Jordanian Desert, discovered in 1961. More than 400 objects, including castings of copper and bronze made by the lost-wax process, can now be seen in the Metropolitan Museum of Art, New York. Fortuitously, these items were found wrapped in straw mat, hidden inside the cave, enabling Carbon-14 dating to show that they originate from 3500BC, or earlier. This region of the Levant was known to have a highly developed agriculture with the extensive use of tools by farmers in Israel and Jordan and an advanced civilization, producing fine terracotta work, sculptures and fine wall paintings. It has been suggested that this treasure was hurriedly hidden having been removed from a nearby shrine at Ein Gedi, near the Dead Sea in Israel.

The Nahal Mishmar findings support the theories that casting began in the cradle of civilization of the Middle East, around modern day Iraq, Iran and the Eastern Mediterranean, about 6,000 years ago. The first castings were produced from the melting of copper ore, followed by alloying of copper (Cu) with arsenic (As) and tin (Sn). Cu – 4 to 12% As items were identified at Nahal Mishmar and contemporary finds). Early workers surely found that Cu was not an easy material to cast, with sluggish fluidity, and made for tools too soft to hold a decent cutting edge. The discovery of alloying with As and Sn provided a greatly improved result, with improved castability, and a useful improvement in hardness permitting a cutting tool edge of practical use. This led to the onset of the Bronze Age, largely in recognition of the spreading of this technology across the known world.

BRONZE AGE

This enabled the use of fires of sufficient heat to melt these bronzes, greatly assisted by the alloying with As and Sn, which reduces the melting temperature. Original moulds were undoubtedly made from stone, with recesses carved into the stone faces into which the liquid metal was poured – skills in handling stone having been developed over the many millennia preceding the

◆	5000–3000 BC	Copper-based experimental work during Chalcolithic Period; Middle East.
◆	3500 BC	Early documented finds of castings; Nahal Mishmar treasures, Jordan, Middle East.
◆	3500–2500 BC	Lost-wax casting origins; Middle East.
◆	3000–1500 BC	Bronze Age, origins; Middle East.
◆	1500 BC	Iron Age (wrought iron); Middle East.
◆	645 BC	Sand moulding; China, Far East.
◆	600 BC	Cast iron first produced; China.
◆	225 BC	Colossus of Rhodes – giant bronze casting destroyed; Greece.
◆	1225 AD	Great Buddha of Kamakura cast, 120 tons; Japan.
◆	1400 AD	Great Bell of Beijing cast, 46 tons, (still sounds!); China.
◆	1500	Sand moulding origins in the West; France.
◆	1570	Whitechapel Bell Foundry established; London, England.
◆	1709	Coke used to fuel furnaces for cast iron; Coalbrookdale, England.
◆	1735	Great Bell of Kremlin, 193 tons(!), but cracked; Moscow, Russia.
◆	1752	Liberty Bell, Philadelphia, USA; cast in London; recast 2002, London.
◆	1779	Cast iron first structure, Ironbridge; Shropshire, England.
◆	1863	Metallography invented, Henry Sorby; Sheffield, England.
◆	1884	Aluminium produced by electrolytic refining.
◆	1895	Eros, first aluminium public statue; London.
◆	1913	Stainless steel invented; Germany and England.
◆	1924	18/8 stainless steel by W.H. Hatfield; Sheffield.
◆	1948	Ductile cast iron (SG iron) developed; USA.
◆	1965	Scanning electron microscope (SEM) invented; Cambridge, England.
◆	1970–present	Many new casting processes and theories developed; worldwide.

Table 1 A brief history of metal casting.

first casting of metals. Various stone 'patterns' have been found, some with a simple recess for use as open moulds, accepting the molten metal, to produce a free surface solidification method of casting. These stones could also be fashioned on several sides, providing a multi-tool approach, to make the most efficient use of stones such as steatite – convenient for carrying perhaps? Where a stone is used to form the upper half of a mould, as we would expect to produce a closed mould, these are known to archeologists as bivalves.

The early fires, providing rudimentary furnaces, used charcoal as fuel and indeed (in the West) this persisted until the industrial era before more efficient fuels of coal and coke were exploited. Similarly, with the use of forced draught, originally simply pumped by human power, blowing through pipes. This was still being observed in the Medieval period by the Conquistadors during their pillaging of Latin American gold and silver casting treasures.

Besides direct casting into stone moulds, it is now considered that the lost-wax process was also well developed in the Bronze Age. While there is clear evidence of early casting in the Middle East, it was thought that suppliers of tin, for instance, originated from Afghanistan and Cornwall, England. However, it now seems that stream deposits of these elements (Cu and Sn) were available in Mesopotamia (Iraq), Egypt and Anatolia (Turkey). Items such as the small silver-bronze statue of a stag, from the Hittite civilization of 2000 BC at Alaca Höyük (Ankara, Turkey), were clearly made by the lost-wax process, although direct evidence of moulds and equipment have generally eluded researchers. However, in 1972 at Gussage, Dorset, England, an extensive excavation uncovered invaluable evidence of an Iron Age foundry, from around 1000BC. This provided several thousand fragments of ceramic moulds from the lost-wax process, with many bronze products for horses and chariots, such as bridle bits, showing an advanced industry of lost-wax casting was well established in England at least 3,000 years ago.

The earliest bronzes were copper-arsenic alloys, containing Cu–4% As; but up to 12 per cent As was also used, throughout the Middle East and as far west as Great Britain. This alloy can often be recognized as arsenical copper by a silver coloured surface, resulting from the inverse segregation of the low melting point, As-rich, phase appearing on the cast surface. This can confuse these with silver or silver-plated work. The phenomenon is similar to that of tin sweat, as observed in the tin bronzes (Cu-Sn). The subsequent discovery of the tin bronze alloys may have originated from ores containing both elements, Cu and Sn, in the natural state.

It should be remembered that the following ages, such as Iron Age, added another layer of technology, and bronze has continued to the present day as a familiar material of choice for casting. This is not only for the many and varied statuary and decorative items, but also critical engineering products. Often chosen for the excellent corrosion resistance in marine applications, it is almost exclusively used for the wonderful bells still being produced by specialized foundries such as the Whitechapel Bell Foundry, able to trace a continuous casting history from 1420 to the present day (see Chapter 4). We now move to the geographical spread of the early casting practice.

FAR EAST

The origins of casting in China, India and Southeast Asia are thought to be around 2000BC, some 1,000 years after the Middle East. It was once assumed that knowledge had slowly diffused towards China, but a study of the dates when Chinese foundry sites began indicates a progress westwards rather than the expected eastwards development profile. It is perfectly possible that casting developed independently in China, where it was certainly the only significant method for producing metal artefacts before ~500BC.

As the detail work of early Chinese bronze artefacts was so extensive it was originally assumed lost-wax was the predominant technique. However, more recent finds at Anyang provided unused ceramic piece-moulds. This method could deploy a number of piece-moulds to cast separate parts of a large statue often in delicately thin hollow sections. These were eventually joined together either by direct casting-on of the adjacent piece, or by a sophisticated stitching method, somewhat analogous to that of the present day for the joining of cracked cast iron vehicle parts, such as a cylinder block considered a problematical fusion weld repair. This enabled some impressively gigantic religious effigies to be constructed, in the manner of later works such as the Great Buddha of Kamakura, Japan. Built in 1252, the Great Buddha comprised some 120 tons of bronze, the alloy being Cu – 9% Sn, 20% Pb; which still survives, despite its location in an earthquake zone.

The early alloys used in China tended to be leaded tin-bronzes (Cu – Pb, Sn), used for improving castability through their greater fluidity, enabling thin sections to be safely reproduced. While this could be considered a problem with leakage at moulding joints producing flash on the mould line it could be used to advantage, either requiring only a simple operation to remove the flash, or it could be incorporated into the design, for instance along folds in the subject's clothes. Interestingly, a reproduction bronze sword was recently cast by an Oxford academic, using a bifold mould to produce an item with jointline flash that could be readily removed with minimal post-cast work.

When an early bronze casting site, c. 2000BC in Thailand, was excavated it revealed evidence of the lost-wax process, from the unused ceramic bivalve mould found buried with the foundry man, having one half placed in each hand.

SOUTH AMERICA

While there appears to have been no casting activities in North America by the indigenous population before the eighteenth century colonization from Europe, and the subsequent explosive growth of casting to support the Industrial Age, the same is not true in Latin America.

12 • Introduction – The History of Casting

Copper was discovered, exploited and exhausted long before the European explorers set foot there in the Middle Ages. By that time their metalworking expertise had reached an impressively high level, and castings had been produced not only in the copper-base alloys (bronzes) but also in the precious metals of gold (Au) and Silver (Ag). Tumbaga being an alloy commonly used containing, in varying amounts, gold, silver and copper. Following Tumbaga casting, the item was 'pickled' in an acid that attacked the copper and silver, leaving a gold-rich layer on the surface – effectively a gold plating. Termed *mis en couleur* (depletion gilding), this produced a gold appearance that drove the European explorers to distraction, and the wholesale plunder of these priceless artefacts.

AFRICA

While the early casting history of Egypt can be more closely linked to the developments as noted above in the Middle East, present knowledge of West African casting begins from the Middle Ages onwards.

Perhaps it is the predominance of blacksmithing and small-scale forging that has obscured the origins of castings from the western and central part of the continent, but we begin with the most notable Benin Bronzes, made by the lost-wax process. These are indeed very fine examples of the intricate and highly controlled casting art. Several fabulous bronze statues, such as the head of Queen Iyoba from the Medieval period (sixteenth century), were made for the Benin Court in Nigeria. Discov-

Figure 1 The Grayer-Anderson Cat, currently residing in the British Museum. (Author's sketch)

ered in the Benin expedition of 1897, a particularly fine example can now be seen in the British Museum in London.

In Nigeria and Ghana, zinc was alloyed with copper, producing Cu-Zn (brass) and, once again, the lost-wax process was used. Ghana is known for its gold weights, in fact these are normally brass with sufficient zinc to produce a golden colouration. Also developed was a clever arrangement of crucible and mould contained within a unified structure, based on the lost-wax process. When charged with Cu and Zn, and moulding de-waxed, it could be heated to liquid and inverted to fill the mould, while isolated from the atmosphere. This forms the approach preferred in present times in the pursuit of the defect-free casting.

Zinc refineries recently discovered that operated in the seventeenth century at Zawar, India, are thought to have supplied the long-range trade routes to West Africa, as one source of raw material.

CAST IRON

Remarkably, for such an important material, cast iron was not produced in the western world until some 1,000 years after its introduction in China, around 600BC. The early Chinese cast

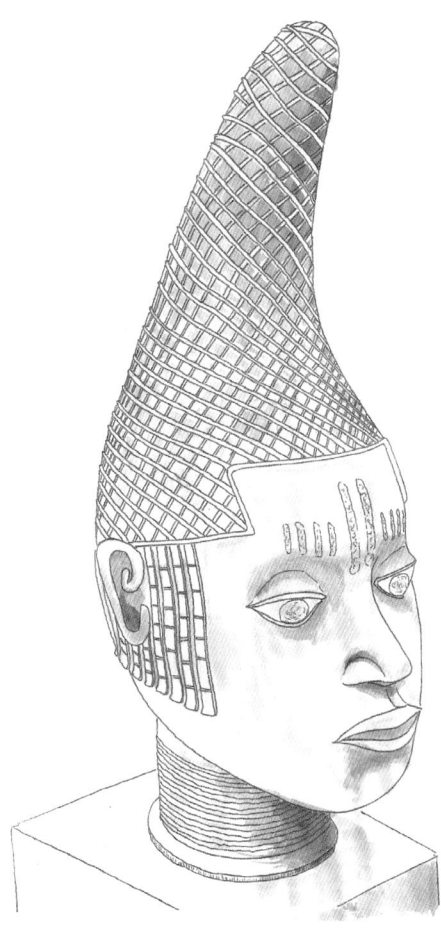

Figure 2 Bronze investment casting of Queen Iyoba, Benin tribe, Nigeria, fifteenth century, presently in the British Museum. (Author's sketch)

Figure 3 West African warrior casting, c 1800AD, now in the British Museum. (Author's sketch)

iron is known to be high in phosphorus (P) and sulphur (S), the latter arising from melting in coal-fired furnaces. This composition results in exceptional fluidity with a melting point near of that of bronze and, like the Far Eastern bronzes, it is noted for the thin sections and fine replication of castings – contemporary cast iron being used not only for common artefacts but also decorative and statuary works.

While cast iron may well have appeared in Europe in the Medieval period, it was generally regarded as a source for producing wrought iron, the precursor to our ubiquitous modern-day 'mild steel'. This was obtained by a long process of refining the cast iron to remove almost all the free carbon responsible for its lack of ductility and toughness. These properties were, even in early times, recognized as important in forged product, free from the sudden failure characteristic of brittle materials, aka cast iron.

Rather ironically, until the nineteenth century invention of the processing of iron ore in the Bessemer Converter, the route to manufacturing steel involved the aforementioned removal of carbon from cast iron to make the ultra-low and ductile wrought iron – only to add back small controlled amounts of carbon to make steel. Such was the means to produce the first steels in Europe – the Huntsman cast steels of 1740. Typically, cast irons contain around 2–4% C and steels 0.1–1% C; carbon being an extremely powerful element when combined with iron, influencing steel behaviour. This ranges from the lower strength,

Photo 3 Ironbridge, Coalbrookdale, Shropshire, UK.

highly ductile, mild steel (< 0.2% C), to the high strength and low ductility, heat treatable, high C (~1% C) steels.

It was not until Abraham Derby began producing cast iron in volume during the eighteenth century at Coalbrookdale in Shropshire that the use of cast iron in the western world took off. Testament to this pioneering work is the famous Iron Bridge, the western world's first major cast iron structure, built in 1779 to span the River Severn gorge, and still standing today. Darby was fortunate in this iron processing, having used coke as furnace fuel, the local iron ores contained sufficient manganese (Mn) to combine with the excess sulphur (S) from the coking coal. This produces benign MnS inclusions, thereby scavenging the S and allowing the great productivity gains of coke as a fuel, which soon replaced the use of charcoal as it was less efficient and of dwindling supply.

The excellent 'castability' of cast iron enables its use in a very wide range of applications, and it proved its worth with the rapidly growing need for heavy machinery to power the Industrial Revolution. The explosive growth of industry was well under way in Great Britain as the nineteenth century dawned and water power was steadily displaced by steam. However, the inherent lack of ductility of cast iron, making it unsuitable to accommodate tensile stresses for fear of sudden failure on overload, was recognized by the more knowledgeable Victorian engineers, deploying it only in compression loading for safety. It was not understood until the advent of modern physical metallurgy, in the late nineteenth century, that the problem with these cast irons lay in the manner in which the carbon was formed as microstructural long graphite flakes. These render the structure brittle, as will be explained in Chapter

Photo 4 Ironbridge, detail of cast iron bridge, built 1779.

5. Means were later developed to overcome this problem, for designs involving tensile loading, by converting the graphite into non-damaging microstructural 'rosettes' as 'Spheroidal Graphite', or Ductile Cast Irons – arriving in the late 1940s for some extremely demanding applications such as motor vehicle crankshafts.

Following Ironbridge – notably successful as it was designed to maximize the use of cast iron members in compression, thus avoiding significant tension loading – architects found many uses for cast iron as a structural material, including the United States Capitol Building dome, painted to resemble masonry. Unlike bronze, of course, cast iron usually requires a protective coating such as painting to avoid corrosion; or copper-plating, in the case of the great staircase casting of the Chicago Stock Exchange. The effect of corrosion in cast iron can be deliberately harnessed by allowing a light rusting, then applying a hydrogen reduction process to produce a surface oxide of Fe_3O_4, a durable, velvety finish suitable for attractive interior works.

PRODUCTS

The production of smaller items, from hand tools to domestic artefacts and decorative work, has been practised, as we have seen, since the earliest days of casting. Larger items present particular problems of scale, solved in the manufacture of massive statuary by making them as an assembly of parts, as described earlier. However, particular products, such as bells and cannons are required to be produced as a single item, and naturally even larger examples were sought for more ambitious designs.

BELLS

Large bells have, since antiquity to the present day, presented problems and opportunities for foundries. Even today, long established processes are in use in the developed world to satisfy the niche demand for high-class bells – still remarkably prominent in our consciousness – such as the sound of Big Ben ringing out from the Palace of Westminster, London (cast by Whitechapel Bell Foundry, see Chapter 4, 'In Memorium – The Whitechapel Bell Foundry').

The sheer size of these large bells is awe-inspiring, such as the Kremlin's Great Bell, cast in 1735 at almost 200 tons, although it is cracked and non-functioning. In contrast, the Great Bell of Beijing, at more than 46 tonnes, of a Cu – 15% S, 1% Pb, bronze, is said to still be capable of generating a deafening 120dB, audible at 12 miles (20km). Cast around 1440AD, in the Ming Dynasty, it contrasts in shape, material and composition with Western European bells, typically Cu – 25% Sn. The Liberty Bell of Philadelphia, USA, and its recently made replica (both from Whitechapel), is a Cu – 23% Sn alloy and at 5 tons relatively small compared to the above bells. However, after pouring at 1,100°C it still required a full week to cool to room temperature! Although bronze is by far the most popular material, white cast iron bells have been cast in China and Russia; and cast steel bells became a product of Sheffield, England, after Huntsman's work in the eighteenth century.

GUNS

The military use of large cannons meant that considerable effort was deployed in the development of castings to satisfy the desire for ever-grander weapons. Even the great Leonardo da Vinci had to abandon his grandiose project to produce a massive equestrian statue when its colossal consumption of bronze was redirected to the Florentines' armoury projects.

Early guns were made from multiple parts, and used a variety of materials, or were cast with large cores that proved difficult to extract before they damaged the casting during cooling. Vannoccio Biringuccio was a pre-eminent metallurgist of the early Renaissance Period. His seminal work *De la Pirotechnica*, published in Venice posthumously in 1540, provided extensive information on the casting of guns and bells. Considered to mark the beginning of materials science and its technical literature, it pre-dated the next important metallurgical study, of *De Re Metallica* by Georgius Agricola, printed in 1556. These works contained information on the copper-base alloys of bronze and brass, mining, refining and the explosives used in the operation of the guns. The latter work remained so influential in Central Europe that it was eventually translated into English in London in 1912 by a prominent mining engineer, one Herbert Hoover, later to become the president of the USA.

In 1715, the Swiss engineer Johan Maritz developed a sufficiently powerful boring machine to enable gun barrels to be cast solid, without a core. Machining the bore conveniently removed the central planes of weakness and segregation, significantly improving the end result. Further work by the likes of Krupp in Germany and Armstrong in England continued the development of gun barrel machining concurrent with an improvement in casting technology that eventually discarded the bronzes in favour of the higher strength steels of the early twentieth century. Of historical interest are the great national armouries, such as the Royal Brass Foundry, part of the Woolwich Arsenal of south London, which was closed in the 1990s, but the detailed records of gun manufacture from the previous two centuries are still available in its archive.

SCULPTURES

Statues have been produced since the earliest times by casting, preceded by plaster and other non-cast materials, although many of the large cast metal statues have been destroyed, often through the need to reuse valuable raw material. Surviving examples are now more commonly found buried sub-sea or excavated from burial sites, including Egyptian tombs. Even early statuary was often constructed not by castings but used copper sheet, formed and supported by an internal framework. Ancient Egyptian statues, for instance, can be difficult to categorize as wrought or cast, due to the effects of centuries of weathering. Some Greek cast bronzes, such as the Charioteer of Delphi, have survived and can be found in museums

Photo 5 Bronze statue – Nelson Mandela, College Green, Westminster, London.

Photo 6 Bronze statue – Winston Churchill, Westminster.

around the world often, it seems, on the opposite side of the world to their place of origin.

While bronze has been, and continues to be, the most popular material for cast statues, lead and silver have also been used extensively, albeit for smaller work. It is unlikely that gold has been used extensively, for obvious reasons. Although many examples appear to be gold, it is usually as a result of surface treatment, of which there are many varieties. Studies of the famous Roman bronze horses in Venice demonstrated that a bronze with a lower tin content was preferred for successful gilding by amalgam. A coppery colour of the, low Sn, base metal bronze is therefore an indication that a gilding process has been undertaken.

There have been some enormous statues produced since ancient times, perhaps most notably the Colossus of Rhodes that was more than 30m (100ft) tall, destroyed by earthquake in 224BC, which lay in pieces until being sold for scrap in the seventh century AD!

Although famous landmarks, such as the Statue of Liberty in New York, has the appearance of a copper casting, it is actually an enormous and complex structure clothed in wrought copper sheet. By contrast, the much smaller, but well-loved statue of Eros, residing amidst the swirling traffic in London's Piccadilly Circus, was the world's first aluminium public statue, commissioned in 1893. Its most recent significant repair, in 1986, produced valuable insights into the method and materials of construction, as some over-exuberant swinging on its flying leg had resulted in fracture. The base material is

18 • Introduction – The History of Casting

Photo 7 Aluminium statue – Eros, Piccadilly Circus, London.

pure aluminium, or as near as this was possible in the 1890s. Earlier repair work had infilled the hollow body and limbs with an Al-12% Si alloy, in an effort to improve a not particularly strong structure. However, it was found that this later additional core had barely joined to the original material, thereby adding little to the mechanical strength. Numerous problems were associated with the TIG/GTAW (*see* Chapter 6) repair, corroded internal supports and solidification cracking of the weld, as is familiar in full-scale casting. Careful rebuilding and NDT (*see* Chapter 6 'Non-Destructive Testing') gradually restored the piece, and provided the mechanical strength necessary to withstand again the rigors of environmental pollution and unprotected display in central London.

1 Fundamentals of the Casting Process

LATENT HEAT

The 'states of matter' are controlled by temperature and pressure, thus at room temperature (RT) and one atmosphere pressure this is known as STP – standard temperature and pressure. Almost all common metals are solids. Only a couple of the metals are liquid at RT, but this includes mercury (Hg), widely deployed in sealed glass tubes as thermometers.

Adding sufficient heat to a solid body causes it to change state from solid to liquid, but requires extra heat energy at the boiling point, known as **latent heat** to effect this change, without temperature rise, as in Figure 4. For common solid materials, such as metals and ice, this is a **reversible** process as these changes of state can proceed either way, by adding or removing heat energy.

A similar process is involved to effect change from liquid to gas, but the latent heats are considerable larger. Similarly, from gas to plasma, except that this change requires extremely large quantities of heat, or electrical excitation, to reach the plasma through an ionization process, as described later.

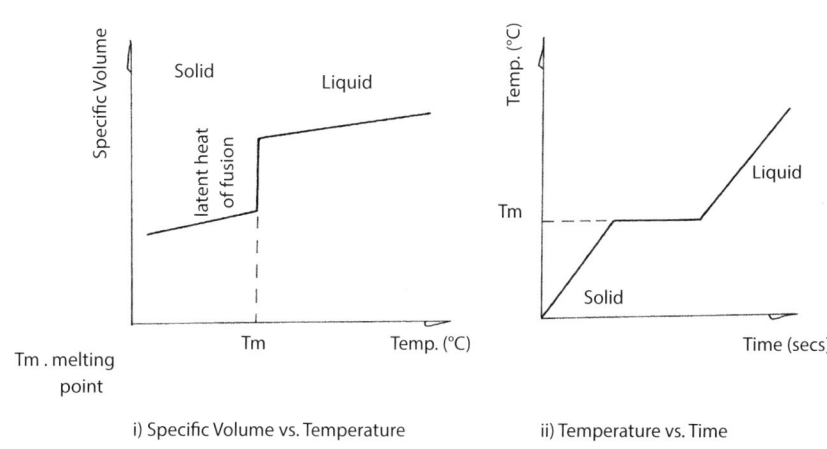

i) Specific Volume vs. Temperature   ii) Temperature vs. Time

Figure 4 Metal states: solid to liquid.

STATES OF MATTER

The four fundamental states of matter are familiar in everyday life, although not necessarily always recognized as such.

Solids

Figure 5 shows these states as solid, liquid, gas and plasma. In fact, these all play their part, directly or indirectly, in the business of casting. Put simply, the solid state is the casting's end product, being formed fundamentally as a structure comprising (normally) an extremely large number of minute grains formed from regular, crystallographic, arrays of the individual building blocks of molecules, as in Figure 6. These grains of highly ordered crystallographic structures possess what is known as long range order, in that each grain is (almost) perfectly composed in a regular array. The imperfections can be ignored at present, but are briefly discussed later to explain why the theoretical strength of most metals is not achieved. Nevertheless, it is self-evident that metals can be extremely strong, thereby providing the practical materials utilized in the products of the

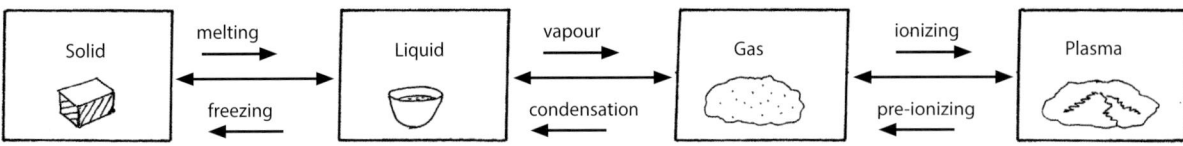

Figure 5 The basic states of matter and phase transformations.

modern world, so familiar that we take them for granted. Importantly, the difference in strength and properties can, within each alloy system, be very considerably changed during the casting process.

For non-engineering castings, such as statues or many household artefacts, the mechanical properties of the casting are usually not of particular concern, and success is measured by producing a cosmetically acceptable solid structure, if sufficiently free from surface defects. However, for items that are required to withstand the rigours of engineering applications, such as those found throughout our motor vehicles, the process of casting requires considerable knowledge and understanding to provide the necessary mechanical properties. And these properties are, firstly, controlled by the casting process as the molten metal flows from furnace to mould and eventually solidifies into the final shape. This is where an understanding of the fundamentals, from **fluid flow** to **nucleation** in the **solidification** process, leading to a suitable **microstructure**, are appropriate. This sequence also determines the **casting defects**, entrapped or escaping from the casting, which will also determine its suitability. These aspects are reviewed later and form the difference between these modern-day castings and their predecessors in the several millennia of casting manufacture until the dawn of the 'scientific era'. For our purposes, this was around the late nineteenth century, as the physical sciences steadily eroded the subject's status as a 'black art', a consequence of a lack of understanding that included the behaviour of the four states of matter. This enabled castings to play their part in the enormous technological advances of the twentieth century. It becomes clear that the apparently simple process of casting benefits from this fundamental understanding of **liquids** and **solidification** to achieve the full potential of strong (metallic) materials. This is explored further in the next section on the **control of structure**.

Liquids

In contrast to solids, where in metals there exists a long-range crystallographic structure providing a settled overall shape, in a liquid this structure is no longer regularly defined. Figure 6 shows a molecular arrangement of loosely held atoms free to swim around and adopt the shape of a vessel, or disperse across a surface in the absence of containment. Thus, the familiar filling of a jug with water, that could have been produced by melting the solid (e.g. blocks of ice) with sufficient heat to reach the melting point and then overcome the latent heat of fusion.

The characteristics of liquids, such as water, are relevant to the foundry worker as some molten metals have a similar **fluidity** to water, as seen later.

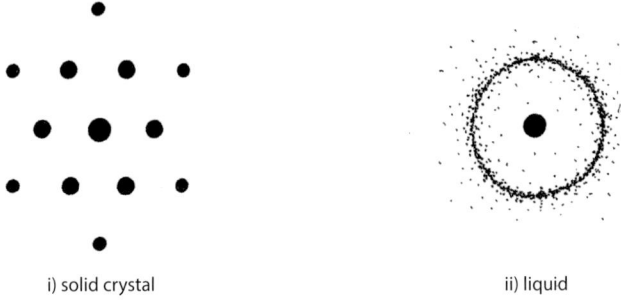

Figure 6 X-ray diffraction patterns – crystal and liquid.

Liquid	Density (lb/in³)	Kinematic Viscosity (in²/sec)
Water	36.1	1.6
Aluminium	86.6	2.0
Cast Iron	220.0	1.6
Steel	254.0	1.4
Magnesium	57.8	1.3
Copper	288.0	0.6

Table 2 Kinmatic velocities for molten metals.

the effects of creep (Photos 8 and 9). In metals, such as lead piping at ambient temperatures, it can take many years; or observed as the flow of ice in the slow movement of glaciers as they progress at the stately rate of metres per year down the high mountain ranges.

Photo 8 Matterhorn, Switzerland; showing fracture, crevasses and slow movement of glaciers down the mountain.

In fact, cast iron has a **viscosity** index identical to that of water, Table 2, enabling the use of transparent models of **moulds** and **gating systems**, to observe water flow in the analysis of casting processes.

Water, for example, exhibits a distinctively different profile to mercury.

Liquids have a ready facility to flow, an important feature shared with gases, used in pouring or otherwise transferring molten metal into

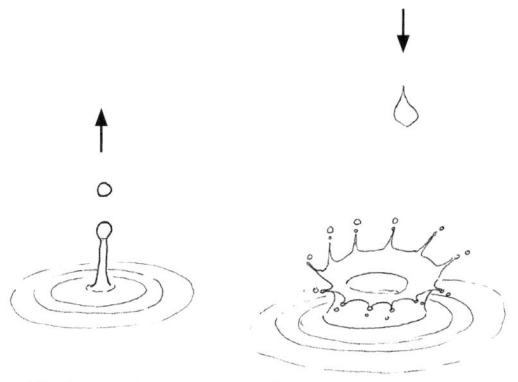

a) Surface tension – water drop impact

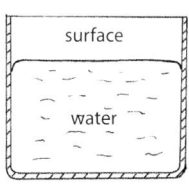

b) Surface tension in a container

Figure 7 Surface tension: (a) the impact of a water drop, and (b) in a container.

Photo 9 High altitude glacial movement, Tête Blanche, Swiss Alps.

Liquids can be regarded as incompressible fluids, comprising mobile atoms held together by intermolecular bonds that allow filling of a vessel – but retains, under gravity, a distinct free surface with an associated surface energy. **Surface tension** (see Figure 7) is a characteristic of the liquid, as seen from the meniscus, surface profile, made with the wall of the container.

the casting mould. The manner of this flow is understood in the study of fluid dynamics. Whilst this is a deep field of knowledge, a general grasp of its basic features enables the foundry worker to produce gating systems suitable for advanced projects. Note that whilst flow is a readily observable feature of liquids (and gases), it can also occur in solids under sufficient pressure, as seen from

Density is another important measure, as weight per unit volume (kg/m3) of liquids. Liquid density is actually nearer to solids than gases in this respect; one of the factors determining flow characteristics quantified through the Reynolds number (Re); for Re = $\rho v d/\mu$ (unit less) – where ρ is density (kg/m3), v is mean flow viscosity (m/s), d is pipe diameter (m) and μ is dynamic viscosity (N S.m2). Experiments have shown that Reynolds numbers of $\leq$

22 • Fundamentals of the Casting Process

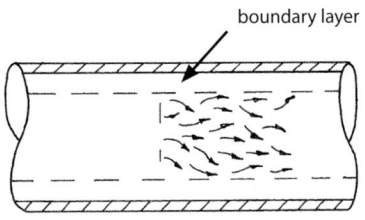

R$_e$ <20,000 – stable boundary layer

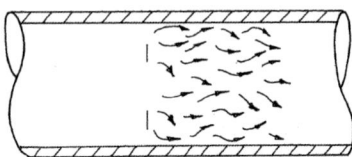

R$_e$ >20,000 – absense of boundary layer

Figure 8 Turbulent flow in pipes.

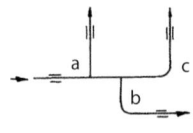

flow loss coefficients   a = 2.0
b = 0.5
c = 1.0

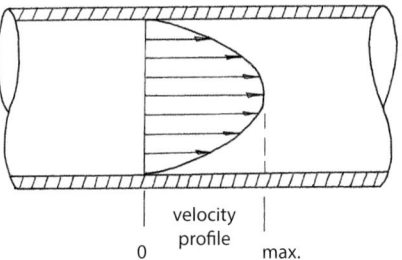

Figure 10 Laminar flow in pipe velocity gradient.

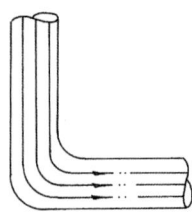

i) Laminar flow smooth curve

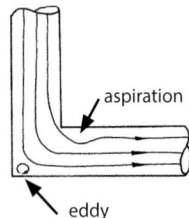

ii) Air aspiration and eddy currents

Figure 9 The effect of increased flow rate on a liquid.

2000 produces laminar flow of water in pipes, ≤ 20000 turbulent flow with boundary layer intact and ≥ 20,000 turbulent flow with disrupted boundary layer (*see* Figure 8).

Laminar conditions, as Figure 9, are familiar when observing water flowing from a tap, initially as a low rate proceeding in an orderly, smooth flow. As the flow rate increases this pattern changes to irregular, essentially chaotic, turbulent conditions. The Reynolds number also details the onset of boundary layer failure, as noted above. The flow along a passage, normally either a pipe or similar for modelling purposes, has a velocity profile (*see* Figure 10) that is important in casting as the sides of the mould provide a resistance to flow, with the fluid velocity increasing to maximum at the centre. The curves in the runner system and mould also strongly affect flow into the mould, and are dealt with in detail in gating and mould design (*see* Chapter 4, 'Design for Castings').

The flow characteristics of each metal alloy for casting is an important factor determining successful filling of the mould, and a practical test, shown in Figure 11, provides a measure of how the liquid metal will, in practice, flow down a standardized spiral tube.

While cast iron has a fluidity equal to water, and largely for this reason has been regarded as 'God's gift to the foundry man' (*Campbell, 2011*), the molten casting alloys often encountered, range from this ideal to far less accommodating slurries. Clearly, this has an important impact on how gating systems and mouldings are designed. Similarly, it would be preferred to have laminar flow and very low Reynolds numbers, but this can mean that the flow approaches stagnant, slow rate conditions. These are just one of the foundry worker's constant concerns – producing misruns.

Furthermore, greater fluidity, achieved by increasing the temperature at pouring, is not generally metallurgically satisfactory, impacting on the microstructure formed from solidification (see this chapter, 'Control

Fundamentals of the Casting Process • 23

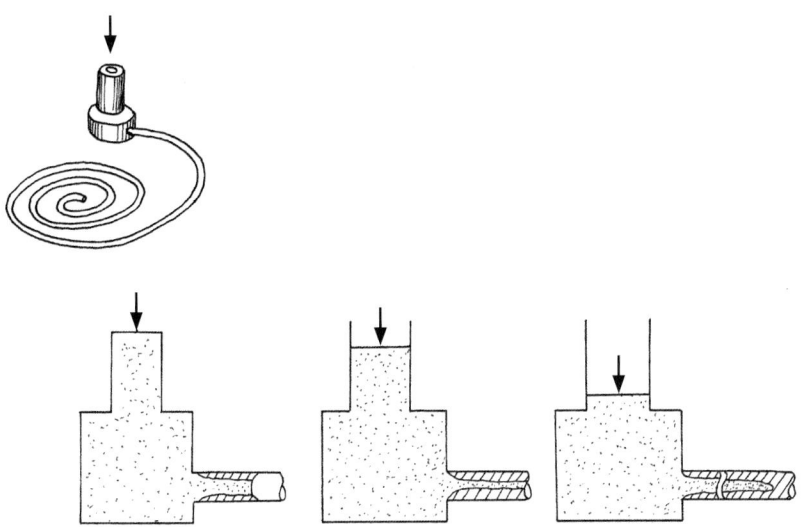

Figure 11 Fluidity test for casting metal.

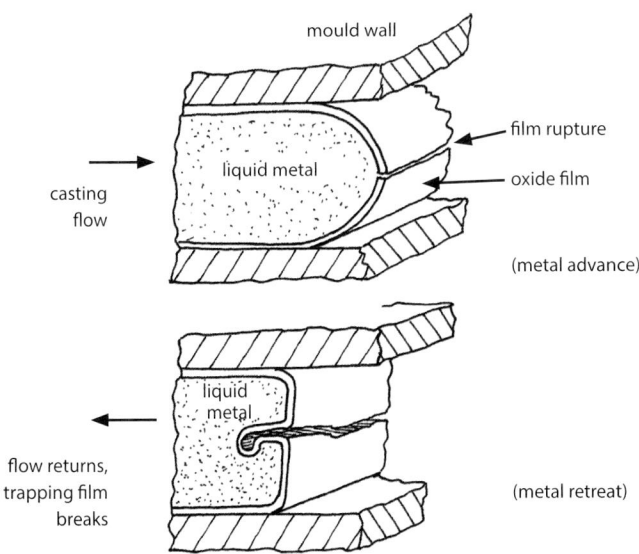

Figure 12 Bifilm theory – rupture and folding leading to trapped oxide film defect site. (Based on Campbell, 2011)

Simply put, this involves the entrapment of the extremely thin surface films, ever present on the casting fluid. This is familiar in conventional processes open to the atmosphere, bifilms finding their way into the bulk of the melt. They can form around liquid laps during turbulent flows, or around inclusions/foreign matter, as Figure 12. Once trapped in the fluid flow, then into the mould, these minute films can provide the source of familiar defects, such as the microporosity, that has previously been attributed to other mechanisms.

These bifilm defects are now considered responsible for many of the minute internal flaws understood to occur even in apparently high-integrity ingots that subsequently are formed into wrought product, such as steel plates or forgings. The fact that these flaws are often below the threshold for detection by commercial NDT methods has led to the common assumption that such small defects do not exist (see Chapter 6). Methods to overcome such problems have been developed in recent years, such as the Cosworth Process (see Chapter 3), where the casting fluid is pumped from below the free surface up into the gating system and mould, with special precautions, to promote laminar flow and produce a significantly improved final casting microstructure, see Figure 13.

Gases

Whilst the relevance of gases may not be immediately apparent to the study of castings, in particular they can be seen in defects such as **porosity**. This is due to the ability of liquid metals to

of Structure'). The process of transferring the liquid metal into the mould has long been regarded as important, but it is only within the past couple of decades that the fundamental source of significant defects, of vital importance in critical engineering castings, has been established in the theory of bifilms as propounded by leading casting experts (Campbell, 2011).

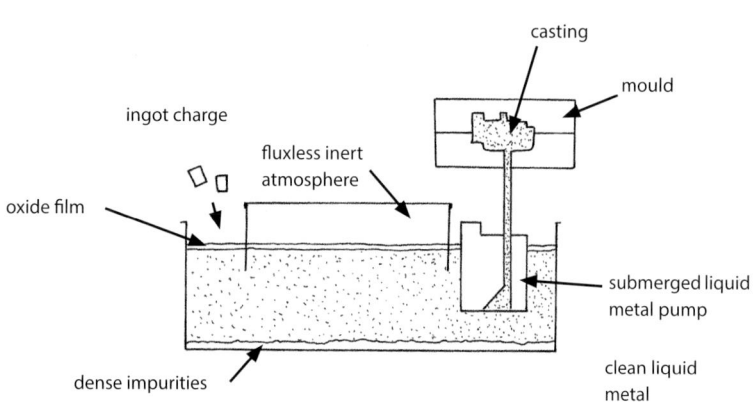

Figure 13 The Cosworth process casting unit (schematic).

dissolve significant amounts of gas, such as hydrogen (H_2) in aluminium, and retain it after solidification in the casting, as Figure 14.

As the state of matter bounded by liquid and plasma, gas is fundamentally different from the lower state of liquid because of its vastly increased interatomic particle spacing, resulting in its characteristic floating around to fill any available space. This particle spacing, in the case of common colourless gases, such as air (a compound including oxygen and nitrogen), makes it invisible to the human eye and, whilst ever present, so familiar as to be ignored. But, like liquids discussed earlier, gases have important roles to play in flow, as described by fluid dynamics. They are also, unlike fluids, compressible.

Gases are omnipresent in our world, including air, clouds, steam, smoke – and the understanding of their behaviour is essential to concepts from flight to heat engines. However, it is only with the advent of modern computing power that the complex mathematical models developed from the eighteenth and nineteenth centuries, particularly the Navier Stokes Equations, can be solved to predict gas behaviour from the trivial to critical, from computer gaming to weather prediction. A fascinating story in its own right, these theories are still developing, even forming one of the seven 'great unsolved proofs' eligible for the $1million prize offered by the Clay Institute, as scrutinized by the likes of Sir Andrew Wiles, famous for proving Fermat's Last Theorem some 358 years after it was originally posed.

Returning to basics, we have elemental gases, categorized as homonuclear molecules at STP, comprising hydrogen (H_2), nitrogen (N_2), oxygen (O_2), fluorine (F_2) and chlorine (Cl_2), the latter two classed as halogens. Included in this group are the monotonic noble gases of helium (He), neon (Ne), argon (Ar), krypton (Kr), xenon (Xe) and radon (Rn); some of which are familiar in casting work, especially repair, by welding, *see* Chapter 6.

The behaviour of gases was established scientifically by the well-known work that led to the familiar laws such as Boyle's and Charles', relating pressure, temperature and volume. It gradually became established that the wide particle separation of gases, far greater than liquids and solids, is controlled by the considerably weaker intermolecular attraction of the Van der Waals Forces, rather than the ionic or covalent bands of the lower states of matter. Observation of visible gases, such as drifting smoke, provides an indication of flow of gases such as air, useful in illustrating the flow of air around the body as in vehicle shape testing in a wind tunnel.

Despite apparently not being of primary concern to the foundry worker, the fact that a gaseous environment is the norm (and why vacuum processing is a desirable, if usually unobtainable, aim), has to be always considered. Particular effects are the surface films forming on the molten metal, with the

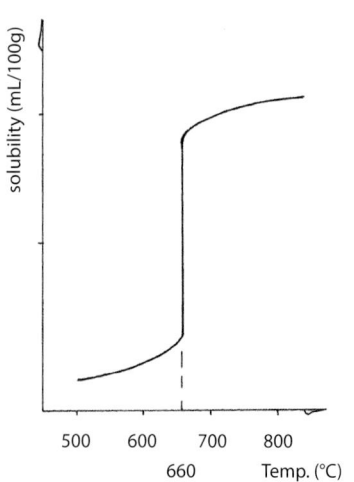

Figure 14 The solubility of H_2 in aluminium.

attendant risk of entrapment in the bulk, such as through the bifilms discussed earlier. Even at the final stage of a casting's progress, where repair by welding is required – a familiar occurrence in practical foundry work using conventional processes, such as sand casting – inert gas, such as Ar, is used to protect the weld and locally heated region (heat affected zone – HAZ) from the unwanted contamination by the various elements present in the surrounding atmosphere (*see* Chapter 6).

Plasma

This is the last of the four 'ordinary' fundamental states of matter of concern in casting, albeit that plasma is principally involved in an important aspect of post-casting processing (*see* Chapter 6). Welding is required post-casting either for local repair of defects, or as means to join the parts of a multi-piece casting, a practice often required in large structures and statues too large or complex to produce as a single piece. Often produced as thin-wall pieces, typically by investment casting, as welding presents by far the most appropriate method of joining. Plasma is formed in the intense arc or arc welding by GTAW (gas tungsten arc welding), SMAW (shielded metal arc welding) or GMAW (gas metal arc welding), and other fundamentally similar manual techniques.

The plasma state is reached through the input of very large amounts of heat energy, or the introduction of a strong electromagnetic field, to change from the gaseous state. Use of, for instance, a microwave generator changes the electron numbers of particles, forming negative or positive-charged **ions**, thereby disassociating the molecular bonding. This electrical charge facility means the plasma is conductive and can be manipulated by electromagnetic fields, unlike the gas from which it came. Thus, plasma can be exploited in neon signs and plasma TVs.

As it happens, plasma is by far the most abundant form of matter in the known universe; although it has been conjectured, but not universally agreed, that the elusive and enigmatic dark matter and dark energy may form all but a few per cent of the matter in the intergalactic universe. What is certain is that the sun and stars are essentially plasma. On earth, plasma is seen in dramatic electrical discharges from small sparks to great lightning flashes, to the familiar re-entry effects on space vehicles or debris; and back to the smaller scale of the welding arc.

In welding, the intense electric arc ionizes the local gas and either produces a stable plasma between a non-consumable electrode and the workpiece, as in GTAW; or the electrode (and shielding flux) is transferred across the plasma to the workpiece in SMAW, as a highly efficient and effective manner of depositing liquid metal into a pool on the workpiece. In essence this can be considered as a miniature arc furnace and the transfer of liquid metal a fundamental form of casting, without a mould. This is not so dissimilar to the methods used early in the Industrial Revolution where liquid cast iron was simply decanted into open channels in the foundry floor, to form simple sections such as beams and plates.

While our understanding of the physics of plasmas has largely been achieved though the study of nuclear fusion and power, it was only in 1879 that Sir William Crookes first identified plasma as 'radiant matter', followed by Sir J.J. Thompson, who first discovered the electron in the early Edwardian period; and Irving Langmuir's observations in 1928 of the Crookes tube, coining the term 'plasma', from the Greek meaning 'adopting the form of [a container]'.

CONTROL OF STRUCTURE

Solidification

We can now examine the actual casting process where the liquid metal is transferred via the gating system to the mould, where the solidification process begins – where indeed the die is cast. Between start and finish, liquid to solid, there are three basic shrinkage phases. This contraction is denoted as a positive change, but in certain cases can be negative (an expansion). These are – liquid

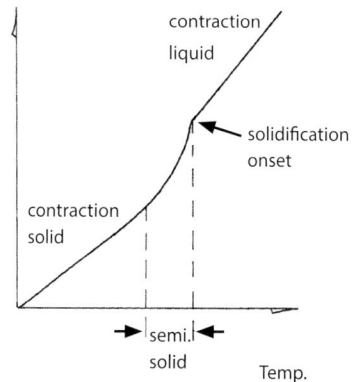

Figure 15 Volume change versus temperature.

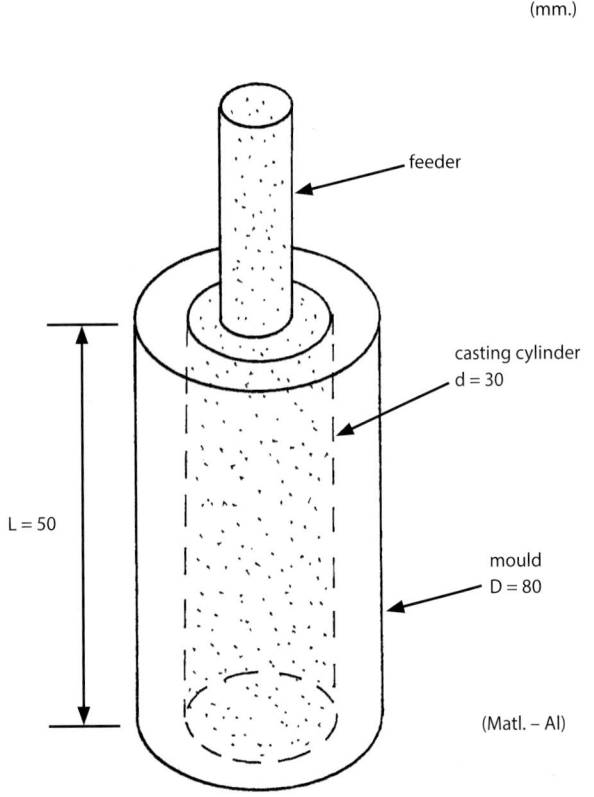

Feeder Size Example:

For Al shrinkage = 6%:-
Cast cylinder, cut off from feeder, would shrink 6% of cylinder volume, (V_c), presenting a cavity volume, (V_s).

So, $V_c = \dfrac{\pi d^2 \times L}{4}$

$= \dfrac{\pi \times (30)^2 \times 50}{4}$ mm²

$V_s = V_c \times 6\%$
$= \dfrac{\pi \times (30)^2 \times 50 \times 6}{4 \times 100}$ mm²

∴ $V_s = 2{,}121$ mm³

A cavity of over 2,000 mm³ would form due to shrinkage if the feeder was removed before solidification, or the feeder was of insufficient size to supply the cooling casting from liquid state.

Figure 16 Solidification shrinkage feeder size.

shrinkage; solidification shrinkage and pattern-maker's shrinkage.

As an illustration of the general shrinkage process, Figure 15 shows this volume change versus temperature, as the molten metal finally becomes a casting.

Liquid Shrinkage

From the properties of liquids discussed earlier, it is clear that as it cools the liquid will occupy a smaller volume. This is seen in the example of Figure 16, so it is not a difficult matter to calculate the size of the 'feeder' sufficient to provide liquid metal that will feed the cooling material, thereby backfilling the voids that would otherwise ensue. The gating design needs to provide not only an efficient feed to the mould cavity, but also sufficient fluid state to compensate for the shrinkage of the cooling liquid and thus avoid cavities. Therefore, this form of casting defect is readily avoidable with proper gating system design, as based on experience or calculation.

Solidification Shrinkage

As solidification begins immediately after mould filling, it proceeds in a manner determined by several factors, including: the rate of cooling; nucleation behaviour; and the temperature gradient as the alloy passes through the 'mushy' state to final solidification. At this stage, most metals undergo a volume contraction shrinkage, as Table 3. However, it should be noticed that grey cast iron actually increases in volume, due to the growth of its characteristics free-graphite flakes.

This stage is important in the avoidance of internal defects, voids. For instance, pure metals and eutectics with a short freezing range are known for forming voids in the last material to solidify, see Figure 17. The principle of directional solidification is employed

Table 3 Solidification shrinkages.

Aluminium	6%
Copper	5%
Magnesium	4%
Zinc	5%
Carbon steel (low C)	3%
Carbon steel (high C)	4%
Cast Iron (grey)	-2%*
Cast Iron (white)	4–5.5%
*expansion	

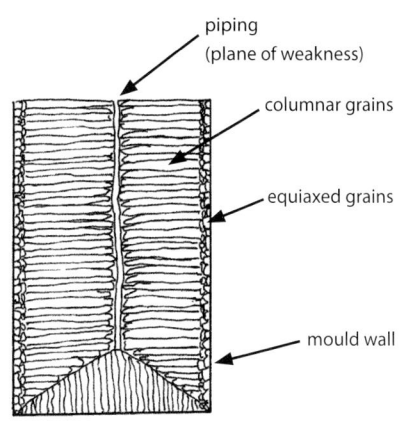

Figure 18 Typical casting ingot structure.

Table 4 Linear shrinkage. allowances (pattern-maker's allowance)

Aluminium	1.0–1.2%
Brass	1.5%
Magnesium	1.0–1.2%
Steel	1.5–2.0%
Cast Iron	0–1.0%

in gating design, to avoid piping, a line of weakness normally formed at the centre of the casting. Liquid is fed from the gating system to transfer the void safety beyond of the finished cast, see Figure 18.

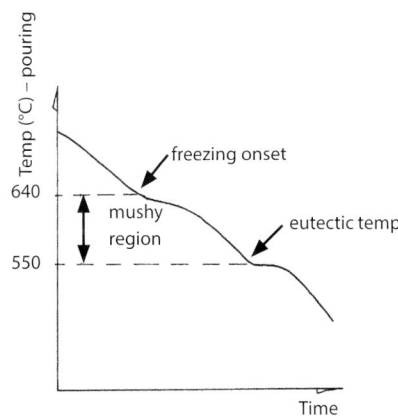

Figure 17 Cooling curve.

Alloys with large freezing ranges are prone to difficulty in the control of micro-shrinkage as the material, still in a mushy state, is pushed ahead of, and trapped between, the solidification fronts that move from the initial solidification at the mould walls into the bulk of the casting. This presents a difficult feeding problem as the last liquid to solidify is cut off from a supply of liquid metal. Late solidification shrinkage can lead to dispersed porosity and consequently inferior mechanical properties, such as in toughness and fatigue resistance.

Pattern-Maker's Shrinkage

This final volume change is that due to cooling from the point of complete solidification, down to room temperature. Therefore, it is governed by the thermal coefficient of expansion, a material constant tabulated in materials data reference works, see Bibliography. This is accommodated by making the pattern (and thus mould) to dimensions that compensate for this change, as seen in the examples of Table 4. As an aid to producing patterns for a particular metal, pattern-maker's rules are produced as scaled rulers that convert pattern dimensions to casting dimensions appropriate for that material. The casting of various alloys can thereby be produced accurately through moulds of slightly different dimensions. While on small jobs this is not usually critical, for large items it is often highly significant, each pattern being only suitable for the particular alloy system.

Cooling Curves

As shown in Figure 19, these curves illustrate the behaviour of the liquid-to-solid transition, which impacts on the solidification process as described above. The initial temperature is the pouring temperature. Increasing pouring temperature improves fluidity but, as noted earlier, there are constraints due to individual solidification and flow characteristics. Consequently, some experience is required to obtain the optimum pouring temperature.

As the liquid cools, the curve dips as undercooling ensues (see Figure 20), prior to the flat region, where the latent heat of transformation is extracted at the melting point prior to solidification, and subsequently cooling, known as the thermal arrest point. This undercooling is connected to the next stages, nucleation and growth, as detailed shortly.

Usually, we are concerned with mixtures (alloys) of more than one element in the melt, and the cooling curves reflect this stage of cooling as the

28 • Fundamentals of the Casting Process

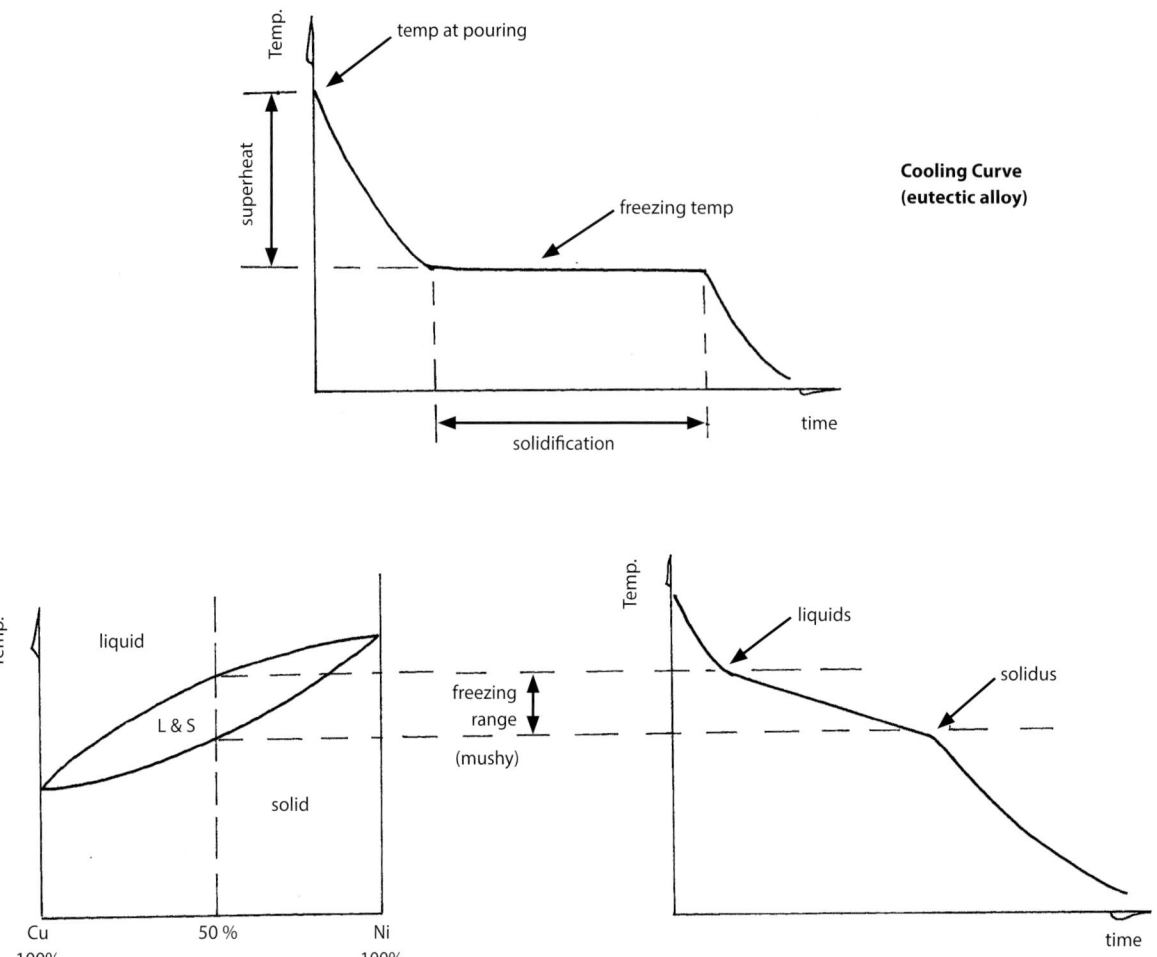

Figure 19 Liquid to solid transition.

Metal	Pouring temperature (deg. C)
Sn alloys	320–400
Zn alloys	350–450
Al alloys	620–730
Cu alloys	900–1200
Cast Iron	1350–1500
Ni alloys	1425–1550
Steels (high alloy)	1485–1600
Steels (low alloy)	1570–1700
Ti alloys	1700–1820

Table 5 Typical pouring temperatures for casting.

'freezing range' (mushy state). Where encountered, it complicates the pattern of solidification, as seen in Figure 19.

The range of solidification is particularly important in the design of feeders and risers, as noted previously, and this can be calculated by the well-known Chvorinov's Rule, stated as:

$$t_S = \frac{B\,(V)^2}{(A)^2}$$

where:

t_S = time to solidification

V = casting volume

A = surface area of heat extraction

B = mould constant – derived from testing

This is utilized in the section on design of gating systems, patterns and moulds (see Chapter 4).

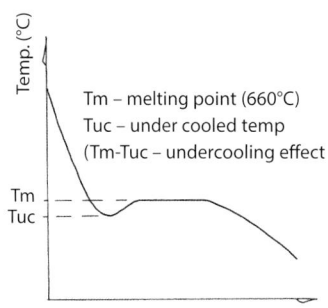

Figure 20 Cooling curve for aluminium.

NUCLEATION AND GROWTH

We now arrive at the crucial point in the casting process, where solidification begins and a metallurgical structure develops. Although it may be possible, in certain alloys, to modify this 'as cast' structure by subsequent heat treatment, it is almost universally the case that the final cast product is structure sensitive in that this original microstructure, as initially laid down during solidification, controls the mechanical properties of the final product.

There are two fundamental aspects to be considered, of basic metallurgical structure; and of internal defects such as inclusions, flaws and porosity. In order to understand the first category, we return to the progress of the liquid shown in the coding curve as it approaches the freezing point, leading to nucleation.

Nucleation from the Melt

Once again, we do not have to look far in our everyday experience to see nucleation in action. The formation of ice on a window pane; or creation of raindrops; the latter often associated with a rising temperature, raising the super-saturated air to form clouds. As the clouds rise, their reducing temperature encourages the excess vapour to nucleate heterogeneously, preferentially, on cloud condensation nuclei – as raindrops.

In castings, the moment of nucleation from the liquid is of considerable importance as it influences the subsequent pattern of growth, for the aim is always, apart from special cases such as single-crystal growth, to provide a final structure with as fine, small-grained, a structure as possible. Fine grain structure is recognized as a major factor in achieving desirable mechanical properties.

Figure 21 shows the well-known relationship between the competing thermodynamic energies associated with the cooling liquid, and indicates

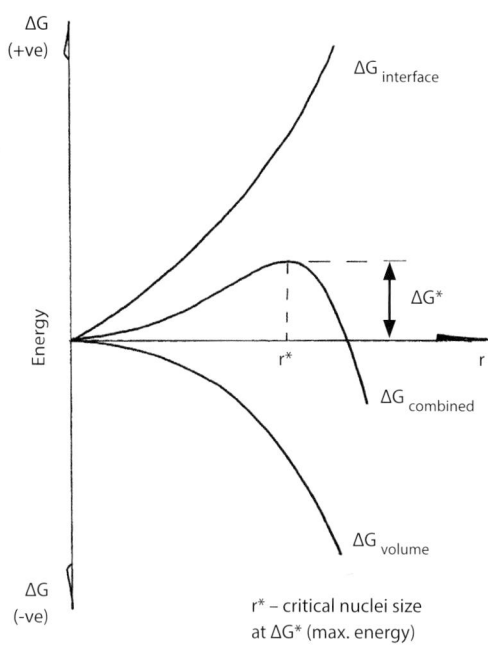

Figure 21 Particle energy balance versus particle size.

the critical size of nuclei for sustainable growth. In practice, minute nuclei are rapidly forming and dissolving until this critical size is reached, where explosive growth can occur and the solidification process is set in train.

The spherical shape of a particle derives from this being the lowest free energy condition, as intuition and experience tells us. However, for this to occur in a homogenous manner, throughout the melt, it requires a higher change in free energy (ΔG) than nucleation from a surface, such as the mould wall, or upon a foreign particle. Thus, in practice heterogeneous, preferential, nucleation is the way that solidification proceeds – as in the cloud example.

The degree of effort required to trigger this nucleation process is reflected in the cooling curve Figure

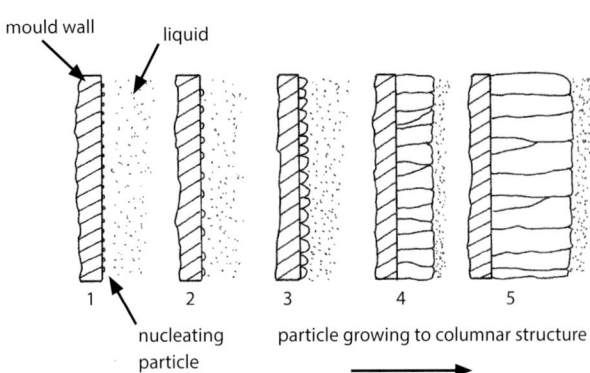

Figure 22 Particle growth from nuclei to columnar grain from mould wall into the liquid.

20, where the dip in the graph indicates the degree of undercooling needed. The ease of formation of nuclei is an important feature, and heterogeneous nucleation is assisted by the shape of a particle as it makes a contact angle to a local surface. A lower contact angle reduces the barrier to nucleation, in a manner akin to the 'wettability' of a surface – the concept is familiar as rain falling on waterproof or non-waterproof surfaces of the same texture. This is the classical nucleation theory, which is quite sufficient for a reasonable understanding in this context. The relationships supporting Figure 21 can be expressed as the balance between the free energy of the cooling liquid (ΔG_v) and that of the formation of a new interface ($\Delta G_{interface}$), as $4/3 \pi r^3 \Delta G_v \geq 4\pi r^2 \sigma$ for nucleation, where r is particle radius, ΔG_v part of the latent heat, σ is surface energy; thus $\Delta G_{interface} = 4\pi r^2 \sigma - 4/3 \pi r^3 \Delta G_v$. This leads to values of critical nuclei size (r*) ~10^{-9}m (1nm), thereby needing ~10^3 atoms for stable nuclei. From the above relationship, the formation of nuclei is strongly dependent on the volume free energy and particle free energy, so increased undercooling and reduced **surface tension** are important factors driving nucleation.

Inoculation

The practical application of this nucleation theory provides for its manipulation by well-established methods, such as inoculation and grain refinement treatments.

Although grain refinement by modification of nucleation activity is a long established and widely used process, its mechanism is still not fully understood. Instead, a more pragmatic approach is sufficient to reconcile what works with certain features of inoculant and master alloy. So, lack of disregistry, or compliance between their crystal structures – appears to be a significant feature. The methods used are either introduction of an inoculating agent into the melt in the form of a fine particle dispersion; or by a solid reaction product, produced internally by phase or chemical reactions.

The agents used are now well established and successful in modifying common alloy systems such as Al-Si, widely employed for aluminium casting for many important applications requiring moderate strength. In general, two classes of inoculant are successfully employed. Firstly, Al_3Ti, Al_3Zr and Al_7cr; or TiC, TiB_2 and AlB_2, the latter either as deliberate additions or through interaction with residual impurities in the melt. These nucleating agents typically enable solidification to proceed with an undercooling of only around 5°C. Practical examples include the addition of ferrosilicon to nucleate graphite in cast iron, zirconium to modify magnesium and copper-base alloys; phosphorus and sodium to change the silicon phase in the Al-Si alloys, as noted above; and titanium to improve nucleation in zinc-base alloys.

These additions provide an extremely powerful tool, enabling the foundry worker to produce a casting with desired mechanical properties, through the control of grain size and with a microstructure that is equiaxed and homogenous, free from the undesirable long columnar grain growth and piping that would ensue were it not for proper intervention, see Figure 18. This leads to the next phase in the solidification process – growth.

Solidification – Growth

As an example of the manner in which a typical melt will undergo growth after the nucleation event, we can consider an alloy (as most practical casts are), of the well-known, heat treatable, Al – 4% Cu. Figure 20 shows the characteristics cooling curves of pure Al, and Figure 17 the Al-Cu alloy. The latter has a wide range of freezing temperatures, resulting in a mushy zone. Growth proceeds through the development of

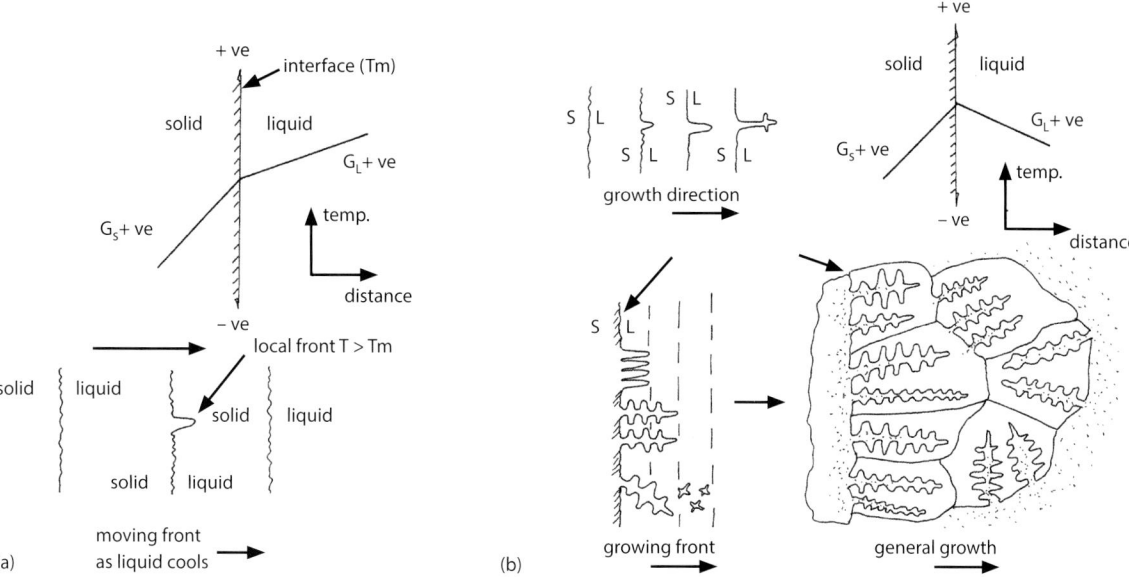

Figure 23 (a) Progress of solidification front in a positive temperature gradient, and (b) solidification in a negative temperature gradient (dendritic growth).

small spikes of crystal growth from the nucleated particle on the mould wall (place of most favourable free energy, ΔG, for formation of a viable nucleus), as in Figure 22.

Figure 23 shows how the energy balance across the interface between liquid and solid controls the way that nuclei are either subsumed, as in Figure 23 (a); or progress to growth, of a dendritic form, as Figure 23 (b). This leads to the two common forms of growth of a particle within the forming grain – dendritic or eutectic – growth.

Dendritic Growth

This is a commonly observed structure that can proceed within the long columnar or smaller equiaxed grains that form according to the macroscope solidification patterns familiar in castings, as was shown in Figure 18, and the control of which has been discussed earlier.

Concentrating on the microscale, the bursting nuclei front pushes forward into the liquid, initially as a tree begins by pushing up a single limb, in a direction favoured by the originating crystallographic contact with the nucleation site, such as the mould wall. Again, this is like a tree sprouting from a rugged surface, but our dendrite is not constrained to progress perpendicularly to the general surface as gravity dictates that trees grow vertically, even on steep slopes. Figure 23 (b) shows this dendritic growth pattern, initially in grains from the mould wall, but subsequently in adjacent grains for an equiaxed structure; or more linearly in the columnar grain structure as Figure 24. In fact, the way that the dendritic structure grows, branching out in a manner recognizable in the three-dimensional growth of trees, is important for the mechanical properties that derive from the spacing of the branches.

The dendrite grows by pushing out this 3D, tree-like structure into the enveloping liquid. And as it does, the chemical composition is continually in flux as one element or other is manipulated within this rapidly growing forest. As the process is usually too fast for the equilibrium conditions of the phase diagram (showing the relative amounts of each element in the alloy), the dendrite trunks can be depleted in some of the elements that freeze last, trapped between the dendritic branches as the grain becomes fully formed. This leads to coring, a problem of segregation, the lack of fully mixed or homogenous, blended, microstructure. This effect is normally alleviated or eliminated by a post-casting, high temperature, heat treatment to allow time for the diffusion of the elements to reach equilibrium.

This differential freezing is seen in the part of phase diagram of Figure 25, typical of Al-Cu alloys, as the alloy composition undergoes solidification through dendritic growth.

32 • Fundamentals of the Casting Process

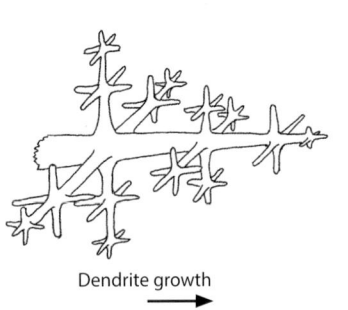
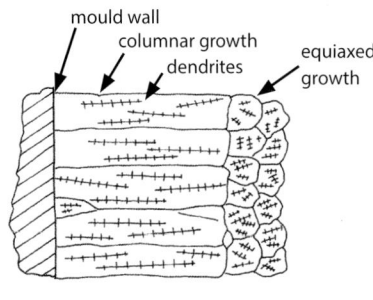

Dendrite growth

Figure 24 Dendrite onset (schematic), and growth from the mould wall. Dendrites in columnar and equiaxed grains.

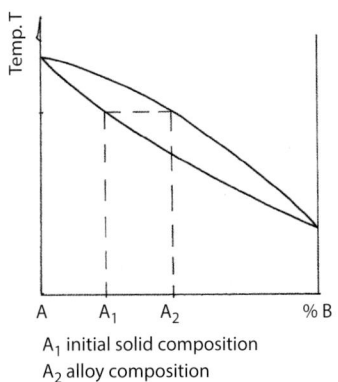

A₁ initial solid composition
A₂ alloy composition

Figure 25 Freezing range of alloy: solid solution phase.

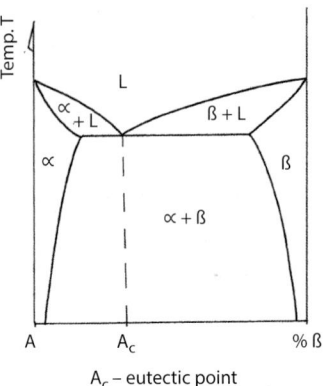

A_c – eutectic point

Figure 26 Phase diagram for eutectic alloy.

Eutectic Growth

Figure 26 shows a common eutectic phase diagram, such as the Al Si binary system. In these systems, the two separate phases grow in tandem from within a grain, most commonly observed as lamellae, or sandwich, development of plates to form a fine microstructure reminiscent of a plywood configuration. In essence, each element grows together with the other to form, in this case, a laminated structure. However, this is by no means the only style of growth, and the concurrent growth of the solid phases can adopt a completely different style of growth, such as rod-like structures in a matrix of the second phase – but the principle remains of concurrent growth. These eutectic structures are generally associated with equiaxed grains.

Dendritic and Eutectic Growth Combined

It is also common to find that growth can begin as a dendritic structure, such as Al Si, where Al-rich solid solutions dendrites form; with the later freezing liquid infilling as a eutectic structure. Similarly, in grey cast irons, where austenite dendrites can form, then infilling by austenite–graphite eutectic grains from the inter-dendritic regions.

Thus, the structure laid down by these initial solidification processes can persist even after post-casting treatments, important when particular mechanical properties are required.

CASTING DEFECTS

Macro and Micro Voids

Macro voids can be considered to arise from shrinkage, as discussed earlier. This is relatively simple to avoid for liquid metal shrinkage (*see* Chapter 4, 'Liquid Shrinkage'), but solidification shrinkage is more difficult to control and we need to consider the role of gas porosity, due to the ability of liquid metal to absorb certain gases. Of particular note is gas porosity in Al alloys, due to the significant solubility of hydrogen in liquid aluminium, as was shown in Figure 14. Thus, sources of H_2, such as surface contamination and moisture in casting equipment, provides the opportunity for gas dissolution into the melt and its capture in the solidifying casting as internal porosity. This can lead to severe consequences for the mechanical properties, and degassing treatments into the melt are often employed, alongside those for grain refinement.

Inclusions

Non-metallic inclusions can also have a severe effect on the mechanical properties of castings, especially toughness, fatigue strength, and even corrosion behaviour. The larger inclusions, detached from the mould (such as sand particles), and slag, are readily seen and good foundry practice should be sufficient for their control. However, there are intrinsic sources of inclusions, resulting from melt reactions, such as in aluminium alloys where alumina, Al oxide, inclusions can occur from melt surface oxygen reactions and their entrapment in the bulk liquid. In steels, inclusions are commonly formed sub-surface in the liquid, from solids of deoxidation treatments. It is possible to calculate the behaviour of such inclusions deep in the liquid using Stokes' law, which provides an inclusion size calculation to permit their floating safely out of the melt. This shows that a large inclusion is far more buoyant, and therefore more predisposed to rising out of the melt than smaller inclusions, utilized extensively in the manufacture of steel castings and ingots. And it is from ingots that almost all non-casting, wrought, product form is made.

Shape control of inclusions can be employed, such as by adding calcium and the rare earths to steels, to improve mechanical properties, through mitigation of the disruption to the microstructural integrity of these foreign particles. Such practices relate to the control of the melt quality. This includes using premium grade material, preferably vacuum melted, clean and dry, before charging the furnace, as discussed later in Chapter 5.

Further Casting Defects

There are several obvious surface defects familiar in practical casting work, often associated with problems in gating systems, and in metal transfer from furnace to mould. The misrun has been mentioned earlier, as an effect where these conditions have not been successfully organized. But this is a practical topic and such failures should not inhibit repeat work with suitable modifications, in the time-honoured trial-and-error manner. A great feature of casting as a process is that it is usually the case that a casting failure provides valuable experience and the material is not lost, being available for remelting for another try, unlike machining operations which are non-reversible.

Laps and shuts are seen, as their names imply, as surface defects, consequences of flow into the mould and primarily concerned with gating design, described in Chapter 4. When pouring the molten charge, there is also the effect of surface films being drawn into the casting bulk as bifilms and responsible for problems, such as microporosity, previously considered to arise solely from gas solubility, as discussed earlier.

As the casting begins to cool towards room temperature the contraction stresses can, while the solid is still locally at high temperature and with a low yield strength, suffer failure by 'hot tearing'. This is often associated with casting shape and mould cooling and considered in the section on gating and moulding design, Chapter 4. It may also be addressed through structure control, being aware of the rate of solidification and the segregation effects, as late-freezing elements are trapped in regions susceptible to severe contraction stresses. A similar approach is needed where, rather than the relatively large hot tears, finer but equally damaging cracks occur. As a crack is, by definition, the illustration of a plane perpendicular to stresses that exceed those sustainable by the microstructure, a means needs to be found to reduce these lower-temperature contraction stresses, or improve the metallurgical structure at the critical condition. Apart from alleviating cooling stresses by mould shape design, attention to structure, such as grain refinement, avoidance of microporosity, and the effects of segregation, may be necessary to address what could be indicative of a fundamental problem.

SUMMARY – FUNDAMENTALS OF CASTING THEORY

◆ While there are still some details of casting theory as yet not fully developed, it is rather a case of 'the more one knows, the more there is to know. . .', an ever-expanding subject. However, the development of casting theory to date means that it can no longer be regarded as a black art or magical process, as persisted from its origins some five millennia ago until the last couple of centuries of scientific enlightenment.

◆ This does not mean that the purely practical approach, concerned simply with process rather than theory, should deter the eager participant. Rather, that theory can sen-

sibly follow practice to illuminate some of the possibilities of this powerful process, with its roots in antiquity, potentially being uniquely fit for the most critical of applications.
- The basics of foundry work begin with an understanding of the four fundamental states of matter – solid, liquid, gas and plasma. These inform the methods to provide the metal melt and means to transfer it through a gating system to the mould. It has, relatively recently, been realized that the bifilm theory (*Campbell, 2011*) holds a key to many of the defects that can afflict castings (such as microporosity), and even persist into wrought products, such as steel plates and forgings produced from a cast ingot.
- As the liquid enters the mould, the process of solidification is seen to be vital to the structure of the final casting, where it is now possible to control the rate and frequency of the nucleation process. This largely determines where and how the grain structure is formed, thus determining, to a great extent, the suitability of the casting to perform to specification. Nucleation can be controlled by attention to well-known principles, usually aimed at generating a fine grain structure for optimum mechanical properties.
- The next stage is growth from the nuclei, of critical importance to the final product, such as the manner of dendritic, tree-like growth within each grain. The spacing of the inter-dendritic arms is vitally important, as are interactions during this phase. Eutectic growth, where the two solid phases sprout in unison, occurs where dictated by the phase diagram of the alloy, and may proceed in conjunction with pre-existing dendritic growth.
- This growth phase leads to final solidification, and can determine the trapping of microporosity and segregation of elements, providing sites of potential defects and weaknesses in the casting.
- The understanding of internal defects in castings is built on the previous theories and practical observations for avoidance of shrinkage cavities, porosity, microporosity, non-metallic and slag inclusions, hot tearing and cold cracks – in short, the soundness of the casting structure.
- Application of this theoretical base is made to all aspects of casting, ranging from selection of materials, pouring temperatures, liquid metal transfer, gating systems, mould design, post-casting heat treatment and casting soundness evaluation (non-destructive testing, NDT) – as expanded in the later chapters.

2 Setting up a Home Workshop Foundry

Photo 10 Initial layout of the micro foundry, solid fuel furnace.

Before entering into a full-scale casting operation it should be appreciated that it is far from a simple activity and circumstances need to be weighed against the difficulties and costs to be overcome in order to reach the ultimate goal of producing one's own casting from raw metal to finished article.

Indeed, the complete process is not going to be a viable proposition unless the elements of casting and requirements of the workshop can be accommodated. It is best to understand this in order to avoid overreaching oneself, but instead tackle perhaps part of the process, leaving other parts – typically the mould making, melting and casting – to a professional foundry. Even should this be the case, a sound understanding of the background theory and practice of casting is invaluable in tackling the extremely wide range of items that can only be produced satisfactorily by casting, such as the restoration of historic and classic vehicles (motorcycle cylinder barrels, crankcases) or domestic furniture (fire grates, railings).

For the undaunted, read on, as it is possible to achieve surprisingly successful results even given considerable constraints of space and resources, as will be seen in the case of Dave's 'micro foundry', producing bronze from sand castings in half a garage using only a 12v power supply, in an urban environment. Beware though, as such a set-up requires careful assessment of one's capabilities. However, given more space and resources the game becomes more amenable and difficulties reduce considerably.

Unlike setting up a woodworking or metalworking home workshop, where a remarkably agreeable and productive operation can be set up in a relatively simple garden shed, at least for producing reasonably small articles – for a casting workshop, a more substantial base is a prerequisite. While it is not possible to produce a layout that is suitable for all purposes, a review of the following elements and requirements should enable a workshop to be planned that is appropriate to the items required as final castings.

From the disparate activities outlined below, it may be considered best to concentrate on certain aspects, such as drawings and pattern making, essentially requiring woodworking skills and facilities.

Elements of the Home Workshop Foundry

Patterns
Wood and woodworking tools.

Moulds and Cores
Sand, measuring and handling tools, coreboxes, weights.

Metal
Furnace charge, i.e. raw material.

Melting
Crucibles, handling tools, furnace and power sources, temperature measuring equipment.

Casting
Mould set-up, pouring.

Finishing
Removal from mould, clean up tooling, analysis.

Records
Notes on process, remelts, details for improvement conditions monitoring.

Requirements of the Workshop

Space
Room to make patterns; moulds; cores; raw materials – sand and metal for melting; tooling for various operations; protective clothing; suitable building and safety precautions – heat resistant, non-flammable flooring, dry conditions – awareness of moisture control.

Power and Tooling
Means of operating power tools for pattern making and finishing ops; furnace power – electric/gas/solid fuel.

Working Conditions
Workshop enclosure, accommodating heat, fume control, spill control, safety equipment.

Setting up a Home Workshop Foundry • 37

Photo 11 Later micro foundry layout, gas furnace and holding oven, ready for casting. (Photo: Colin Mills)

DETAILS OF ELEMENTS AND REQUIRMENTS

Patterns

For sand casting, it is normal practice to produce wooden patterns and these need to be designed in order to produce a finished casting as near to the desired shape as possible, consistent with enabling removal from the sand mould without collapsing it. The first constraint is that re-entrant profiles cannot be accommodated without damage to the mould on removal of the pattern. Any given item needs to be assessed in order that the pattern will enable satisfactory runners and rises to be produced in the mould, and molten metal flow provided for a sound casting – this is dealt with in the section on design (*see* Chapter 4).

It is sometimes possible to simply employ the existing part as the pattern, where a replica is sought. This clearly avoids the need for producing a wooden pattern, and much can be gleaned from a careful examination of the original casting – for instance the centre line, where usually some telltale joint line is found marking the line of the cope and drag.

Starting from scratch, it is preferable to produce a dimensional drawing of the pattern, not usually difficult for a simple item; incorporating sufficient taper to allow removal from the mould. For more complex parts, this requires some considerable skill and it soon becomes apparent why pattern-makers are held in high regard in the industry, and why professionally made patterns are expensive. However, cast items are often of very high value, and this style (sand casting) employs a reusable mould. Fortunately, such a pattern can be used to make almost any number of castings, thereby reducing the unit cost.

It is apparent, therefore, that pattern making can be treated as a separate activity, with drawing and woodworking undertaken in the woodwork shed, should one be fortunate enough to have such a facility or opportunity to use one. While wood is the most common material for our purposes, it may be perfectly possible to make patterns, especially of the smaller type, using a proprietary plastic-based moulding material, such as the two-pack modelling materials that, when mixed, can be roughly shaped, dried and finished, by machining or hand working to the desired shape. (*See* Appendix for details of materials.)

Once produced, patterns should be sealed or lightly painted, where absorbent, and stored carefully, providing assets for future use. Should it be intended to provide a pattern for a professional foundry to make the mould and casting then it is wise to discuss and agree details, otherwise problems are to be expected. (*See* Chapter 7 for

Photo 12 Preparing for casting, sand mould and investment mould in foreground. (Photo: Colin Mills)

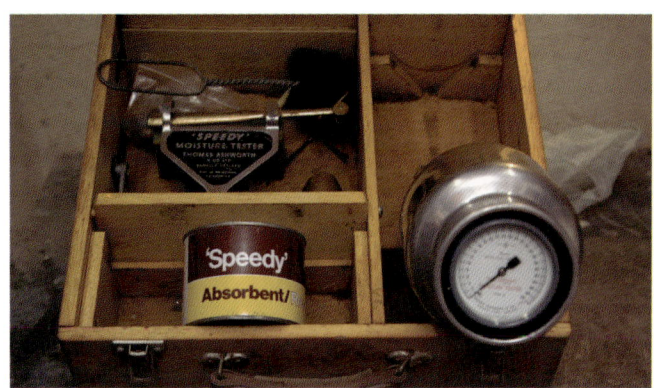

Photo 13 Kit for sand moisture testing. (Photo: Colin Mills)

Photo 16 Dusting the pattern, in the drag. (Photo: Colin Mills)

Photo 14 Sand casting mould preparation, powder dusting for mould and pattern release. (Photo: Colin Mills)

Photo 17 Preparing runner and riser cups. (Photo: Colin Mills)

Photo 15 Placing cope into position. (Photo: Colin Mills)

Photo 18 Preparing runner and riser cups. (Photo: Colin Mills)

Setting up a Home Workshop Foundry • 39

Photo 19 Sand mould, ready for pouring. (Photo: Colin Mills)

Photo 21 Gas-fired holding oven and round furnace. (Photo: Colin Mills)

Photo 20 Commercial foundry moulds, ready for pouring. (Photo: Colin Mills))

Photo 22 Careful sand work – making feeder channels. (Photo: Colin Mills)

Photo 23 Drawer of self-made sand-moulding tools. (Photo: Colin Mills)

Photo 24 Making sand funnels for runners and risers. (Photo: Colin Mills)

an example of such a small jobbing foundry.)

Moulds and Cores

The next step is production of the mould, requiring sufficient room and dry conditions, with a workbench that can accommodate the cope and drag boxes, plus sand and associated equipment. This is ideally undertaken near to the melting furnace area, but requires only limited space, typically the size of a kitchen table. Photo 12 shows the micro foundry, sufficient for small to moderately sized (say, a few kg) castings.

The workbench allows the cope and drag to be filled with sand, stored nearby, and tested for moisture content, as shown in Photo 13. Into the core boxes are introduced the pattern, dusted as shown in Photos 14, 15 and 16; tamped down; and assembled as Photos 17 and 18. The runners and risers are made, and the boxes are ready for final preparation prior to casting (Photo 19), although often this is some time before everything is ready and therefore careful storage is required. Especially important is dry storage, and sufficient room is needed for several core boxes if a furnace charge is planned to produce several castings, *see* Photo 20.

Cores are made in a similar manner, but are sometimes subject to a drying process, as in Photo 21. Accommodation in to the mould is seen in Photo 22. Tooling associated with the moulding process is relatively simple; Photo 23 shows some home-made examples. These should all be kept in easy reach of the moulding table, as in Photo 24. (See also Appendix II, Practical Casting and Process Notes).

Metal

This is the raw material that will form the furnace charge, thereby determining the chemical composition of the final casting, in much the way that the baked cake comprises the original ingredients. Similarly, the end result may not be in the expected condition, as a consequence of the interim reactions. Provided that mechanical properties are not critical, and operational stresses low – which is the case for many components in every-day domestic use – then the final casting composition is sufficiently close to that of the furnace charge. This is the case for the common copper-base alloys of bronzes and brasses; aluminium for aluminium-silicon casting alloys; and the grey cast irons cast from common artefacts of cast iron scrap. Indeed, this is how many of the long-experience, low-tech, jobbing foundries operate perfectly satisfactorily, provided that the above constraints on properties and non-critical applications are recognized. After all, vast quantities of castings have been produced without benefit of the technology of chemical analysis, microstructural examination, mechanical testing and non-destructive testing (NDT), which have only been developed since the early twentieth century and still remain out of reach in many parts of the globe.

This marks a clear divide in the world of castings, between those of the former, non-critical, category and critical items that require significant analysis in order to match application demands. For instance, a ductile iron car crankshaft can only be supplied where a full understanding and technical support is available, with a consequent dramatic increase in cost. However, providing the right level of knowledge and controls are exercised, the applications of such castings are virtually limitless, although not necessarily economically viable. On the other hand, a lack of understanding of the potential of castings can miss opportunities of great economic benefit.

The advance of casting theory, such as bifilm and fluid flow, lead towards expensive methods of pouring in controlled atmospheres; but for practical work in small-scale operations, the

Photo 25 Gas-fired furnace, mounted on castors, showing gas burner, and blower part-removed. (Photo: Colin Mills)

Furnace

The basic choice of a furnace is: electric; solid fuel; or gas powered. Electric-powered furnaces, of the induction type, are the industry standard, but considered prohibitively expensive for the home workshop. Resistance furnaces are available commercially, or it is possible to home-construct, but this is a specialist area requiring significant cost and expertise to produce a unit capable of handling alloys with higher melting requirements than Al, circa 750°C. (*See* Suppliers.)

Note that the high energy demand and cost is a significant factor to be considered when assessing the use of an electric furnace, especially given the requirement of approaching 1,500°C for cast iron melting (1,450°C being a general rule of thumb value); see Photo 25. As an indication of energy costs, at the time of writing, in the UK; the last twenty-minute phase of heating, at full power, for a 500kg melt in a small commercial foundry's 0.5MW induction furnace – costs around 25p (£0.025) *per second*!

Solid fuel provides a promising alternative heat source, in the form of smokeless coke and a forced-draught furnace. However, unless the small foundry is located well away from built-up areas, then the inevitable fume emissions are likely to present problems. If no such restraints exist, then it is possible to construct a viable furnace, as shown in Photos 26 to 32 using a simple refractory-lined container, with a grid for a bed of coke, and small fan-assisted draught introduced below the coke bed. This can be highly effective in

ancient method of melting and gravity pouring into moulds is normally the only one available, and quite satisfactory for our purposes.

There are often further minor additions to the melt, such as degassing tablets, and Al Si modification treatments, prior to pouring, as described in Chapter 1. These items obviously need to be dry stored and made ready for rapid use, near the melting equipment.

As applies to all equipment and furnaces charges, scrupulous care is required for moisture control, as a means of safe working and avoidance of explosion risk, as noted in Chapter 3.

Melting

The melting equipment forms the heart of the small foundry, comprising furnace; power supply; crucible(s); and handling tools for skimming the melt, lifting the crucible, and pouring. For the small foundry, these are all of limited size and weight, with all operations manually controlled. Normally, a minimum of two workers are required, especially for the safe lifting of the crucible for furnace pouring of the molten metal from crucible to mould(s).

42 • Setting up a Home Workshop Foundry

Photo 26 Construction of heat-insulation lining, for solid fuel furnace, employing steel dustbin as base container.

Photo 29 Plan view of solid fuel furnace, after firing.

Photo 27 Plan view of original furnace, during lining with proprietary refractory.

Photo 28 Steel-fabricated grid to support bed of solid fuel (coke).

Photo 30 Solid fuel furnace in action.

Setting up a Home Workshop Foundry • 43

Photo 31 Solid fuel furnace at full power, using forced draft from simple fan air-blower.

Photo 33 Gas-fired furnace, burner removed, ready for lifting out of crucible for pouring.

Photo 32 Roof vent for furnace.

producing sufficient heat, even for cast iron, but suffers from emissions and difficulty in close regulation of the heat generated and time-cycle of operation – being essentially similar to a domestic fire in control characteristics.

The gas-powered furnace presents the best solution for small-scale work, as shown in Photo 33. The self-constructed furnace is produced from a domestic metal waste bin, with substantial refractory lining and ports to accommodate

Photo 34 The gas burner for the furnace.

Photo 37 Gas burner for holding oven.

Photo 35 Detail of furnace burner showing the copper gas jet in the steel holder.

Photo 38 Detail of holding oven burner, jet hidden by brass coupling.

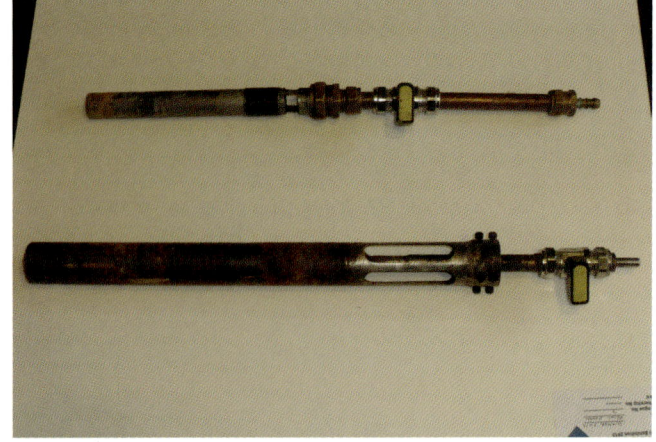

Photo 36 Gas burners for furnace and holding oven (top).

Photo 39 Furnace (right), and holding oven (left) with investment mould. (Photo: Colin Mills)

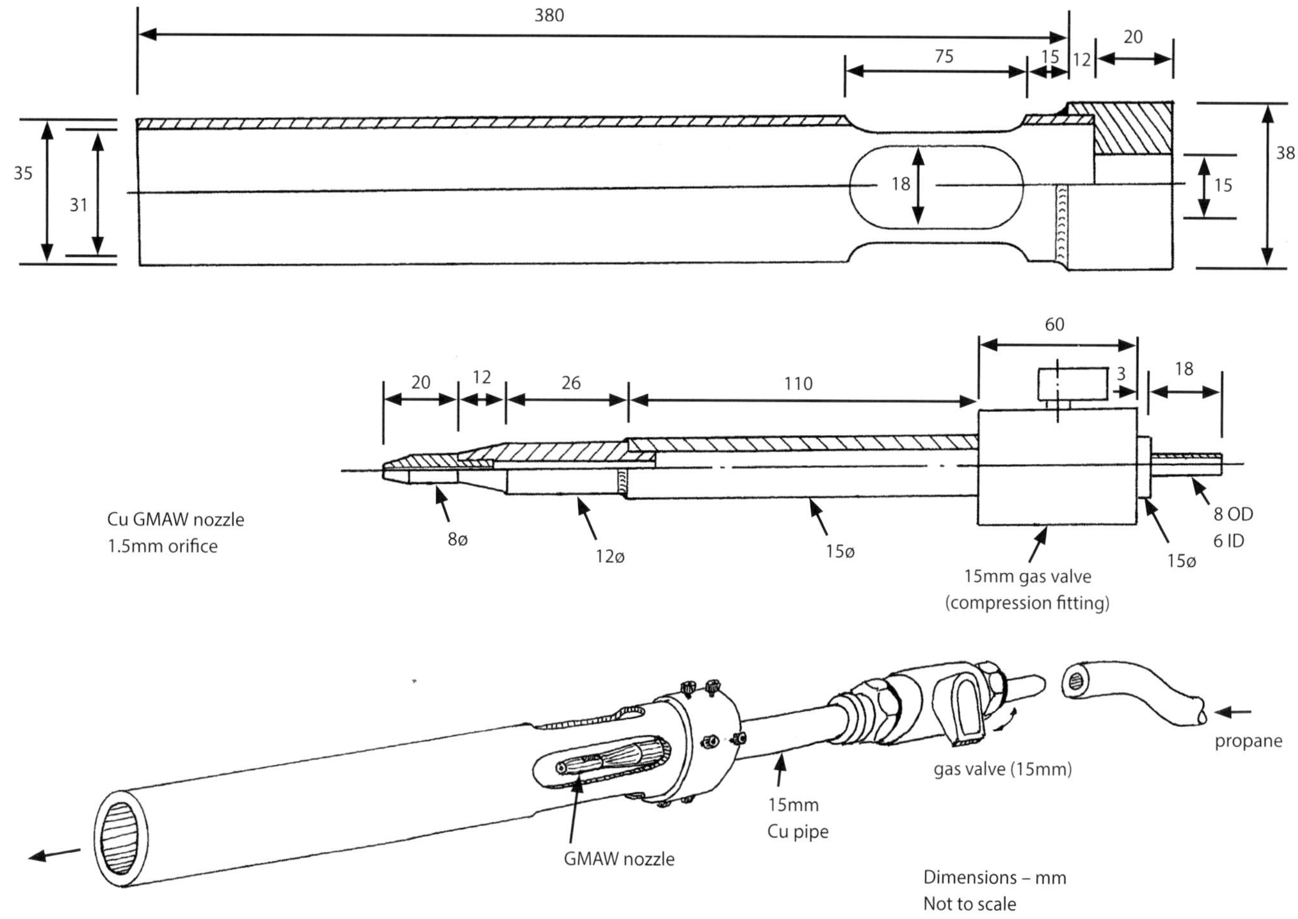

Figure 27 The construction of the furnace gas burner.

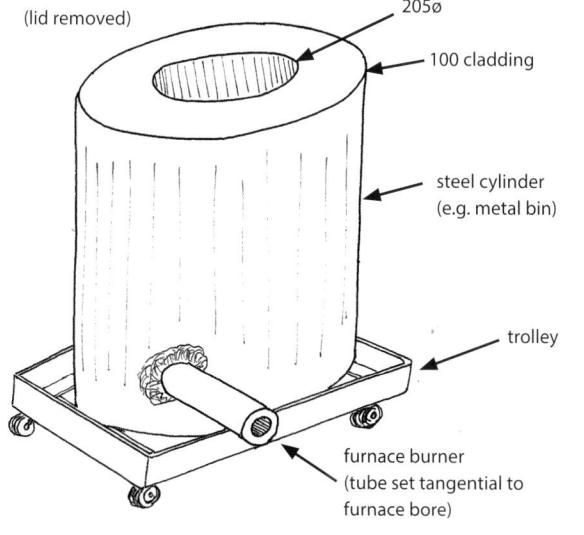

Figure 28 The casting furnace for the gas burner.

the gas burner. Details of the gas burner are shown in Photos 34 and 35, and also in Figure 27. The burner is fed from a readily available large domestic gas bottle, assisted by a low-pressure fan to enhance heat output. This arrangement provides a rapid and controllable heat source, successfully melting the copper-base alloys. Although not seriously deployed for cast iron work, this has proven within its capability.

The advantages of gas burners are: very clean operation, compared to solid fuel; lower operating and installation

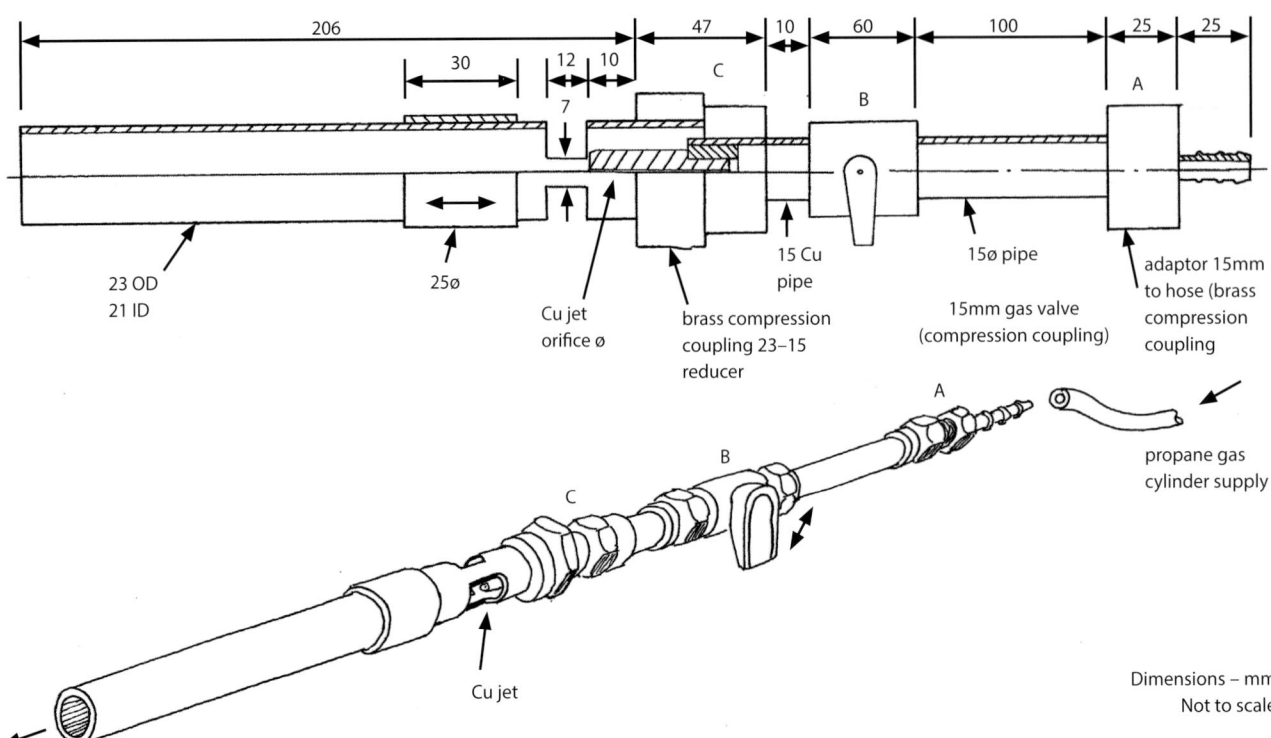

Figure 29 Heat treatment oven gas burner.

Figure 30 Heat treatment gas oven.

costs, compared to electric; and highly controllable heat input, rather like cooking with a gas cooker. Construction of the furnace, shown in Figure 28, utilizes a convenient metal cylinder approx. 1m high by a 0.5m diameter, with a substantial lining (~50 to 100mm thick), built up by plastering layers of refractory lining, to make a remarkably heat-insulated furnace casing. Alternatives are many, including heat-resistant brick constructions – ideally suited to operations with less constraints on working space.

The furnace requires a port through its body and lining, so that the burner can be introduced, held during firing, and later removed for maintenance. The setting angle, as shown, is used to provide the swirl effect that most effi-

Setting up a Home Workshop Foundry

Photo 40 The micro foundry in later guise, preparing for pouring. (Photo: Colin Mills)

ciently heats the crucible and charge. A simple lid with a non-flammable plate, lined with refractory, provided with suitable venting and cap, plus a means of introducing a chromel-alumel thermocouple for charge temperature monitoring – completes the furnace. (See Appendix II, Practical Casting and Process Notes).

Photos 36, 37 and 38; and also Figure 29, show the burners; the larger for high temperature use with the melting furnace; and smaller, used for lower temperatures with a baking oven and temperatures below ~800°C. This oven is useful for drying, and even stress-relieving or tempering alloys for more advanced metallurgical work, see Photo 39 and Figure 30. (Also, see Bibliography.)

REQUIREMENTS OF THE WORKSHOP

Space

The space required for a viable foundry is to a great extent governed by the two factors – the metal to be used and the physical size of the final casting.

For the lower melting point alloys such as aluminium and the precious metals, the lower temperatures (< 1,000°C) mean that heating requires less power and likely a lower specification furnace. If combined with a small product, then the space required can be reduced to table-top dimensions, for domestic artefacts such as jewellery and small sculptures.

For working in the copper-base and cast irons, the temperatures are significantly higher and serious furnaces are required for all but the smallest work. Physical size is likely to be more significant, with weights of several kilograms requiring space for floor-standing furnaces, tables for mouldings, and several square metres of floor space for setting the moulds and safe pouring to be undertaken. (See Photo 40 for the micro foundry layout, representing something of a lower limit of working and storage space.)

Power and Tooling

The normal minimum requirement could be considered a mains supply of electric power, of 450, 240 or 110v. However, it is possible to operate in more remote locations or those without power grid connections, with some ingenuity, on a self-contained eco system based on a 12v battery arrangement, as shown in Photos 41, 42 and 43. This has proven a viable proposition where it was not practically possible to connect to the UK's 240v, single-phase domestic grid. Developments in low-power LED lighting, electronic voltage transformers and solar power recharging, coupled to low-cost, high-capacity, lead-acid vehicle batteries, have proven sufficient to power the micro foundry. Such a unit could even operate in the bush!

Photo 41 Power supply for the micro foundry, entirely from 12v battery power. (Photo: Colin Mills)

Photo 42 Charging control from solar panel to 12v battery system. (Photo: Colin Mills)

Photo 43 Roof-mounted solar panel for battery system.

Photo 44 Sand casting core boxes, fabricated from steel angle section.

Similarly, the gas-powered furnace can operate from portable gas cylinders, although for anything but the smallest work, the larger cylinders are an economic and practical necessity.

Tooling associated with foundry work, with the exception of woodworking tooling for pattern making, is simple. This comprises casting boxes (*see* Photo 44) and simple tooling for handling sand, shovels and trowels, plus tamping tools, for compacting the moulds (Photo 45). One particular piece of testing equipment that is often found to be very useful, unless one has extensive experience of sand preparation, is the sand moisture meter.

As the moisture content of the sand mix is critical at around 3 per cent, a meter is useful to ensure there is sufficient water content to keep the delicate sand profile intact, while avoiding excess moisture. This leads to dramatic gas evolution during the rapid solidification of the casting, and severe porosity.

Working Conditions

As noted at the outset, foundry operations inevitably generate heat, dust and fumes, and the workshop needs to be able to accommodate this – perhaps coming as something of a shock to the office worker used to safety measures commensurate with the ultimate risk of paper cuts or coffee spills . . . Essentially, this is an ancient, rather messy, potentially dangerous, but dramatic, exciting, frustrating, and maybe even rather rewarding experience – that can uniquely produce an artefact to restore a priceless machine or make something that could last for generations.

Photo 45 Ramming-up tool, cast in the micro foundry.

Therefore, the basic construction of the workshop needs to be reasonably non-flammable, with flooring able to tolerate molten metal spills without ignition – which is why all manual, working foundries liberally utilize dry sand underfoot to avoid such contact with concrete, and disastrous consequences – don't try it!

Clearly, adequate ventilation is required at all times when heating and casting, but this can normally be accommodated with simple precautions for sufficient airflow, without draughts, or compromising subsequent processes. Refer to the Appendices for safety aspects.

3 Methods of Casting

The intrinsically wide range of items possible from each type of casting process is likewise further expanded by the many and varied individual processes now available. This section is concerned with identifying these different processes and includes some, whilst not of direct concern to the small scale or home-based worker, nevertheless worthy of attention as the industrial route through which items of significant interest are produced.

Arguably, we stand at a potentially critical point in the history of casting. From the origins described earlier (*see* Introduction), beginning around 4000BC, we have progressed from Stone Age moulds; to Bronze Age lost-wax processes; Medieval sand casting; Industrial Revolution with early cast irons; and the post-industrial era of scientific revolution from the nineteenth to the twenty-first century – and often back to lost wax.

With the digital revolution of the late twentieth century (remarkably, digital computing has only been around since the 1950s), we are now poised on the edge of the additive machining (AM or 3D-printing) revolution that has only appeared in the twenty-first century and has yet to expand into the mainstream for which it is destined within the next few decades. With any new technology, it is always rash to predict the future, as famously the CEO of IBM's forecast made in the 1950s, of a 'global market of only a handful of computers'. The important point is to try anticipating the impact on the *local* area of interest – for instance, we need no reminding of how rapidly the photographic world has succumbed to digital processes. With casting, it is arguable that direct production, such as by direct laser metal printing of metal castings, for our purposes, is unlikely to have an impact for several decades. What, however, is already with us in the advanced technological world, is the present capability of using AM to produce either patterns direct from CAD software, for investing patterns in investment casting (aka lost wax); or the direct production of sand-based moulds straight from CAD (virtual) models, with no intermediate stages of pattern making, or moulding production techniques as described in the following processes. This also opens the way for considerably improved gating systems and almost limitless complexity of casting. However, the vital point is that this remains a fundamentally recognizable casting system, for metal is being melted and poured into the, albeit digitally produced, mould. It is then broken out, and subjected to NDT and finishing operations. This is, surely, the future but not necessarily a frightening nor unrecognizable one. There are parallels to be drawn from CAD-CAM, where software can now drive computer-controlled machines in the home workshop. Not necessarily displacing the Myford ML7, but just another tool in our ever-growing toolbox.

So much for the future – of immediate interest is the past development of processes and those available at present. The most common process worldwide is undoubtedly sand casting, accounting for some 90 per cent of all castings and so examined here in some detail. But to put things in perspective, we can categorize casting processes into three, thus:

i) Single-use moulds – multi-use patterns.
ii) Single-use moulds – single-use patterns.
iii) Multi-use moulds.

Often, parts i) and ii) are termed expendable moulding and part iii) non-expendable moulding, for reasons that are self-explanatory.

Les Hall, Master Pattern-Maker

Les Hall, as a spritely nonagenarian native of Cheshire, England, is testament to a passing – or maybe already passed – generation of highly talented craftsmen with a lineage directly to their forebears in the pre-Victorian era of the world's first Industrial Revolution. They embody a wide range of skills that deserves more recognition in a world focused on the energy of youth but lacking the long training necessary to produce the practical skills associated with once familiar professions, such as pattern making for the foundry industry.

Les at home, March 2017. (Photo: Colin Mills)

While it is now possible to produce the – still essential – foundry pattern by adopting the technology of the present day, such as 3-D printing and robotic manipulation for industrial production, there will always remain a place for the more direct approach to the unusual project for the likes of Les. The process of innovative design benefits from a more immediate 'feel' of the work, through practical handing of pattern materials – plaster, wood, metal – than can necessarily be obtained through the seductive facilities of the virtual image, enabled with ever-increasing computer power. Les scores with an ability to span a range of processes; from developing a pattern that can immediately produce a successful mould, envisaging materials and planning, through stages such as machining and completion within tight schedules, to successful installation. Such an example occurred at a late stage in his career when Les, as a self-employed craftsman, undertook the complete task of producing a batch of two-dozen replacement aluminium castings for sea-borne action in the Falklands War. Against 'impossible' deadlines, he organized the whole process from his Cheshire home. Patterns he produced himself were sent to the foundry, tested, machined, and on the aircraft for Ascension Island within the few days allotted, in time for a critical action.

Les in his home-based pattern-maker's shop. (Photo: Colin Mills)

This neatly encompassed a career begun during the Second World War as an apprentice at Kearns Machine Tools in Broadheath, Cheshire. The stress and strains of a wartime manufacturing environment were reinforced with a keen understanding of the competing demands of precision and production to critical schedules when, literally, the roof was falling in – experiences never lost in a long working life.

During the 1940s and 50s, a keen competitive spirit in the industry was evident with Manchester renowned for its large machine tool firms such as Kearns, and vitally important were the foundries that supplied the large castings upon which they relied. These firms achieved a good reputation for producing a wide variety of large machinery, with which Les became familiar, enabling processes to be developed for producing large complex parts efficiently. This is critical for a business to operate profitably; in the words of Nevil Shute '... an Engineer – someone who can do for ten bob what any fool can do for a pound. . . .' A good example was the making of a 3m diameter gear wheel in cast iron. The pattern was made, instead of the complete wheel with its many identical gear teeth, as just a quadrant. This required the pattern-maker to produce only a fraction of gear teeth; and the quadrant was rotated on its centre, in steps around the casting core box until the full wheel was rammed-up in the mould. This reduced the pattern cost dramatically, just one of the novel process methods used to drive commercial success.

By 1947, Les had also worked at Coventry, in the Midlands, experiencing the different manufacturing approaches required in the motor and aero industries, with their smaller-scale product than the machine tool industry. This was an industrial boom time as the world recovered from the devastation of the Second World War, and Les was headhunted to set up, from scratch, a new factory in Salford, Manchester, for the Birmingham-based Wright and Platt Co. Ltd, a very large foundry business. Left to organize the complete project, it was six months before the owner drove up to Salford in his Rolls-Royce to congratulate Les on a factory ready to start manufacture. From there, Les also had to operate as the sales department, steadily building the business over the next ten years where at its peak some thirty-two pattern-makers were employed.

On the death of the owner, Les decided on a change when a good customer, Bill Cooke, asked him to manage his Eagle Brass Foundry in Salford. Although not a foundry-trained man, Bill had taken on the firm from his father, and was keen on the non-technical side of the business, leaving Les a free hand. It was a period of great activity and contracts were established with a wide range of clients, including work producing patterns for the first ductile iron (SG) crankshafts employed by Ford Motors of Dagenham, followed by other critical work for Ford. Despite employing some 500 of its own pattern-makers, to supply the Ford Dagenham Foundry, in England and Germany Ford still required the services of highly skilled suppliers such as Les to produce patterns for production. These were made and tested to tolerances of ±0.003in (0.075mm), and kept as master patterns from which replicas were made at Dagenham for use in the sand moulds of the high-volume car production line. The many other contracts included Rolls-Royce in Derby, involving aerospace standards.

However, during the 1960s, foundries were closing rapidly as the effects were felt of de-industrialization in the UK, and after a takeover Les found himself looking for a job. Finally, after an interview at a Gloucester foundry for a foundry manager's job in Bolton, Lancashire, he was greeted by the apologetic owner with, 'You are the sixth foundry manager I've interviewed this week.' This was enough for Les, who immediately set up as self-employed, based at his home in Sale, Cheshire, with a garage converted to a pattern-maker's shop. Gradually, he returned to a stage of full employment, producing patterns and managing projects right up until his eighties when his wife Ann's final illness curtailed full-time work, but he has never entirely stopped his pattern making activities.

Les's workshop with some simple commercial patterns for a local foundry. (Photo: Colin Mills)

Interestingly, work that had come his way in this latter period include an order for a cast iron coffin from a client of the Whitehead Foundry, Broadheath. Once it was confirmed it was not a practical joke, Les obtained ideas for likely designs from Gresty, the local undertakers. The client, based on a farm near Sutton, Macclesfield, even came to see Les for a 'fitting', agreeing the design. Duly completed patterns from Les's workshop were used for six-piece castings at the Whitehead Foundry, then assembled as directed. Following the client's death, permission from the local church was successfully obtained by the family for burial of the casting, but at more than 6cwt (~330kg) Les anticipated a significant mechanical handling problem in the old churchyard . . . Actually, when it came to the funeral, the family resorted to more normal practice at the funeral, and the cast iron coffin is now believed to be safely buried, with its owner's personal artefacts, but at the farm. Another unusual job was the casting in aluminium of presswork for a bra supplier in the Philippines, who wanted to make the product at sight. Les's customary ability to be unfazed by the unlikeliest of jobs again saw the project duly completed and, by all accounts, it is still producing highly successful results. . . .

Perhaps the most technically demanding project in a long and distinguished career followed the fire that started at 5pm on 16 September 2003 at the National Motorcycle Museum in Birmingham. With no sprinkler system, it was not until 6.30pm that the blaze was brought under control, causing the loss of some 150 extremely valuable machines. As a long-time Velocette enthusiast, it was to Les that Ivan Rhodes, president of the Velocette Owners Club and famous guru of the marque, brought the task of remanufacturing the complex cylinder head from the priceless 1935 supercharged 500cc Velocette racer, universally known as the 'Dog Kennel' model, derived from the unusual appearance of its cylinder head. Only five examples still exist, two in Australia, two in the UK, and one in Japan, so rebuilding the destroyed machine was worth a great effort. One part that could not be found from extensive searches for spares was the overhead camshaft (OHC) cylinder head, a highly complex and elegant design, characteristic of the renowned Velocette works. It was a small, family-owned and run firm from its inception in 1907 to its demise in 1976, which remarkably still holds the world 500cc record, gained in 1961 from the first-ever '100mph for twenty-four hours' on a motorcycle.

The original Velocette factory drawings for a similar 350cc machine were provided for Les to analyse, and after considerable work he produced a series of patterns, including modification for the destroyed 500cc version. The cylinder head was successfully cast in LM25 aluminium alloy at a foundry in Accrington, Lancashire. Returned to Ivan Rhodes, it was used in the complete rebuild of the destroyed machine, which was then started, tested, and finally delivered for display at the renovated museum when it re-opened some years later. It is a permanent exhibition of the skill and craftsmanship of Les, Ivan and their ilk.

This latter story touches on Les's other lifelong passion that began when, in the post-war years of 1949 to 1951, he rode two-up from Cheshire and around the Continent, on holidays with 500cc BSA and Triumph bikes – including a 2,400-mile tour taking in as many Alpine passes as possible. These mountain rides encountered forty-eight hairpin bends, on roads only tarmacked at the bends, where the pillion rider had to survey the oncoming traffic while the pilot concentrated on keeping the bike on the track and not off the edge of the mountain! These trips were still remembered vividly well over half-a-century later, and it came as no surprise that latterly Les had established a stable of three Velocettes. He still retains his faithful 500cc MSS Velo, used for the six (!) End-to-Ends (Land's End to John O'Groats, nearly 2,000 miles of riding from home, as a round trip), as charity rides with friends, for Parkinson's relief. These outings have raised some £114,000, and were undertaken at four-yearly intervals, until 2013. The Les Velo, naturally, incorporates several of his own castings, from patterns made from his own workshop.

Les with the much-travelled Velocette. (Photo: Colin Mills)

The Les Velo, own castings for magneto, dynamo and regulator. (Photo: Colin Mills)

SINGLE-USE MOULDS – MULTI-USE PATTERNS

Sand Casting

While there are a number of processes that all involve sand, we begin with the original, and still widely used method, commonly known as green sand moulding. Green sand is discussed further in the section on sands, but in essence it refers to sand that, blended with a binder such as water, can be used directly for making the mould.

The sand is basically a refractory material in granular form, such as silica, zircon, chromite or olivine sand; see later 'Sand'. The process typically begins with two, or more, core boxes. As shown in Photo 51, the upper box is called the cope and lower the drag. The sand is mixed carefully with a precise proportion of binder, such as water, clay or proprietary additive, in order to provide sufficient strength of the sand moulding to retain its shape, ready for receiving the casting fluid. This can be considered somewhat akin to building a sandcastle on the beach, but the amount of binder is critical to the success of the casting operation.

In the pattern plate method, the lower moulding box (drag) is inverted with a board separating the two boxes, with the pattern set on the board, then the drag is filled with sand and packed around the pattern. The drag is then inverted and the sprue (feeding passage) and riser (fluid out flow) placed in the chosen position on to the pattern. The cope is then filled and packed with sand, the two moulding boxes completely filled with sand packed around the pattern, sprue and runner. The pattern board is removed from the drag, and the communicating passage made by carefully scooping out sand between the sprue, riser and pattern, making a cavity when the pattern is removed. The cope has the upper half of pattern removed, revealing the connecting sprue and riser holes. The cope and drag are reassembled, with the space enlarged at the entry, ready to accept the casting fluid. After pouring, solidification and break out from the mould, the sprue, runners

Photo 52 Newly cast firegrate in cast iron, feeder still hot.

Photo 51 Sand moulds, cope lifted to permit removal of the pattern. (Photo: Colin Mills)

and casting are now ready for cutting off. The casting is ready for use or finishing operations, and the remainder of the material for return to the next furnace charge, with limited waste. *See Photo 52.*

The detailed sequence of producing a mould by the basic method, using for a pattern an original piece for replication, is shown in Chapter 7, 'Case Studies, Processes and Projects'.

This relatively simple method is identical to that used from the earliest days of sand casting. As described here, it utilizes a pattern split along its major axis and mounted on a board, producing a top and bottom half-pattern. Often made in wood, this pattern is reusable, aligning top to bottom to make a matching product with minimal centreline indications. There is a degree of skill and expertise to be developed in preparing the pattern; sand compositions; sand packing; and gating system, comprising sprue, runners and connecting passages. The system of gating is discussed in detail later (see Chapter 6), as in some alloys and products it is necessary to arrange considerably more complex routes for directing feeders and chills to avoid defects such as microporosity.

This is the principle of a reusable pattern to provide an imprint in a disposable sand moulding, comprising a mould produced in two, or more, parts; sufficiently robust to accept liquid metal and yet be able to be destroyed to reveal the final casting, with recycling of the various elements for the next cast. It makes simple sand casting a highly versatile technique, able to handle all of the common alloys, ranging from approximately 30g–5 tonnes (1oz–10,000lb).

Used commonly for cast iron, carbon and stainless steels, aluminium, copper-base, magnesium and nickel-alloys, sand castings can be produced in wall thicknesses down to 3mm (⅛in), of all common shapes, but with drafts of 2–3 degrees. Surface finish is dictated by the type of sand and is generally inferior to some of the more sophisticated processes, but a well-executed sand casting can have a surprisingly attractive surface finish, the general range being 2.5–25 microns (100-1000μ in) RMS.

Sand casting is characterized as a low-cost, relatively low production rate process. Set-up costs are the lowest available, making it highly competitive for small-batch production where a high level of accuracy is not required and sufficient machining allowance is built into the pattern making. Thus, it is often likely to be the first, or only, choice for the home workshop foundry.

Green Sand and Dry Sand Moulding

Green sand is the most basic sand casting method as described above, and it is even possible to mechanize the process, with automation achieving a rate in excess 250 moulds per hour. However, there are some intrinsic limitations with regard to surface finish and dimensional tolerancing, which can imply additional costs due to post-casting operations, hand working and machining, to achieve an acceptable product. For the one-off, typical of the home workshop, this is often not a significant problem. Here, it can be perfectly acceptable, perhaps even preferable, to

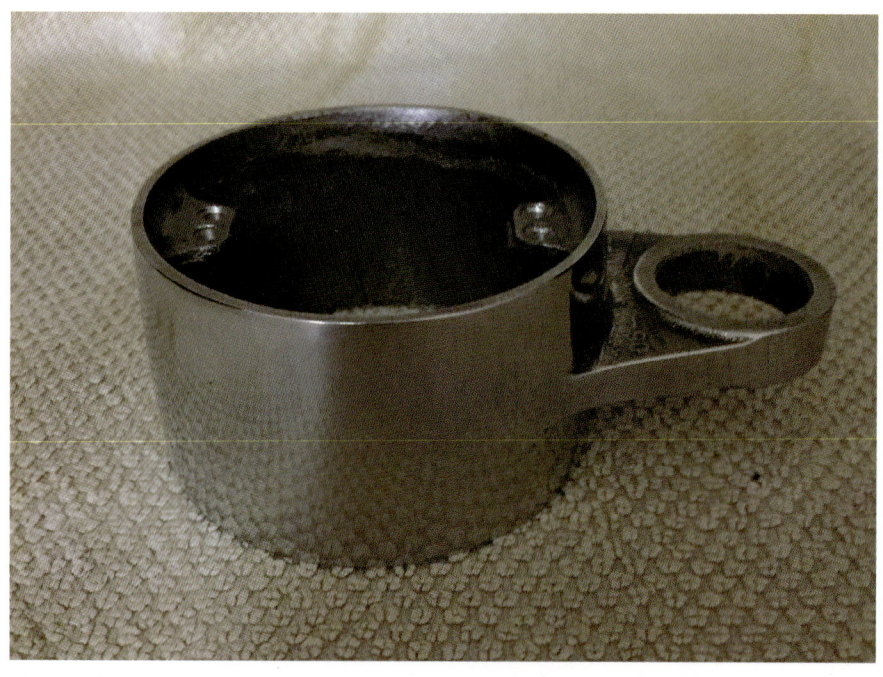

Photo 53 Aluminium Norton speedo holder casting, from home foundry.

Photo 54 Aluminium Norton speedo fitted.

undertake relatively time-consuming cleaning and polishing operations that would be non-viable in a high labour cost industrial environment. Photos 53 and 54 show the fine product that can be achieved with a relatively small degree of post-casting hand work on an aluminium sand casting produced in a home foundry. In volume production, this could be made by an entirely different casting route, requiring far higher set-up costs and consequently a high volume to reach break-even sales.

One route to improved green sand moulding is the dry sand method, where the mould is heated to around 200°C ± 50°C, baking until almost all moisture is removed. This has the effect of strengthening the mould and reducing gassing and porosity problems, enabling these more robust moulds to be stored safely long before use. The disadvantages of a time-consuming and costly drying operation, however, often makes this a less attractive prospect. An alternative, drying only approximately 12mm (½in) depth from the mould cavity, using gas torches, leads to the skin dried mould process.

For the casting of steel the higher temperatures, compared to cast iron, mean that the skin dried process, plus a refractory, high silica, wash of the casting cavity is normally applied. Use of the more expensive zircon sand and additional binders, such as linseed oil, may also be preferred. As pouring temperatures increase, so does the need for improved moulds, beyond those adequate for the ever-popular cast iron.

Sodium Silicate – CO_2 Moulding

This is the first of several sand enhancement techniques used to provide moulds superior to green sand types. The sodium silicate method is also known as 'water-glass' as it has 3–6 per cent water added to the sand. An inorganic liquid binder that remains passive when mixed by the usual means, this pre-mix can be stored safely ready for use.

Once formed into a mould, the blended sand is infused with CO_2, an odourless and non-flammable gas, to provide the reaction:-

$$Na_2SiO_3 + CO_2 \rightarrow Na_2CO_3 + SiO_2$$

Hardening to a strength of ~0.3MPa (40psi) is achieved within seconds, and after ageing at room temperature for twenty-four hours, can reach 0.7–1.4MPa (100–200psi). A problem can arise in the loss of 'collapsibility' after casting, making breakout difficult. Therefore, further additives are often included to encourage burnout during pouring, sufficient to assist subsequent collapsibility.

As with other processes, this one can be used equally effectively for the making of cores. Also, this blended sand may be used in particular areas of a green sand mould, perhaps where improved surface finish or dimensional control is required. It can even employ metal patterns containing passages through which the CO_2 can be pumped, when the mould is complete. Care must be taken to avoid contamination of stored blended sand with surplus CO_2, due to this rapid setting facility, particularly as it requires no heating for the reaction, normally regarded as a positive benefit.

No-Bake Moulding

These methods are known as 'no-bake', 'air set' or 'chemical bonding of sands', relying on alternative blendings to the sodium silicate type. They also produce a reaction at room temperature, employing two more components to produce a hardened mould in a few minutes to a few hours after mixing. This enables sufficient time to produce the mould before the compound hardens.

Again, these are applicable to moulds and/or cores. When aged, they are often treated with a refractory wash to the casting cavity, ready for pouring.

Although a slower method than green sand moulding, no-bake adding around 25 per cent to the time to prepare a mould, there are significant

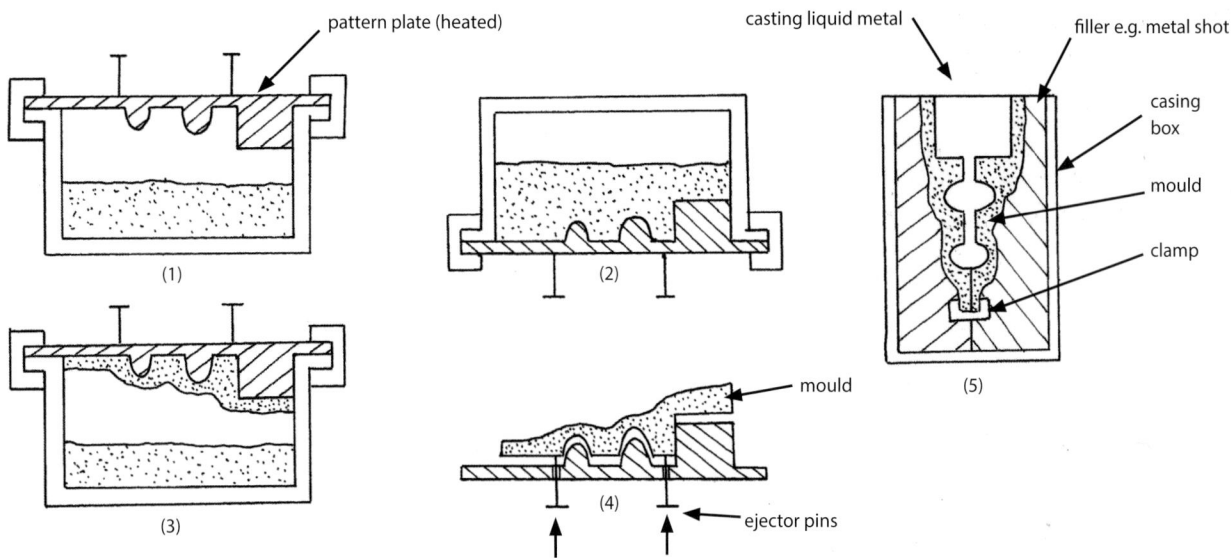

1. Pattern clamped into box containing sand and resin mixture.
2. Moulding box inverted – sand mixture adopts pattern plate profile as shell.
3. Box returned to original orientation – surplus sand falls leaving shell.
4. Shell ejected from pattern plate.
5. Shell halves clamped and encased in casting box ready for casting.

Figure 31 Shell moulding process (schematic).

benefits with improved surface finish; thinner sections; reduced draft; and greater dimensional control. A wide range of alloys and designs are possible and, in contrast to sodium silicate, the breakout facility is unimpaired and has good collapsibility. No-bake, however, requires good venting of the mould in order to allow escape of the binder additives that, on decomposition, can evolve water vapour, hydrogen and hydrocarbons – all potential sources of defects in the casting.

Shell Moulding

While this still utilizes sand, it is rather different to the preceding techniques, producing a high-integrity shell, based on a thermo-setting resin, to receive the casting fluid. The shell is supported in boxes filled with sand, metal shot or even small stones. This process is also known as Croning shell moulding after its German inventor Johannes Croning, who patented the process in 1943.

- The first stage is to provide a metal pattern, often using cast iron. The fine-grained silica sand is then treated with a thin layer of thermo-setting phenolic resin and liquid catalyst, to be heat cured. This sand blend is then used to build up a layer over the metal pattern, causing partial curing of the mixture, as the pattern is held at 200–300°C (392–572°F). This is effected by blowing or dumping the sand on to the pattern until some 10–20mm (⅜in–¾in) of cured sand 'shell' has been obtained.
- Next, the pattern is moved to allow the unbranded sand to fall away, leaving the shell and pattern ready for further heating in an oven, to complete the curing of the blend.
- When fully cured, the shell is removed from the oven and separated from the pattern. These shells have a strength of around 2–3MPa (300–450psi).
- The shells are now glued together or clamped ready for pouring. As shown in Figure 31, these shells may be placed inside boxes, packed to support the poured casting.
- The shell surface, provided by the

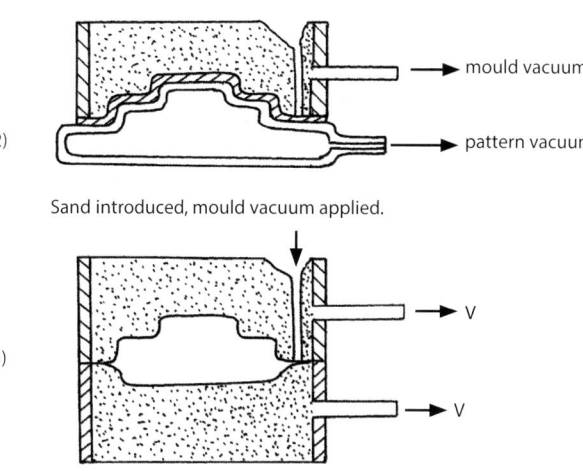

Figure 32 Vacuum moulding process (schematic).

cesses with minor variants to those described above, often developed for particular applications or to overcome specific problems such as casting defects, the three remaining sand processes are noted.

Vacuum Moulding

Also known as the V process, this is different in that it uses no binder, but instead applies a vacuum to hold the sand in position before and during casting, as Figure 32.

The first requirement is the provision of a pattern, which also contains air passages through which evacuation of the mould cavity is made. Complexity of cast shape is therefore dictated by constraints on producing the pattern, with internal air passages. The pattern, for imprint into both cope and drag boxes, is then covered by a film of plastic. This sheet is drawn into intimate contact with the pattern, as the vacuum is formed.

Next, the pattern is enclosed within a special vacuum vessel, into which is entered the unbonded sand, vibrated to fill around the heat shrink plastic-covered pattern and sprue, complete with pouring entry funnel. When ready, a vacuum is applied inside the vessel, thereby compacting the sand against the pattern. Now the pattern vacuum is released and pattern removed, with this thin plastic film still in situ and the sand intact. Both cope and drag are now ready to be brought together and clamped ready for pouring.

A vacuum of around 500 Torr is maintained in both cope and drag while the pouring begins, which vapourizes

fine sand and cured additives, produces a fine surface finish of 0.3–0.4 microns (50–150μ in) RMS, very low draft of 0.5 degrees and thickness down to 1.5mm (¹⁄₁₆in). Castings from 30g (1oz) to 12kg (30lb) are common. Dimensional accuracy is also very high, with a tolerance of around ±0.1mm (0.04in), due to the mould forming around the metal pattern.

This is the process that provides great benefit with regard to appearance and reduction of post-casting operations for fine, relatively small, products. It is essentially a high-productivity process, suitable for medium-batch production of fine castings, but with high set-up and operational costs compared to its less sophisticated alternatives. The thin shell is advantageous, allowing the gases at pouring to escape. The burnout of resin binders provides excellent mould collapsibility, and removal of the casting. Combined with the facility of long-term storage of pre-prepared shells, this makes it a strong candidate for industry.

Note that it has been found far preferable to orientate the joint line of the shells in the vertical plane, rather than horizontally where there are insurmountable problems with sprue design, leading to entrainment defects.

While there is a proliferation of prothe plastic film, filling the cavity and replicating the vacuum-supported moulding cavity of unbonded sand. When cast, the mould collapses spontaneously, making breakout a trivial matter. With no additives used in the sand, there is freedom from sources of porosity. Absence of water vapour and the decomposition products of binders make for a potentially low-defect cast. However, the time incurred producing the vacuum means that it is a slow process, and therefore often used for prototype or special work.

The Cosworth Process

This became a commercially important process during the 1980s, following problems that the Cosworth engineering concern was experiencing with its world-beating engines that had claimed more than 150 F1 Grand Prix victories between 1967 and 1984. The increasing demands on the complex aluminium alloy cylinder heads, which incurred ever greater stresses, encouraged research into more advanced casting methods, which eventually led to the formulation of a complete process for a range of critical aluminium casting applications.

This began by tackling the sources of porosity and microstructure control, as described in Chapter 1, 'Fundamentals of the Casting Process', with emphasis on reducing turbulence and fluid surface-oxide films. These are sources for the bifilms that can become entrained in the melt, and hence result in microporosity and planes of weakness from linear films, seriously affecting ductility and fatigue performance.

The method also succeeded in avoiding pretreatment of the melt with deoxidants and modifying agents, resulting in a considerably purer melt. In order to achieve these aims, as seen in Figure 13, use is made of a furnace with controlled atmosphere to reduce the oxide films on the fluid surface. The mould is fed from a central position in the furnace melt, via a special submerged pump that provides a finely controlled fluid flow, as a bottom-feed, into the moulding cavity. This route eliminates several of the problems of entrapment and distribution of bifilms that exist in conventional gravity-fed processes.

The mould is produced from furan-bonded zircon sand, which avoids the problems of the thermal dimensional change of mould and cores, that reduces dimensional control and restricts the reduction in wall thicknesses experienced with silica sand. These characteristics are often sought in high-performance, low-weight, castings of this ilk. The increased cost of zircon compared to silica sand is claimed to be offset by the above advantages, leading to reduced post-casting machining, and also the high level of reclaimability of the sand.

The process, as described, has claimed advantages of some 25 per cent reduction in casting cycle time, plus highly significant subsequent heat treatment times. Typical alloys of the LM25 type (Al – 7Si-Mg) have been produced successfully with greatly reduced microporosity, and finer dendrite arm spacing microstructure, as a direct result of the improved feeding control compared to conventional processes. With the latter, it is necessary to adopt elaborate and expensive chilling and feeding methods to obtain similar microstructures and mechanical properties. The overall result is an improvement of production yields from 55–85 per cent, machining allowances of only 1.5–2mm (0.06–0.08in) and weight reduction of 10–12 per cent.

The FM Process

Whereas the Cosworth process was designed for aluminium, the FM method was developed by the French firm Pont-à-Mousson for making thin-wall ferrous castings. 'FM' comes from *fonte mince*, thin iron, and uses a bottom-filling method with similarities to the Cosworth process.

FM can accommodate a variety of sand moulds, from green sand to shell mouldings, with positive pressure applied to the fluid metal, and negative pressure to the mould, so permitting rapid filling. Handling grey and ductile irons, steels, nickel-base superalloys, and stainless steels, it can be a versatile process with a capability for producing wall thicknesses down to 2.5–3mm (0.10–0.12in).

SAND

Whilst we use the generics sand and sand casting, it would be more accurate to refer to the sand as an aggregate; for it is always a combination of sand and additives, such as binders, that form this moulding material. Aggregates could then also cover the non-sand materials used for non-permanent moulds. There are many aggregates that can form a temporary mould, accept the cast, and be subsequently destroyed – even including the metal shot and binder used in some ferrous castings.

Before examining the main types of sand widely available – silica, zircon, chromite and olivine – we need to recognize the four main functions of the sand when used in a moulding. These are: refractory, cohesive, permeability and collapsibility.

Refractory

Refractory properties determine the ability to retain shape and surface coherence in the presence of the sudden and dramatic onslaught of the fluid metal as it rushes through the gating system, into the casting void and on to final solidification.

Cohesive

Cohesive properties are essential to retain the mould's image of the casting pattern and gating systems, without collapse before, during, or after removal of the pattern and other moulding equipment.

Permeability

Permeability is the ability of the sand mould to allow the escape of the gas, evolved from the fluid and its sudden filling of the casting cavity, while retaining the required shape and surface finish of the casting.

Collapsibility

Collapsibility is required in order to retrieve the casting after completion.

The ideal is for the sand to fall free of the castings with minimal effort, but this can often be difficult while achieving the former requirements for a sound casting. Nevertheless, there are additives and processes where this can be achieved – a not insignificant criteria for sand and process selection.

From the above requirements placed on a sand aggregate, selection of the best system requires some compromise. In practice, solutions have been found to provide remarkably good castings in a wide variety of non-ferrous and ferrous materials.

Mixing

In industrial applications the mixing of the sand-and-additive(s) aggregate is made in machines known as Mullers, in a manner analogous to producing concrete from sand, cement and ballast in a concrete mixer. For the home workshop, this is a process that can be achieved by using premixed sands and/or substituting hand mixing for machine (sometimes amusingly referred to in industry as 'man-draulic' processing).

Testing

The next requirement, having produced the aggregate – for instance a green sand mixture of 89 per cent silica sand, 8 per cent clay and 3 per cent water – is to ensure, ideally by testing, the following properties: grain size; moisture; permeability; and compressive strength. Realistically, small-scale operations can be expected to achieve little better than a nominal testing, but a grasp of grain size and moisture content is important for consistent results. With experience, a sufficient idea of permeability and compressive strength can be also reasonably gauged.

Grain Size

This is measured by passing a known amount of clean and dry sand through a series of sieves of decreasing mesh size and then weighing that retained in each sieve to calculate an American Foundry Society (AFS) number, with which foundry workers are familiar. Where metrication is the norm, a good rule of thumb conversion from AFS to μm (m x 10^{-6}) is:

$$\mu m \sim \frac{15000}{AFS\ No} \quad \text{e.g. AFS 100} \sim 150 \mu m$$

As a general rule the range is around AFS 50–AFS 200 (300μm–75μm), *see* Bibliography, *Campbell, 2011*.

Moisture Content

This is normally done using a special piece of equipment that measures the electrical conductivity of a standard compacted sample of sand. It is possible to achieve this from first principles, by measuring the weight loss in a 50g sample of sand before and after drying at 110°C, for sufficient time to remove all the entrapped moisture. This is, as noted above, an important measurement as a consistent, low value, of moisture is required to avoid defects such as porosity arising from excessive moisture. However, insufficient moisture also affects cohesiveness and thus increases the risk of mould collapse

Photo 55 Speedy sand moisture tester. (Photo: Colin Mills)

Photo 56 Speedy, weighing unit of sand. (Photo: Colin Mills)

Photo 57 Speedy, accepting sand sample. (Photo: Colin Mills)

before casting is completed (*see* Photos 55 to 61).

Permeability

The mould needs to be able to cope with the evolution of gas during casting and allow escape through the walls to avoid gas trapped as porosity. Figure 34 shows the basics of a permeability tester, which takes a standardized sample of compressed sand and measures the effects, either flow rate or pressure drop, when a $10g/cm^2$ air pressure is applied. This is normally calibrated to provide a direct readout as an AFS permeability number.

Compressive Strength

Finally, a measure of strength or hardness is usually obtained by testing a compacted sample, for green compressive strength as a simple compression test. Fracture of the specimen usually lies between 10–30psi (0.07–0.2MPa), indicating a near-optimum content of water and clay for a simple green sand sample. A hardness test, using a special indenter with AFS green hardness number, can also be used as a measure of strength.

Silica Sand

The universal availability of silica sand has led to its widespread adoption throughout the foundry world, but more recently concern has been raised about the potential danger of silicosis from its dust. While a cheap and abundant material with good resistance to the trauma of suddenly encountering high-temperature, low-viscosity, metal – it does have a serious limitation for controlling dimensional accuracy and differential thermal expansion. This is due to the alpha-quartz to beta-quartz phase transition at ~530°C, of ~2.5 per cent volume change. A problem can arise when a core and mould see different temperatures, as for an aluminium casting where a core sees the full fluid temperature, well above the silica transition temperature, while the average mould temperature would often only reach 50 per cent of the pouring temperature, leaving it below the transition temperature (530°C). Thus, a length change of 1 per cent greater in core than mould could occur, amounting to a damaging 5mm in a 500mm long core. This could lead to the core pushing through a casting wall; and potentially even more severe effects in the, higher temperature, ferrous alloys.

Ways have been devised to reduce this effect, such as in Swedish silica sand with some 25 per cent of feldspars. This improves matters, although it is less suitable for high-temperature alloys. Other methods have been reported, but it is probably best to use alternative sands if a likely problem with differential expansion of core and mould is anticipated.

Zircon Sand

Zircon has distinctly different characteristics to silica sand, which often makes it an ideal choice for the manufacture of cores, and even for moulds, although the significant increase in cost compared to silica can make it

Photo 58 Filling unit with proprietary measuring compound. (Photo: Colin Mills)

Photo 59 Clamping sand and compound in the pressure cylinder. (Photo: Colin Mills)

Photo 60 Pressure unit showing sand moisture content. (Photo: Colin Mills)

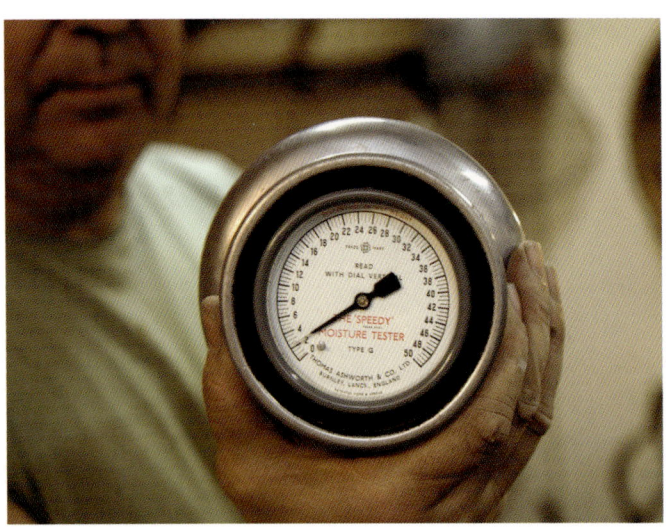

Photo 61 Detail of Photo 60. (Photo: Colin Mills)

castings, which has both the advantage of promoting improved microstructures while making the casting of thin sections less difficult.

The high density, twice that of Silica, can be a disadvantage in the more mechanized systems with the greatly increased weight of drag and cope, but this is generally less of a problem, compared to the cost factor, for the small-scale operator. Again, the erosion of patterns due the abrasiveness of zircon sand is more of a problem for larger batch manufacture, insignificant for normal small-scale work.

less attractive where qualities such as dimensional accuracy are not vital.

A light-coloured sand, generally comprising fine rounded grains, perhaps its most important feature is its low linear coefficient of expansion and, unlike silica, lack of phase transformations that makes it particularly useful in maintaining dimensional stability during casting. With a density near to that of aluminium, it is ideal for cores in aluminium castings, having a neutral density that aids stability during pouring into moulds with complex cores. A high thermal diffusivity, greater than silica, can provide a chilling for

Chromite Sand

Chromite has, like zircon, a very low coefficient of thermal expansion and good chilling characteristics, making it popular for use as a facing aggregate with silica, for steel castings.

However, after recycling, it can be prone to chromite glaze, where a surface decomposition of the chromite mould facing can lead to fayalite (Fe_2SiO_4, melting point 1,250°C) formation, leading to a loss of fine surface finish. Recycling of the fayalite-contaminated sand can lead to further problems. The chromite tends to oxidize at steel pouring temperatures, to Fe_2O_3 and Cr_2O_3, which, combined with carbon from organic binders, can lead to surface defects of the casting. Finally, the grain shape tends to be less rounded than zircon, leading to large volume loss during recycling a silica–chromite aggregate.

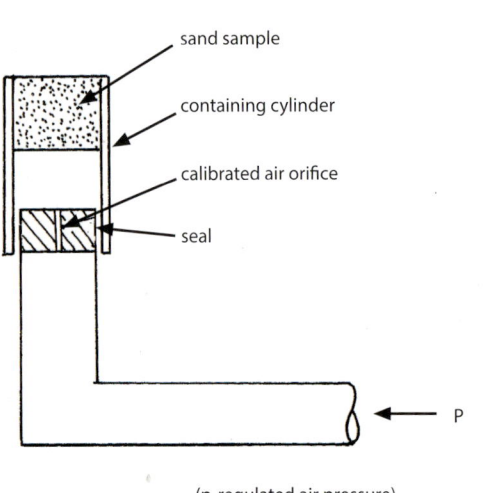

Figure 33 Sand permeability tester (schematic).

Olivine Sand

Olivine has the advantages of low thermal expansion and, unlike chromite–silica, no reaction when combined with chromite for high-alloy steel and high-manganese steel castings. It is also considered to be safe.

Unfortunately, olivine is not compatible with the most popular binder, furan no-bake (FNB). It requires use of phenolic-urethane no-bake (PUNB), a specially formulated binder, with consequent handling complications. Olivine is also similar to chromite with regard to its less rounded grain shape, derived from its source as crushed rock, making it less attractive for handling and moulding.

These disadvantages can outweigh the positive aspects sufficiently to make olivine less popular than the other alternatives.

There are a number of other refractory elements, often chosen because of local availability; as well as bonded aluminium shot and steel shot, for aluminium and steel castings. Carbon, in the form of aggregate powder, has been used for expendable moulds, but is more important for permanent moulds, machined from the solid. This has been used for zinc–aluminium alloy castings, even for steel railway wheels by a special process.

PLASTER MOULDINGS

This is a process capable of producing, generally smaller, castings of a near net shape, with dimensional accuracy, shape complexity and fine finish, that is greater than any of the sand moulds described hitherto.

It is, however, limited by temperature to the non-ferrous alloys of aluminium, copper and zinc. Magnesium is not suitable, due to its risk of exploding when in the presence of water retained in the plastic mould.

The advantages of producing near net shape can readily be seen in the manufacture of small, complex-geometry items, such as aluminium impellers with curved vanes typical of water pumps. The machining of vanes and bosses would be very costly, and therefore the ability to use them 'as cast' is of great benefit, even for one-offs. In practice, ~90 per cent of plaster castings are under 10kg, but the process has been used for aluminium castings approaching 2 tonnes (~2 tons), although usually only up to ~30kg (~70lb).

Plaster castings can be likened to those possible with investment casting (see Chapter 3), with the advantages of: fine surface finish, 2–4µm (75–150µin) RMS; intricate designs, with negative draft when using flexible rubber patterns; dimensional accuracy, approaching that of investment casting; thin sections of 0.5–1.00mm (0.02–0.04in); slow cooling of casting, due to low thermal conductivity; and ability to incorporate multiple chills rapid cooling, required for local improvement of microstructure and mechanical properties.

The disadvantages of the process are: high cost, due to the length of preparation time of the plaster, from mixing to pre-process drying, plus expensive equipment; use of multiple set-ups, unless very low-volume production is required; and lack of mould permeability, apart from the foamed plaster process, requiring vacuum and/or pressure assistance to remove the gasses generated in casting, which cannot escape through the mould as in sand casting. Normally, a metal mould is used. If a wooden pattern is used, it needs thorough sealing to prevent contamination by the plaster slurry.

There are four types of plaster moulding: conventional; match plate pattern; Antioch process; and the foamed plastic process. These are dependent on the use of plaster as calcium sulphate.

Plaster

Calcium sulphate exists in three forms, often known as gypsum. When raised above ~120°C the resultant water loss produces the form known commonly as plaster of Paris. When this is raised above ~160°C, it becomes anhydrous calcium sulphate (Ca SO_4). When plaster of Paris is mixed with water, it will set to a solid after a short time, thereby providing a material that can conveniently be cast around a pattern to form the mould. Subsequently, the plaster mould must be heated in an oven to remove the excess moisture. The low heat capacity of the plaster makes it a slow cooling material, which has the advantage of promoting metal flow into thin sections, but where faster cooling rates are required then chills are incorporated into the mould for differential cooling and microstructure control.

Mould drying temperatures vary widely but commonly are between 120°C–250°C, although in certain cases up to 850°C has been used. Once the temperature has been proven for each case, it needs to be controlled accurately, to ±5°C, for consistent results.

Patterns

Aluminium alloy is normally used for patterns and core boxes, otherwise brass or zinc can be employed. Alternatively, flexible rubber patterns may be used, with up to 30 degree negative draft possible, thereby enabling the casting of highly complex designs.

Epoxy resin has also been successfully used for patterns requiring a high level of dimensional accuracy. Wood patterns need to withstand the pouring of the liquid plaster slurry, which may be satisfactory for limited use, but relies on a good sealant to protect the pattern from damage, so metal patterns are preferred in production work.

Casting Metals

The aluminium alloys are the natural choice for plaster moulding, and copper-base alloys can be cast successfully, with some limitations. Copper-base alloys are restricted to ≤ 5% Pb, with greater amounts leading to inferior surface finish. As noted earlier, magnesium is not suitable for casting, but zinc-based alloys, typically Zn -10 Al – 0.05Mg, are widely used for intricate castings.

Conventional Plaster Moulding

This begins with the common preparation of the plaster, which follows the route:

- Dry plaster elements mix
- Add these to water
- Soak, then mix (2–5 min each process)
- Coating of patterns (for later removal)
- Pour in plaster as slurry, sets ~15 min
- Pattern removal, and heat moulds to dry
- Add cores and assemble moulds ready for casting

When ready, the moulds may be preheated to around 120°C, ready for pouring. However, due to the low permeability of the moulds (< 2 AFS plaster, compared to > 80 AFS sand), it is normally necessary to apply a vacuum to the mould, or pressure to the casting metal, gravity pouring usually being insufficient.

Match Plate Pattern Mouldings

This is essentially similar to the conventional process, but by using metal match plate patterns, very high dimensional accuracy and surface finish are possible, see Figure 34. This is usually applicable to larger items, with patterns weighing typically from 10–200kg (20–450lb). The arrangement of the pattern, mounted on a metal plate, typically 10mm (⅜in) thickness, requires precision in assembly of cope and drag. With these moulds, it is common to produce vent holes as the slurry is poured for mould separation and compressed air. Drying is generally 120–200°C for twelve to seventy-two hours. Pouring is usually pressure assisted, due to the aforementioned low permeability of the moulds.

Antioch Process

The Antioch process was developed to overcome the lack of permeability of the conventional moulding process, providing a value of 15–30 AFS, compared to the usual 1–2 AFS. This is achieved by manipulation of the drying process with dehydration and rehydration. An advantage is that moulds made by this method do not shrink, undergoing a very small expansion, unlike the conventional process.

While a more time-consuming and expensive preparation is required, it results in a mould that can accept pouring, as for a sand casting, usually without need for preheating. If very thin sections are employed, vacuum assistance may be required.

Foamed Plaster Moulding

In this process an improved permeability is achieved, while also providing an improved dry strength of the mould, compared to the Antioch method. This is produced by applying a foaming agent, such as alkyl aryl sulfonate, during preparation of the slurry.

Permeability of 15–30 AFS is normal, and air bubbles just below the mould surface provide a means of gas escape without loss of surface finish. As for the Antioch process, normal foundry pouring methods can be employed successfully.

Ceramic Moulding

Ceramic moulding shares with investment casting many of the advantages of a true near net shape process with

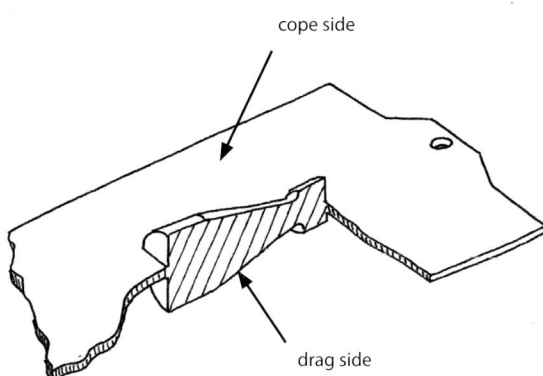

Figure 34 Match plate pattern

high dimensional accuracy and fine surface finish, often with minimal or no subsequent machining. It has a further significant advantage over plaster casting because it can handle the higher temperatures required for the ferrous alloys, including low- and high-alloy steels and the 'exotics', from titanium to high-nickel alloys. The size range is also advantageous, from small items to the very large, essentially limited only by handling and material costs.

When originally devised, the major disadvantage of the process was the high cost of the moulding material, an aggregate ceramic slurry. However, the two processes described here, Shaw and Unicast, provide solutions to this, for sufficiency large items. These employ a mould with a backing that provides the support for the critical inner ceramic shell, thereby dramatically reducing material and recycling costs.

The Shaw Process

This can either use a complete mould from the refractory ceramic, or a composite with a ceramic inner, around 10mm (⅜in) thick, supported by a backing moulding to lower material costs and recyclability, as above. This latter method requires double the simple two-part (cope and drag) moulds, making four moulds – the backing, then inner.

Small items can be most economically produced from the simple, homogenous mould with the ceramic slurry poured around the pattern in the container. The slurry comprises finely pulverized zircon and/or calcinated mullite, typically in a 3:1 ratio of former to latter, with added binder of hydrolyzed ethyl silicate in the ratio of ~1 part binder to 10 parts refractory aggregate.

Prior to pouring, the pattern is treated with a wax silicone release agent, then the slurry is gravity poured into the container to invest the pattern and form the mould. The chemical gelling action is complete within minutes, producing a stiff rubber-like mould that can be stripped off the pattern, without loss of integrity of the mould, while enabling complex shapes to be produced.

The next stage is burn off, where the green mould is fired by igniting the volatiles given off from the gelling reaction. This local heating of the mould surface generates a very fine, three-dimensional network of cracks, in effect a micro-crazing of the surface, sufficient for permeability without impairing the surface finish. The micro-crazing also has a stress relieving aspect that maintains the dimensional stability that is an important aspect of the process.

The composite method is shown in Figure 35. The initial stage is to pack the backing refractory, a sodium silicate-based aggregate, produced to a pattern with allowance for the ceramic shell slurry to be poured in to fill the mould to the final pattern. This uses a slurry similar to that of the solid-body mould. Prior to pouring the slurry, the sodium silicate is treated with a CO_2 gas to harden, as in Figure 36, step 2.

The stripping and firing stages are similar to the previous method, and finally drag and cope are accurately assembled ready for pouring of the casting metal.

The Unicast Process

While apparently very similar to the Shaw process, Unicast has the important difference in the method of moulding stabilization, before fully set. This eliminates movement of the mould on difficult to cast long, thin sections

– and produces high-quality product. The other significant difference is the order of preparation of the two-stage backing/ceramic mould. In the Unicast process the order is reversed, with the ceramic shell being produced before the refractory backing.

The advantages of the solid-body ceramic process makes it of potential interest for small-scale and prototype work of complex parts that are difficult to machine and expensive to make, such as turbine parts subject to high-temperature operation. These benefits include: the simplicity of tooling for pattern making; short method, planning, cycle time; near net shape of product reduces or eliminates machining operations; wide range of casting metals, ferrous and non-ferrous; conventional method pouring can be used without mould preheat; and overall costs can be lower than alternative processes required for high-quality work.

SINGLE-USE MOULDS – SINGLE-USE PATTERNS

Investment Casting

Also commonly known as lost-wax casting, from the early workers where the wax pattern was melted out and absorbed by the porous shell hence lost, investment casting is now firmly established as the precision casting process *par excellence*. This is a single-use pattern process, but although a relatively slow and expensive process, it can achieve commercial viability

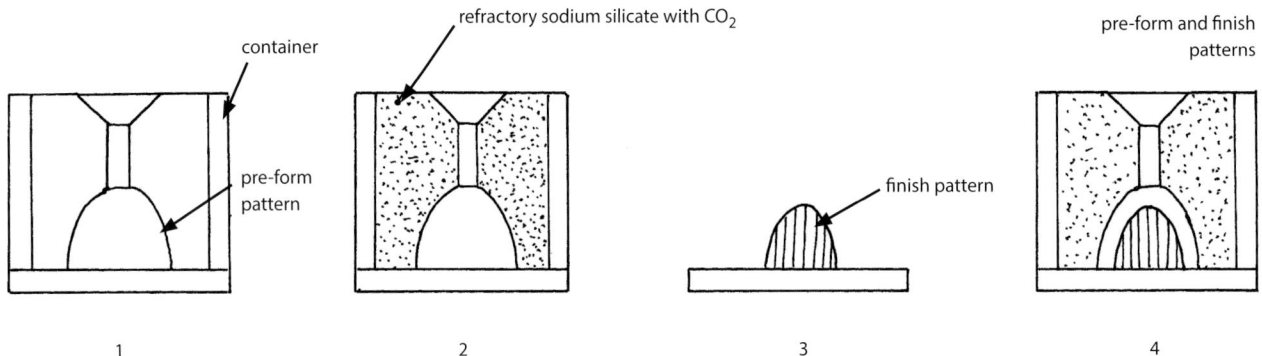

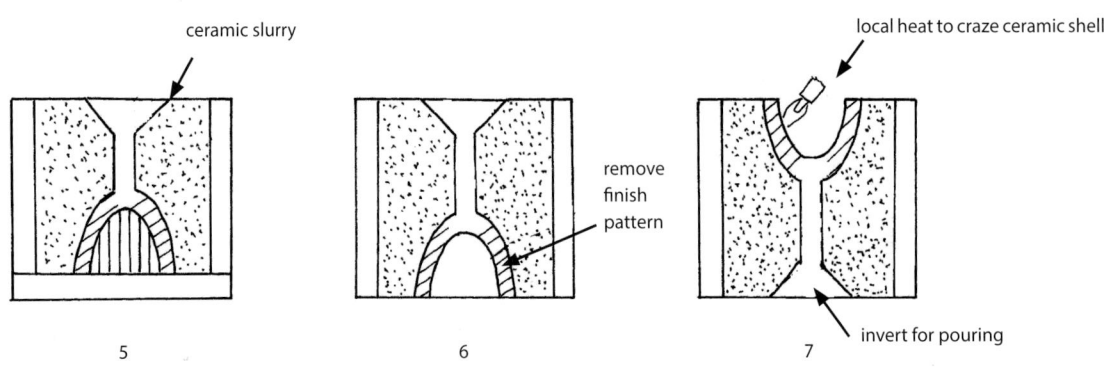

Figure 35 Shaw composite mould process producing a shell.

with multiple moulds combined from a single pour. The benefits of near net shape, dimensional accuracy, and superbly fine surface finish, have been recognized since the earliest times, as outlined in the History section. Perhaps somewhat surprisingly, it is a process that has only become prominent in the industrial and medical world since the second half of the twentieth century, particularly from the Second World War and the 1940s, where dramatically increasing demands on materials and designs were being made by the remarkable advances in technology stimulated by global conflict.

Perhaps the most spectacular opportunities afforded by investment casting have been in the aerospace industry, where it is undoubtedly the case that jet engine development could not have been achieved without the extraordinary achievements of investment casting technology in turbine blade technology. The efficiency of the engine is directly related to the temperature of operation and the ability to withstand these high temperatures and stresses for prolonged periods has been established in the 10,000-hour creep test, as described in Chapter 5, 'Materials for Casting'. Investment casting is able to accommodate the exotics, including the high-nickel alloys, cast as a single crystal (for ultimate creep resistance), and incorporating an amazing array of minute internal cooling passages. The result is a small blade, many of which are assembled for the hot stage of the engine, now running at around 1,700°C, which is substantially beyond the nominal melting point of alloy (figure 63)!

This ability of the process to handle any of the castable metals means that it is used for alloys that could not be cast successfully with other processes described earlier, and it can also reduce or eliminate expensive machining operations, becoming ever more important as ultra-high strength and wear-resistant alloys are required by advancing designs.

Apart from the fundamental characteristics of removal of the pattern by dissolving it from the mould shell, the process has many similarities with that of the ceramic moulding process described earlier. It is basically a fine shell surrounded by a courser refractory backing, into which the casting fluid is poured, to produce a casting with ultra-fine finish. However, the ability to produce a pattern in a material such as wax or plastic enables complex shapes with no limitation on draft for removal, nor centreline marking from split moulds, as for previous methods.

This is a process predominantly employed from the very small (a few grams) to moderate-sized product, typically below 10kg (20lb), taking advantage of detail design and surface finish for critical components, from aerospace, petro-chemical valves, racing engines, dentistry, joint replacements, to artistic and jewellery work.

Whilst the aerospace applications tend to be the province of large-scale operations, with large commercial commitments for specialized products, requiring microstructure control for the ultimate of single crystal growth – the other extreme is the low-volume manufacture of cosmetic items such as jewellery. This can employ equipment accessible to the small-scale or home-based worker, with a small furnace for melting precious or semi-precious metals and casting in simplified apparatus containing a simple investment mould made from a handcrafted, wax-based pattern, all the operations being viable in a small workshop, as described in Chapter 2.

The advantages of the process are self-evident, but it is worth noting that for critical, highly stressed designs, the aforementioned fine surface finish and visual integrity of investment casting can belie an internal structure that can be less than flawless. With the understanding of bifilm theory, as discussed in Chapter 1, the common practice of gravity pouring from exposed furnace fluid, and the use of poorly designed sprue and gating systems, can lead to some of the worst practices in the foundry industry for generations and entrapment of the bifilms that can find their way into the individual casting microstructure. This is a cautionary point, see Bibliography, *Campbell, 2011*. While this is appropriate for items where high integrity is vital, such as aircraft landing gear, it is fortunately of no consequence whatsoever for the home worker, where only cosmetic aspects prevail.

The basic features of the process are shown in Photo 62. The first step is to produce the pattern, which can be made, as in the historical process, simply by carving from the wax-based block, to provide the required shape. Common commercial practice is to replicate the final casting as a master pattern in a suitable material such as wood or aluminum. The present state-of-the-art 3D printers present opportunities here to generate either master patterns by powder deposition, from CAD software; or alternatively, the pattern mould directly from the CAD, as has already become common for high-value sand castings, as seen earlier.

The master pattern is used to produce a permanent reverse mould, normally in metal, to form the expendable pattern in wax or plastic. This is the foundation for the investment coatings that make up the shell into which the casting metal will finally be poured.

The individual wax patterns are often connected in an assembly around a tree, enabling a number of castings to be produced from a single pouring and providing surprisingly good productivity for making small items. These individual patterns are melted or glued into the assembly, as in Photo 62, making a sufficiently robust structure that can be taken to the next step – investment.

In industry, it is most usual to use a dipping process to produce the investment shell. Firstly, the fine slurry is used for the pattern immersion, providing the finest finish for the as-cast surface. This is followed by a series of coarser refractory baths to build up a shell, typically of eight coats thickness, ready for firing. The alternative method, often employed in small-scale operations, is to immerse the pattern assembly in a flask of investment slurry that, when set, provides a substantial shell and mould. Normally, the investment slurry flask is subjected to vibration and vacuum in order to remove the trapped gas that would impair the shell surface.

Either way, the next stage, after the setting of the investment shell, is burnout, where the pattern is heated to above its melting point, to run from the shell. The shell is then subjected to high temperature, typically 500–1,000°C, in an oven in readiness for pouring of the casting fluid, whilst the mould is at temperature. It should be noted that the burnout stage presents the shell with its greatest stresses, and danger of failure, due to the pattern expansion on heating. Methods to alleviate this danger include sudden heating to make the pattern surface melt before the bulk, enabling release from the shell; as well as pattern compounds with preferential temperature characteristics.

The mould is then ready for pouring, then breakout, followed by post-casting operations beginning with removal of the individual items from the tree, as described later. For wax burnout details, see Appendix II, Practical Casting and Process Notes.

Evaporative Pattern and Lost Foam Process

These are two forms of a similar process. In the evaporative pattern, also known as the full mould process, the pattern is produced, in its simplest form, by carving from a block of expanded polystyrene (EPS), or expanded polymethylmethacrylate (EPMMA). This simple method can be used to attach, by contact adhesive, various shapes to a make quite a complex structure. This is then placed in a container and backfilled, around the EPS or EPMMA pattern, with bonded sand. The pattern remains in situ while the casting is poured, causing it to evaporate ahead of the fluid metal, providing simply a casting, a vapourized pattern, and loose sand. Like all things that appear to be too good to be true, there are some basic aspects of both this and the more sophisticated, lost foam process, that mitigate against the pursuit of high-integrity castings – despite some justified claims of this as a low-cost, high-value process. Caution should be exercised, until full process development has been achieved, before expecting the level of microstructural integrity regularly achieved with com-

Photo 62 Constructing a wax pattern tree, for investment casting. (Photo: Colin Mills)

peting methods.

Another method of producing the evaporative pattern is by expanding the EPS from pre-expanded pellets and injecting them into a heated split die, usually of aluminium alloy, in order to provide a reproducible EPS pattern, as Figure 36. This pattern comprises, typically, 2.5 per cent polymer and 97.5 per cent air! It is then used in a manner similar to that described above to produce the casting from the sand mould. Evaporation of the pattern is accommodated by the porous nature of the mould but, nevertheless, is a potential source of entrapment and disturbance of casting fluid flow with turbulence and associated structural variability. Early use of silica sand resulted in loss of dimensional control due to the phase change at ~570°C of the sand, noted before, and use of alumina ceramic beads greatly improved matters with the lost foam process application.

In the lost foam process, the EPS pattern is made as before, normally by injecting into the mould, and often consisting of a construction of a number of parts glued together, as in complex items such as aluminium vehicle cylinder blocks. Smaller items may be jointed in a tree gating formation, similar to that used in investment casting patterns. Also, in a manner reminiscent of investment casting, the EPS pattern is dipped in a fine ceramic slurry to produce a thin shell, albeit thinner than that used in investment casting. This structure is then back-filled with sand or ceramic beads sufficient to support the incoming casting fluid, but avoiding crushing of the pattern prior to pouring. Clearly, this requires some practice and expertise.

Pouring proceeds as before, with the EPS evaporating ahead of the incoming casting fluid. Escape of the vapour is effected through the thin shell, but with the same potential difficulties. The process offers many advantages in volume production of complex parts requiring a high level of dimensional accuracy, while wear on tooling is negligible, of great benefit in a busy foundry. Successful results can be obtained with careful attention to process development, but there have been noted examples where insufficient work has been done to overcome the problems of microstructure integrity. This may only be revealed at the final stage of volumetric non-destructive testing (NDT), such as radiography, see Chapter 6. Particular difficulties can arise from the initial gravity filling of the sprue, where turbulent flow can create entrapment of surface films, as noted previously in Chapter 1.

However, this is potentially a process of interest to the small-scale worker, especially where mechanical properties are not of prime significance, as it may offer the ability to quickly and economically produce prototype castings in the light alloys. The replicast process is a variation of the lost foam process, where the EPS pattern is invested with a slightly thicker shell, sufficient to be self-supporting. This is then fired to remove the expanded polymer pattern, presenting a shell that can accept casting fluid in a similar manner to investment casting. While this would appear to offer the best of several worlds, it has not yet reached wide-scale acceptance. The shell is supported in an aggregate-filled container and, with the provision of a well-designed filling system – often overlooked in investment casting practice, including counter-gravity methods – this could yet be seen as an important casting practice.

MULTIPLE-USE MOULDS

Permanent Mould Casting

This is the most basic form of die casting, also known as gravity – or low-pressure – die casting, to differentiate it from the high-pressure die casting, the later usually known simply as die casting.

In the gravity or low-pressure casting into a permanent mould, the process is relatively straightforward, involving transfer of the casting fluid into a permanent mould that replicates the

---

Summary of Investment Casting Capabilities

- Final surface finish, 1.3–4µm (50–125µin) RMS
- High dimensional accuracy (0.1mm in the first 25mm, 0.005in in the first 1in)
- No shape, draft, or complexity, restraint
- No parting line
- No casting metal restriction
- Size 2g–~10kg (0.1oz–20lb)
- Wall ≥ 0.5mm (0.02in)

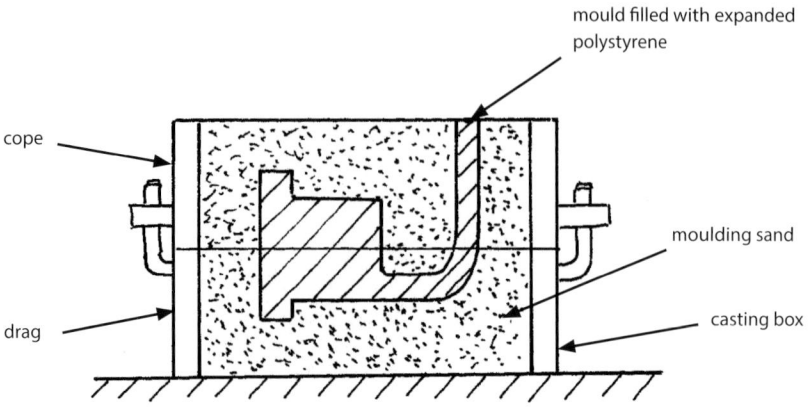

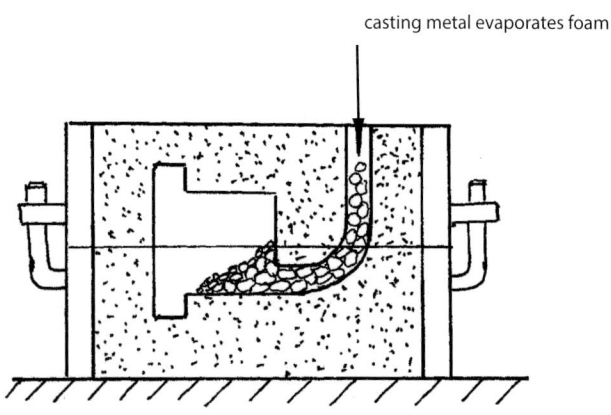

Figure 36 Evaporative pattern process

shape of the product, thereby requiring no pattern as a direct part of the casting process. The production of the die, usually in a split form about a centre-line, can present a difficult and expensive task if the product form is less than simple to machine and prepare, as steel dies are the norm.

The second restriction is casting metals – normally limited to aluminium, magnesium, zinc and copper-base alloys – due to the temperature constraints on the die.

Somewhat counter-intuitively however, this is a process that has been practised, in certain forms, since almost the earliest times of casting – witness the stone die described in the section on 'History of Castings'. Also, with some ingenuity and skill in modelling steel die profiles, it can be adopted in the home workshop for small castings in the light alloys, uniquely practical for making multiple identical parts. A good example is the model aero engine crankcase shown in Photo 63. This was produced by the simple die and gravity-fed process, to produce the excellent finish and good mechanical properties required for a part at the heart of the fundamentally simple, but highly efficient, power unit with a specific power output comparable to an F1 racing car!

Despite the above, all forms of die casting are generally reckoned to require large-volume production to justify the set-up costs, particularly die manufacture, in the industrial environment. Die lifecycles can be expected to range from tens to hundreds of thousands, with the light alloys, but far lower for higher melting point alloys. The process advantages include high dimensional accuracy, good microstructural control, and rapid casting cycles – making it a well-established process for smaller parts in the automotive industry, from pistons and pulleys to engine covers.

A number of variations, assisting metal transfer from furnace to die, have been developed, including tilt pour, where a more controlled transfer can reduce turbulence and increase flow. This is a method that was also critical in improving castings of the difficult-to-cast aluminium bronzes, in the Deville process (*see* Chapter 5); and in solving major problems with the Cosworth process. The low-pressure process, also known as low-pressure permanent mould (LPPM), utilizes 2–15psi pressure, or equivalent as vacuum-assisted filling, to aid the filling process and improve cast integrity through

Photo 63 Crankcase, one-piece aluminium alloy die casting.

increased fill and cooling rates.

One particular feature, common to all die casting processes, is the need to provide deliberate means for gas escape from the mould, in the form of vents. Often this is achieved by allowing leakage of the casting across the moulding joint line, ejecting as a fine flash that can be easily trimmed after ejection from the die.

Die Casting

Die casting is the term universally adopted for the high-pressure type of die- or permanent-mould process, where the casting fluid is injected at > 10,000psi (> 10MPa), so that this forced feeding has a significant impact on the features described for the preceding methods, improving to a condition of near net shape; and often entirely eliminating machining operation, such as the flange faces of internal combustion engine carburettor bodies from the familiar zinc-base alloy die castings.

Clearly, this a process with considerable costs for preparation, and usually the province of high-volume production in an industrial environment. Nevertheless, it has proven highly successful, to the point of ubiquity, for large quantity production of small, high-precision, light alloy products, in demanding applications of well-proven designs. Hot and cold chamber processes are used.

Squeeze and Semi-Solid Casting

Squeeze Casting

These are essentially variants of (high-pressure) die casting. However, whereas die casting can suffer from significant internal porosity – due not so much to entrapped air as to the turbulence during the rapid filling under pressure and the behaviour of biofilms – squeeze casting can avoid such defects.

In squeeze casting the casting fluid is forced, via large gating systems, into the tool steel die at pressures in the range of ~2,000–30,000psi (~12–200MPa). The pressure is maintained during solidification and runners are used to feed the cooling shrinkage, unlike conventional die casting. The gates need to be designed to freeze at the appropriate time, permitting feeding from the runners. The alloys cast are principally aluminium, then zinc, magnesium, and copper alloys; and even certain ferrous alloys are possible.

The system is designed to operate with a low fluid entry flowrate, to reduce turbulence problems and then promote directional solidification in the die, enabling the pressurized runners to feed the cooling shrinkage. This results in achievement of high dimensional tolerances and an improved microstructure, particularly reduction in the microporosity, noted above, that can occur in the conventional die casting process.

Semi-Solid Casting

Semi-solid casting is exploited through the rheocasting or thixotropic methods. These utilize the condition of an alloy where it is cast in a partially liquid and solid state. This presents a liquid with discrete solidification 'islands' that be processed as a slurry.

- ◆ **Rheocasting** During rheocasting, the partially solidified slurry is agitated by mechanical stirring. This breaks up the newly formed dendrites, which form ~25–35 per cent of the slurry. It is then forced, in this partially solidified state, into the die at high pressure. Rapid solidification ensues, as the mix is not superheated, so promoting an improved microstructure.

- **Thixotropic Casting** This method takes the same initial approach as far as the rheocasting metal slurry, stirred in the partially solidified condition to break up the dendritic structure, then cooled to a block of pre-determined size for subsequent die casting. The block is then reheated to the semi-solid condition, ~55–65 per cent solid, making a coherent block of material. This is then placed in the entry chamber of a cold-process die casting machine, then transferred into the die. The low entry velocities avoid the problems of turbulence and subsequent microporosity, and the reduced die temperatures benefit die life, while providing a preferred microstructure. In addition, it is safe to apply subsequent heat treatments, such as solution treatment of high-strength aluminium alloys such as 7075-T6; for use in critical aerospace applications. The previous virtues of semi-solid die casting can also apply, including use of ultra-fine sections, down to ~0.2mm (0.008in).

Centrifugal Casting

There are three forms of this process: centrifugal; semi-centrifugal; and true centrifugal casting.

Centrifugal

This the process of particular interest to the home worker, as it simply utilizes the centrifugal force generated by a rotating device to transfer the casting fluid from a central reservoir to the mould cavities at the periphery of a wheel, via the spokes of a gating system.

It is described in more detail in the section on practical investment casting (*see* Chapter 7), both for producing the silicone rubber moulds, prior to casting the expendable wax mould; and for the actual casting fluid transfer into the investment, for the final casting. This is a practical and relatively simple, low-cost method of forcing the casting fluid from sprue to mould cavity.

Semi-Centrifugal

This uses some relatively complex, expendable or reusable, patterns. These are fed, singly or as part of an array, from a central reservoir via the sprues, spokes, to the mould. The rotation of the assembly provides the centrifugal force to transfer the casting liquid. However, the slower speeds and feeding forces differentiate it from true centrifugal casting, as the essence is enhancement of the sprue feeding into a relatively conventional mould. It is widely used for producing, typically, pulleys, impellers and gear blanks.

True Centrifugal Casting

This is used to manufacture product such as pipes and gun barrels, where the casting fluid is sent into the mould, rotating at up to 3,000rev/min, impacting on the outer surface, and requiring no internal constraint. Normally, cylindrical exteriors are produced, but regular profiles, such as hexagonal, can be readily accommodated, whilst the bore is normally finished by machining.

High recovery rates of ~90 per cent are achievable, as no runner and risers are required, and consistent results make this a process long established for the manufacture of vehicle brake drums, cylinder liners and pressure vessels; as well as using composite layering to optimize strength, corrosion resistance, and cost, for industrial products.

Continuous Casting

Continuous casting is an important industrial process, used for making extensive lengths of raw material stock, in a manner analogous to extruded product. It can provide tubing or gear forms that will subsequently be cut to length, and finish machined. The scale of equipment required to accommodate large volumes of casting fluid – and arrangements for pouring into a die, with extremely long product lengths generated as the solidified metal passes through the die and down the shaft for automatic cut-offs – make this a process appropriate only to industrial-scale operations.

Emerging Processes

There are further processes, either at development stage, or not yet widely adopted, including, counter-gravity low-pressure casting (CLA process); directional solidification; and monocrystal; beyond the scope here, but accessible from the Bibliography, *ASM Metals Handbook, Volume 15*; and *Campbell, 2011*.

4 Design for Castings

This chapter brings together the four elements of riser design; gating design; casting design; and dimensional allowances; introduced in other sections of the book and revisited in order to apply to the practical aspects of producing castings.

Design is applicable to self-produced castings; or product to be made to one's own requirement and specification, but designed and cast elsewhere.

RISER DESIGN

The need for riser design is evident from the details in Chapter 1, 'Control of Structure'. The cooling casting encounters distinct phases of volume change that can have a profound effect upon the product, as liquid shrinkage and solidification shrinkage (also known as pattern-maker's shrinkage).

Liquid Shrinkage, Design

Dependent on alloy and superheat, this is shown diagrammatically in Figure 37, for a mild steel casting. Values of shrinkage for this case are ~1.6 per cent per 100°C superheat. For grey cast irons, this shrinkage can vary from ~0.7–1.8 per cent per 100°C superheat.

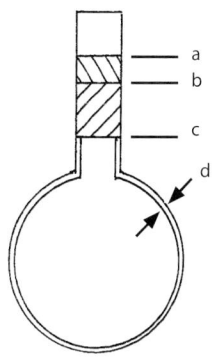

Figure 37 Shrinkage of a low C steel (schematic).

a – original level – liquid
b – liquid shrinkage (1.6% per 100°C pre-heat)
c – solidification shrinkage (3%)
d – solid shrinkage to RT

Solidification Shrinkage, Design

Table 3 in Chapter 1 shows examples of this shrinkage in some common metals. The usual shrinkage behaviour of most alloys is sometimes reversed (i.e. an expansion) in grey cast irons, during this phase, so care and experience, or experimentation, is needed when casting these metals. Indeed, it may even be possible to incorporate the liquid shrinkage within the gating system, and thus eliminate the risers. Clearly, this requires considerable experience and control.

Mould Dilation

Mould dilation is another feature of the solidification process, resulting in an increase in mould volume due to the loading imposed by the metal impacting on the mould. For a grey cast iron, precipitation of the graphite flakes can lead to some 15 per cent increase in the feed metal available in the solidification expansion and mould dilation. In the copper-base alloys, this may be only 1 per cent for green sand mould dilation. As it is difficult to predict accurately, experience is the most effective method of attaining the optimum design of riser. Generally, it is sufficient

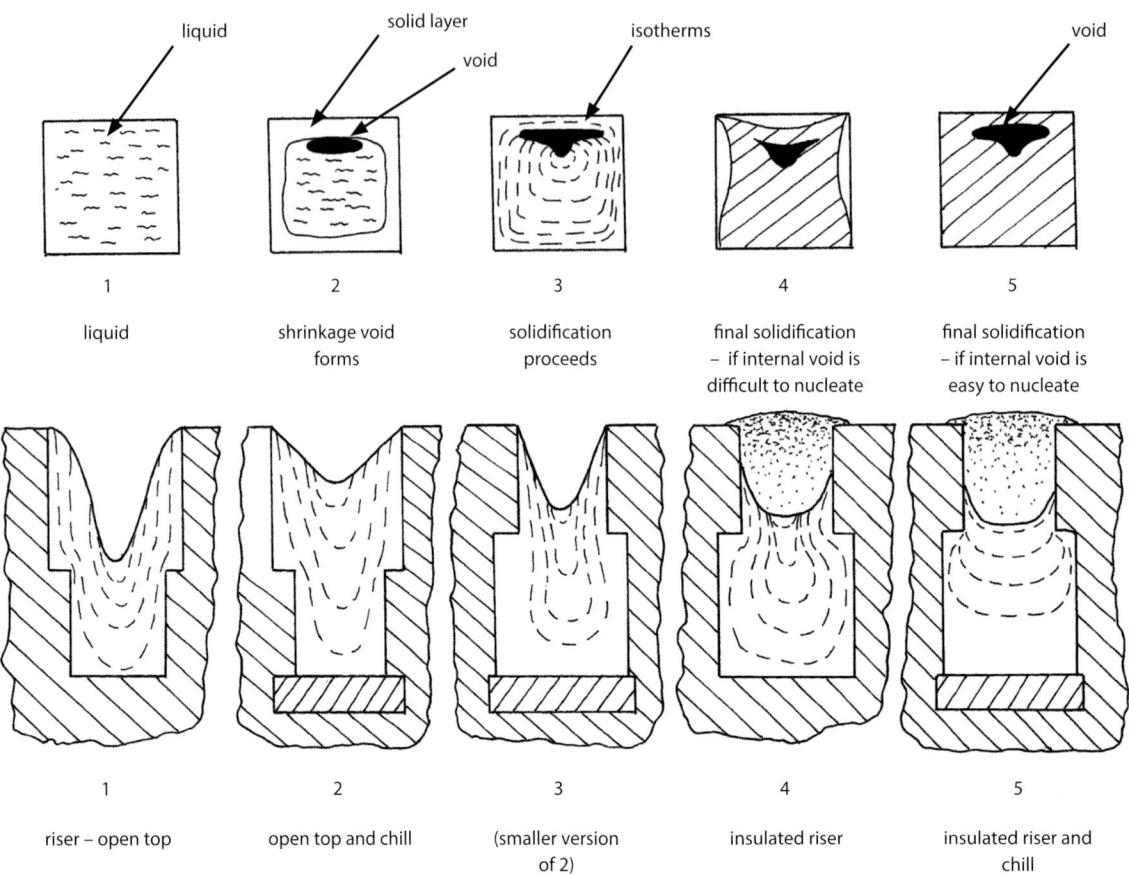

Figure 38 Riser design.

to err on the large size, as normal practice is to weigh in the riser, as removed after casting, for the next similar cast.

Casting Geometry and Riser Positioning

The unique product will naturally dictate the riser shape and location, relating to the avoidance of shrinkage cavities and defects caused by insufficient feeding of the cooling casting, as Figure 38. While shape decisions can be guided by theory, trial and error is perhaps the best guide to positioning, in order to establish practical experience.

Type of Solidification

Solidification proceeds in progressive and directional modes, according to the geometry of casting and riser; and the freezing range of the alloy. The effect of short, medium and long freezing ranges is shown in Figure 39. The directional solidification is from the mould walls, producing different as-cast structures, and segregation at the casting mid-points.

With a uniform wall thickness casting, the objective is to restrict the freezing distance in order to avoid the plane of weakness associated with centreline shrinkage. These solidification modes can result in the defects shown in Figure 40, and for critical work it is preferable to cut a sample casting along the centreline, to check for such problems.

However, the norm for castings is for non-uniform wall thicknesses and sections. Hence, the large sections can

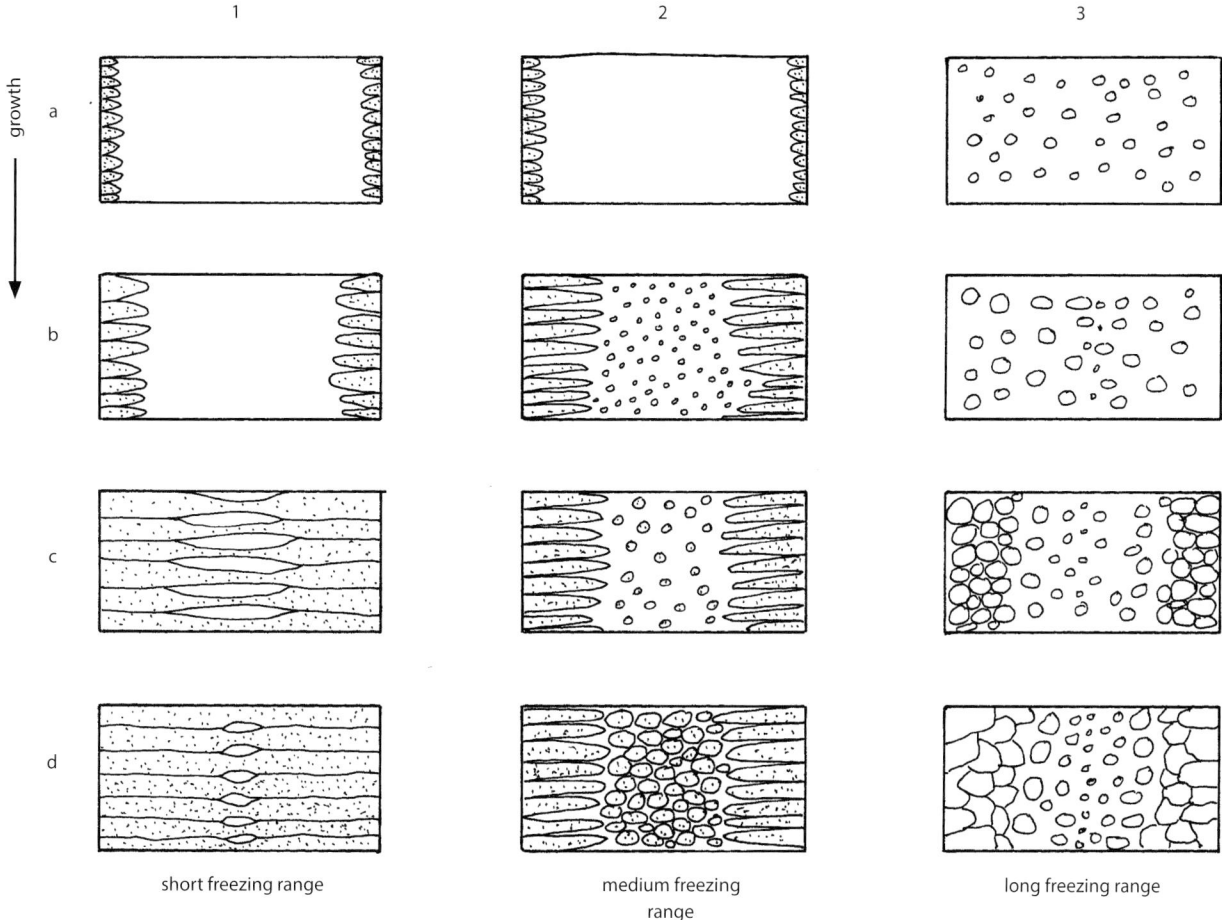

Figure 39 Solidification of alloy types.

often be utilized to feed the smaller ones, but an understanding of solidification is required – often apparent with a careful examination of the drawing, and proven with sample cast sectioning. An example of feeding/chilling/heat application, or control, is shown in Figure 41, using these devices in order to feed late-solidification areas.

GATING DESIGN

Gating is the important means by which the liquid metal is conducted, in a controlled manner; from the mould feeder, to the casting, and onward to exit at the riser(s). It should be appreciated that this is a rapid process, often taking only seconds from beginning to end, and therefore reactions are fast – with all the expense and time-consuming business of heating the furnace charge to a superheated liquid, and all of the mould preparation – and proven, successfully or otherwise, in the blink of an eye as the liquid rushes through the gating system and into the mould cavity.

Mould Filling Perameters

Normally, a fast mould filling is sought because in thin sections the rapid loss of heat from the liquid, through the mould walls, can lead to a premature freezing before the cavity is properly

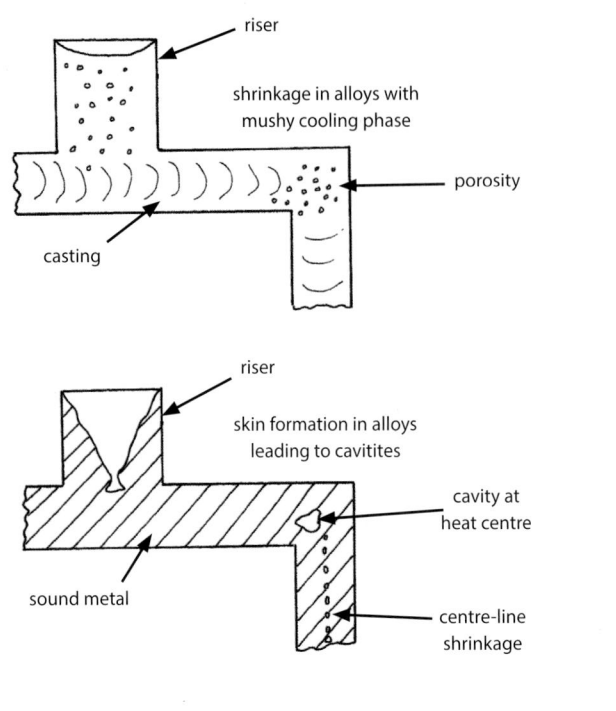

Figure 40 Shrinkage cavities in alloys (typical).

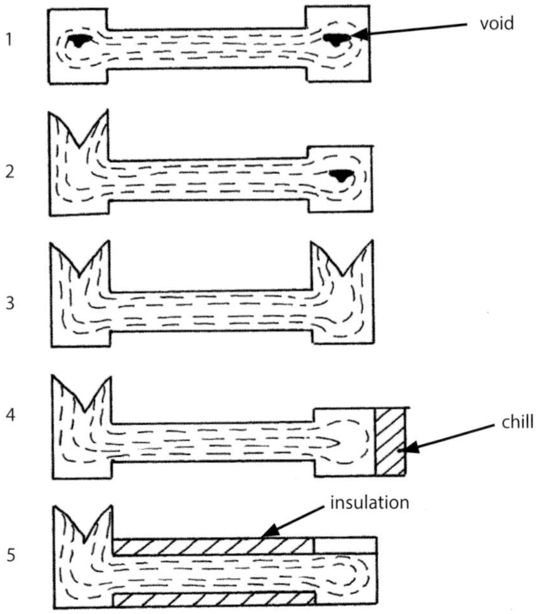

Figure 41 Two heavy sections and connecting member shrinkage effects.

filled. The resulting surface defects, such as scabs and cold laps, require reworking, as described in Chapter 6, 'Post-Casting Processes'.

One method of reducing this effect is to increase the superheat at pouring, but this risks introducing problems with gas absorption and erosion of the mould walls.

Liquid Flow

The liquid flow through the gating system, essentially a pipe-conduit arrangement connecting feeder to mould cavity, has been touched upon in the section on behaviour of liquid metal flowing through pipes. The behaviour of, for instance, liquid en route to producing cast iron, is similar in fluidity to that of water. Therefore, the geometry and rate of flow determines if lamellar-, boundary-, or turbulent-flow will occur in the gating system, during the casting process. Whilst generally a good plan to design for lamellar flow as an ideal, in practice casting flows inevitably involve turbulent flow in the bulk fluid, where not of great concern. However, of crucial importance is the flow rate on pouring, at the liquid/free surface interface. And for this surface, Re is not an appropriate measure. Instead, we need to invoke the Weber number (We), after Moritz Weber (1871–1951), which relates the liquid inertia to its surface tension, thereby giving a measure described as 'surface turbulence', see Bibliography, Campbell, 2011. The Weber number can be defined as:

$$We = (\rho V^2 L)/\gamma$$

where ρ = density of fluid (kg/m^3)
V = velocity of fluid m/s
L = characteristic length (m)
γ = surface tension (N/m)

Design for Castings • 79

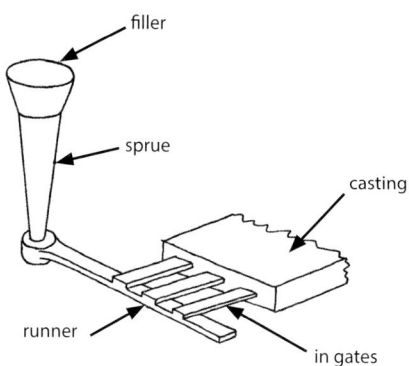

Figure 42 Sample gating system (centreline mould parting)

Design for Fluid Flow

As noted earlier, the principles of sizing a gating system derive from fluid flow based on Bernoulli's theorem, stated as:

Z + Pv + V²/2g + F = K (eliminating w, for weight of the liquid, from each term), where:

Z = Potential head (height of liquid, in m)
Pv = Pressure head (static pressure, in N/m², v is volume, m³)
V²/2g = Velocity head (V is velocity, in m/s; g is acceleration, 9.81m/s²)
F = Frictional loss head (friction loss per unit weight)
K – Constant

For a gating system, the metal flow from ladle to sprue changes from potential energy (due to pouring height); to kinetic energy as it flows through the gating, due to gravity. When filled, the sprue produces a pressure head; and at steady state, potential and frictional heads are approximately constant. So, flow is determined by the remaining factors in Bernoulli's equation, as velocity is low where pressure high, and vice versa.

The Law of Continuity

The law of continuity provides a useful means of analysing the effects on flow rate for changes in section, as Q = a$_1$.v$_1$ = a$_2$.v$_2$, where Q is the rate of flow (m³/s); a is a cross section area of pipe (m²); v is velocity of flowing liquid (m/s). Assuming no losses, and incompressible liquid, it enables flow rates to be

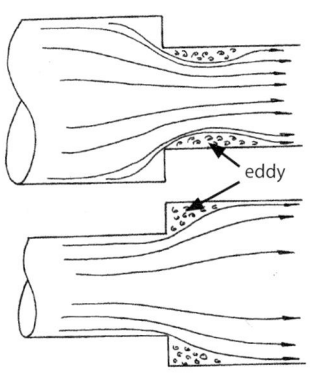

Figure 43 Flow through gating pipework section changes, producing local turbulence.

< 1, of V < 0.5 m/s. For practical guidance with values, refer to Bibliography, *Campbell* 2017.

Mould Surface

Consideration needs to be given to the shape of the gating system in order to avoid damage to the mould surface due to erosion. This also relates to more uniform flow around bends, and section changes, where there is liquid flow, *see* Figure 43.

Purification Methods

Another feature of a well-designed gating system is the incorporation of means to trap unwanted foreign particles, in much the way that grids in domestic drains filter out debris that would later cause a blockage. In castings, this includes slags and solid particles. A popular method is to use ceramic filters, sized to catch these, or even to create a constriction to effect a reduced flow rate; deployed for single use, then renewed for the subsequent melts.

This is a dimensionless parameter, applicable to multi-phase fluid flows with greatly curved surfaces.

It has been found that appropriate We values for successful casting – avoiding surface turbulence – need to be We < 1; whereas, in practice one or two orders of magnitude (We of tens or hundreds) can be found, leading to severe risk of bifilm problems with entrainment and subsequent poor casting integrity. As a general guide, for Al and bronze, this relates to pouring velocities, for We

IN MEMORIUM – THE WHITECHAPEL BELL FOUNDRY

As I sit here on the first day of the New Year in 2017, it seems rather appropriate to ponder on changing times, with the past year having seen political changes not experienced for generations, to say nothing of world conflict to disturb for many years to come. Compared with this historical backdrop, the demise in May 2017, announced on 1 December 2016, of the Whitechapel Bell Foundry, could be thought of as small beer.

But consider – one of only two remaining bell foundries in the UK, the other being the successful Taylor and Co. of Loughborough, Leicestershire – the Whitechapel Foundry was the oldest manufacturing business in the UK, with direct links to 1570, and lineage through master founders back to 1420. The present day bricks and mortar will be protected as the listed site that replaced the old Artichoke coaching inn of Whitechapel Road in 1738, now within a stone's throw of the East London Mosque and the Gherkin.

Photo 64 Whitechapel Church Bell Foundry, frontage on Whitechapel Road, London, E1.

Photo 65 Bell Foundry backyard, January 2017.

Photo 66 Bell Foundry yard.

Perhaps this is just one of the many unintended consequences of the change in east London's make-up through the last couple of centuries; from industrial, to desolate, to gentrified. While it is tempting to obscure the dreadful conditions of earlier times and fail to appreciate the poverty and strife – this was, from before Victorian times to the mid-twentieth century, a world that accommodated Jack the Ripper and the Krays – the cost of its modern success is the steady squeezing out of those businesses and people without a dynamic profitability and generous income.

Undoubtedly, bells were more central to life in earlier times, but their loss would still be a significant deficit in the present day.

The curfew tolls the knell of parting day,
The lowing herd wind slowly o'er the lea,
The ploughman homeward plods his weary way,
And leaves the world to darkness and to me.

The evocative opening of Thomas Gray's famous Elegy on a Country Churchyard, written in the village and church where I was brought up and married, was once the nation's favourite poem, learned by heart by all school children. For centuries the village church bell reliably marked time in an age before clocks and watches, indeed it still does for many in the UK in the form of Big Ben ringing out from the Palace of Westminster, the most famous product from the Whitechapel Bell Foundry. And still of great community interest is the pealing of church bells at times of national importance; encouraging parishioners to services; and individual ceremonies such as weddings. Their loss is unthinkable.

Photo 67 Iconic bell as street furniture on Whitechapel Road, near foundry.

Thus, the state of the bell foundry business has been largely tied to the fortunes of church and state, with the steady rate of ecclesiastical building in the UK in the Medieval period seeing Whitechapel bells supplied in England as far north as Yorkshire and south-west to Cornwall, beginning with the first master founder, Robert Chamberlain of Aldgate in 1420–26, through nine further master founders to Robert Mot (1574–1606), who in turn provides a direct line of twenty-three master founders to the Hughes family in 1904. This final dynasty began with Arthur Hughes, through handovers in 1916, 1945, 1950, 1964 and 1972 involving Albert, William and Douglas, to Alan and Kathryn Hughes, 1997 to 2017.

As will hopefully be perceived from this book, considerable craft and technical skill, involving great experience, is fundamental to the success of any foundry. This is particularly so when making large bells, never an easy task to maintain the business and no surprise at the difficulty of its pursuit in a modern age, where the value of these practical skills is underrated until too late. A brief look at two of the foundry's most famous bells senses this difficulty in sustaining the business, even in less aggressive commercial times.

Design for Castings • 83

Photo 68 Time-clocking at the Bell Foundry, January 2017.

Photo 69 Photograph from the Bell Foundry, Queen Elizabeth II visiting.

Photo 70 Photograph from the Bell Foundry, Queen Mary shortly after the First World War.

The Liberty Bell, 1752

In 1751 the Assembly of Pennsylvania ordered a bell of nearly 1 ton from the Whitechapel Bell Foundry, cast by Thomas Lester, master founder 1738–69. It was shipped from England, arriving in the New World in September 1752, on schedule and in good order.

A report of March 1753 records that, after hanging, it cracked at the first strike of the clapper. As the ship was unable, or unwilling, to take it back from whence it came, a pair of Philadelphia 'ingenious' workmen, Mr Pass and Mr Stow, took the bell for recasting. When they broke it up for remelting it was regarded by them as 'too brittle', and the composition modified by the addition of around 10% Cu, presumably to increase ductility. The resultant casting was deemed unsuccessful, having altered its ringing characteristics – what we now quantify as damping capacity, also known as internal friction, with too high a value of damping capacity deadening sound emission. They subsequently recast the bell, at the original Thomas Lester composition, providing the bell that now hangs in the Liberty Bell Center opposite Independence Hall, Philadelphia.

However, at the threat of English invasion in the War of Independence, in 1777 the bell was hidden in the Zion Reform Church in Allentown, being returned a year later after the English withdrew. Some seven years after its reinstatement the bell was found to be cracked. The cause is uncertain, one likely story being the over-enthusiastic striking of the clapper by several school children during the celebration of George Washington's birthday. Repairs were attempted but failed and its use was stopped as the cracks continued to extend. Such an occurrence is well known in these large bells, which can suffer what we now understand as fatigue failures in a material that has the low ductility and low damping capacity required to provide a sustained ring and tone. A modern scientific analysis would likely identify microscopic structural weakness, such as shown in bifilm theory*, that predisposes the initiation of minute fatigue cracks, leading to failure after extended service.

In 2001 the Whitechapel Bell Foundry received and completed a commission for a replica of the 1752 Liberty Bell, marking the 250th anniversary of the original.

*Note from Professor John Campbell

The bifilm causing failure was huge, following the path of the falling metal stream, from the crown of the bell, across its shoulder, to its skirt. Failure was inevitable after relatively few rings. This performance is, unfortunately, typical of top-poured castings.

Photo 71 Model of the Liberty Bell, USA, in the foundry, 2017.

The Great Bell of Westminster (Big Ben) 1858

In 1834 a great fire ravaged the Palace of Westminster, succeeding in destroying the Houses of Parliament where Guy Fawkes and friends has so famously failed in 1605. Some parts such as the Westminster Hall of the Old Palace, built in the time of William Rufus (1099), were incorporated into the present buildings by the architect Charles Barry. His designs introduced the familiar clock tower, with the specification for an exceptionally accurate clock assigned by one of the finest scientists of the time, Astronomer Royal, George Airy. He demanded it correct to one second per day, an unheard of accuracy at the time.

Despite the competing clockmakers' reluctance to undertake construction of a mechanism this accurate, on the scale and exposed position decreed, Airy remained firm in his demands. This caused parliament to appoint the eminent barrister Edmund Becket Denison, later ennobled as Sir Edmond, Baron Grimthorpe, as co-referee to Airy.

Denison was clearly not an easy man with whom to deal, infuriating all and sundry with a total confidence in himself and his ideas on technical matters far beyond that of a lawyer, no matter how eminent. Remarkably, however, he was often proven right and his absorption with the clock problem led to his design, with Dent and Co.'s manufacture, and the successful testing of the clock.

Photo 72 Letter stamp patterns in the foundry, January 2017.

Photo 73 Early letter stamps.

After the achievement of his clock, Denison applied himself to the bells that, at around the 14 tons specified, were considerably larger than the 10 tons previously cast by Whitechapel for the Great Peter Bell of York Minster. Undeterred, Denison eschewed foundry experience to demand his own design, not only for bell shape, but also an unconventional chemical composition. After some delay, the Stockton-on-Tees foundry of John Warner and Sons cast a bell, somewhat oversize at 16 tons, in August 1856. However, during testing in Westminster Yard, it cracked, failing beyond repair. This led Denison, recently made a QC, to charge the Whitechapel Bell Foundry with this poison chalice of a task.

Master founder George Mears set to using the existing bell for raw material, the breaking up of which took three weeks, to charge three furnaces for the melt. The mould was preheated for a full day, an innovation in bell casting. Pouring, a process usually accomplished in seconds in more familiar castings, took twenty minutes to completely fill. It was then left to cool for twenty days before it could be broken out from the mould. The finished bell weighed in at some 13½ tons, and was rigorously tested to the satisfaction of Denison by May 1858. An indication of the status of the Victorian master founder can be seen in the fine memorial to Mears in the famous Highgate Cemetery, near Hampstead Heath, north London.

The bell's journey, the few miles from the East End to Westminster Bridge, was a major event, drawn on a huge trolley by sixteen elaborately decorated horses, cheered by the crowds lining the route. Installed in the clock tower, the great clock bells first rang out on 31 May 1858. This caused parliament to create a special sitting for naming the bell. After a typically long-winded speech by Sir Benjamin Hall, Chief Lord of Woods and Forests (!), it has been claimed that some wag announced: 'Why not call him Big Ben and have done with it!.' This has not, however, been recorded in Hansard, hence the alternative explanation that it simply adopted the name of Big Ben, the epithet of the then-current ring-fighter champion Benjamin Caunt, who once lasted sixty (!) rounds in a prize-fight with a Mr Bendigo. Caunt, weighing in at 17 stones, then retired at the age of forty-two, and surely justified his fame as Big Ben. Either way, Big Ben it became.

The story hardly ends there, as in September 1858 Big Ben developed a crack. It transpired that Denison had, characteristically, overridden the expert's advice when he insisted on the manufacture of a hammer twice the weight chosen by George Mears. This led to Big Ben being removed from service for three years, replaced by the largest quarter-bell. When returned, Big Ben was slightly modified and the hammer replaced with a lighter one, offset 45 degrees to avoid the damaged area. This has produced the familiar, if technically imperfect, tone heard today.

Photo 74 View of foundry shop-floor, from Bell Foundry display.

Photo 75 Pouring into bell mould, from Bell Foundry display.

Still Denison refused to admit his mistaken design for the hammer, and manipulated a foundry employee to perjure himself in a court case against Mears and the foundry that, despite his legal advantages, he duly lost. He had even stated that a filler had been used to disguise a poor casting, which was conclusively proven incorrect when the bell was thoroughly examined in 2002. Finally, after some twenty years of bad-tempered sniping at the foundry, he overstepped the mark in print, leading to a libel trial that he also lost. A transcript of the trial still exists in the foundry's library records. These records report a demonstration of the principle of bell casting, using a fine model bell that is still held by the company. A profile of this largest bell ever cast by the foundry has been retained throughout its working life, in the casting shop at Whitechapel Road.

Photo 76 Display from Bell Foundry shop, January 2017.

While it has never been easy or comfortable business at the foundry, master founder Alan Hughes explained in *Spitalfields Life* that in earlier times a lead-time, from order placement to final delivery for large church bells, was around eleven years. So orders placed in the good times of church building sustained the works during intervening fallow periods with an obligation to pay up, often counter to the prevailing economic climate. Later, the destruction wrought on bell towers during the twentieth century world wars, provided decades of subsequent work for the foundry. Export far across the world had been significant since the eighteenth century. However, even modern developments in mechanical engineering and foundry processes, periods of popularity for hand bells and campanology, and online stores have proven insufficient to sustain this remarkable business in the manner to which it has been accustomed since the sixteenth century.

Photo 77 A tuned bell display.

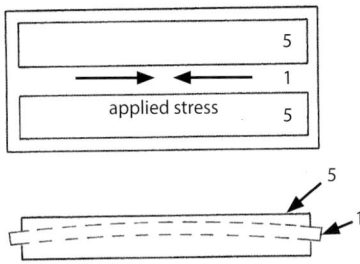

Figure 44 Stresses and strains (distortion) from solidification of different section modulii.

calculated at different pipe sections in a gating system, in order to check that they do not become either unstable, or too low for efficient mould filling, *see* Figures 8, 9 and 10.

CASTING DESIGN

A number of key elements in the design of a casting, as the final product, have already been considered – for it is necessary to understand the complex process of transformation from liquid metal dispensed from ladle or crucible; into the mould via the gating system; filling the mould cavity; and finally entering the riser system. And as this rapid and dramatic sequence of events are set in train, the melt is cooling from superheated liquid to final casting at room temperature – a process that can range from seconds for tiny castings in the light alloys, to many days for massive castings such as the Liberty Bell, see 'In Memoriam – The Whitechapel Bell Foundry'.

These aspects need to be understood at the design stage if the casting is to be successful in meeting the desired shape, composition, surface finish, and freedom from defects, within a prescribed range.

Consider, as noted earlier in this chapter, the effect of shrinkage due to cooling:

◆ Liquid (furnace temperature) to Liquid (at pouring)
◆ Liquid (entering the mould) to Solid (at solidus on the phase diagram)
◆ Solid (at solidus line) to Solid (final temperature ^{N}RT)

In addition to casting design, the initial liquid to liquid – from the superheated, circa 100–170°C above its melting point, down towards its freezing temperature – does not need to concern the designer, this aspect being handled by the foundryman.

For solid-to-solid cooling, from the early stages of solidification, to room temperature, the change in volume is handled by using pattern-makers' rules in order to oversize the pattern/mould cavity to compensate for this shrinkage. This is a well-established practice, to relate the pattern for a particular alloy to finished product size. Therefore, care is required if the pattern is used for another alloy, of a different contraction coefficient, where significant errors in dimensions can cause embarrassment on completion of the casting!

An important aspect of solid-to-solid shrinkage is the effect of uneven cooling, due to variation in section geometry or volume. This is the principal cause of internal stresses resulting in: distortion and warping; stress relief through failure by cracking; or the insidious danger of hidden internal stresses. The latter may provide a stored problem, resulting in failure by fracture during post-casting processing, or service loading leading to sudden and unexpected failure. Internal stresses are normally difficult to impossible to ascertain, requiring destructive testing on sample castings for critical work; or expensive thermal stress relieving.

The concept of **section modulus** (SM) is introduced as of particular interest for the designer. This relates the casting volume-to-surface area, simply as:

SM = casting volume (m^3)/casting surface area (m^2).

The SM can be applied to different parts of a casting to show sensitivity to internal stress and distortion. As the volume increases, so does the cooling time. But as surface area increases, the cooling time decreases, as the mould interface presents more opportunity for heat loss. Therefore, as the volume-to-surface area ratio increases (providing a large value for section modulus), the time for cooling and solidification increases. A larger section modulus equals increased cooling time and slower cooling rate. This can be seen in Figure 44, where section moduli range from 1 to 5, due to the different section thicknesses in the plate. The lowest section modulus (SM = 1) solidifies first and restrains that of the modulus 5, solidifying last. This is likely to cause the distortion shown in Figure 44.

Further to Figure 45, if the central bar is equal to, or greater than, the outside bars then the final RT condition is for the

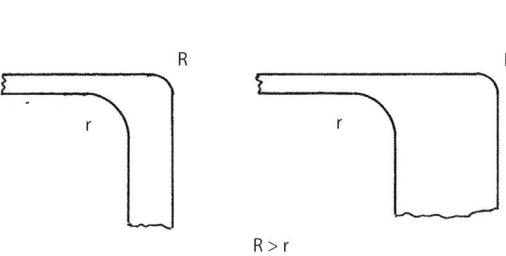

Figure 45 Section effect on casting design.
r, Rare radii, e.g. r=8, R=20

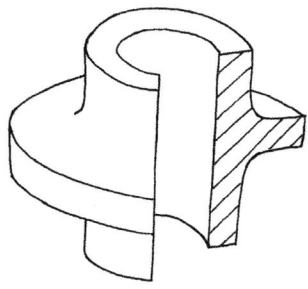

Figure 46 Preferred flange location for optimum casting design

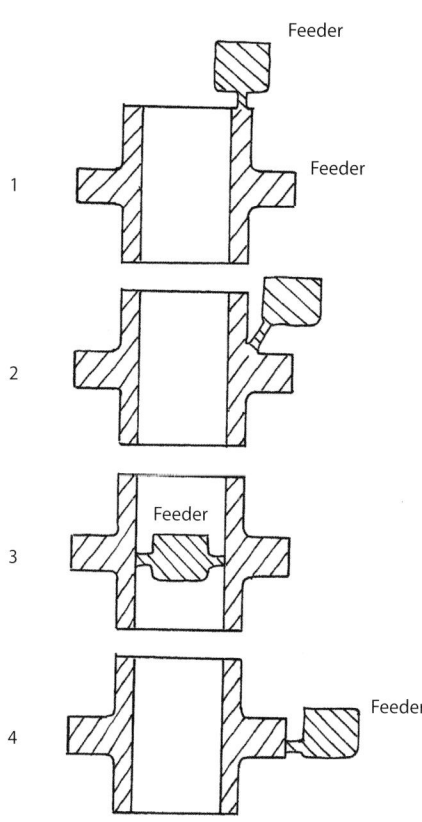

Figure 47 Possible feeder-head positions. (The ideal position may not be practical.)

central bar to retain a damaging tensile stress. This may be accommodated as a residual stress, or be sufficient to generate internal cracks to relieve the excessive stress. This is, unfortunately, a common occurrence in the centre of castings – often containing dangerous hidden cracks and areas of weakness.

The explanation of the above relates to the outer bars contracting on cooling, whilst the centre remains hot and yields at its lower strength condition. When the outer bars have cooled, they then constrain the cooling inner, which is also trying to contract, but is thereby beset with a final tensile stress. As this is the case for most castings, it is an important factor that prejudices the casting integrity unless designed-out.

Liquid to solid cooling presents the greatest difficulty for the designer, with the general principle being that the largest sections solidify last, the geometry of the casting being of great significance. In order to handle the design rules, a number of standardized sections have been modelled, as:

- 'L' sections (plates making L)
- 'T' sections (plates making T)
- 'X' sections (plates making X)
- Cylinders
- Plates
- Plates to cylinders

L, T and X sections are shown in Figures 46, 47 and 48. It is possible to use Chvorinov's Rule (see Chapter 1, 'Cooling Curves'), to calculate the total solidification time for a casting, thus:

$$t_S = B \cdot \Sigma(V_i/A_i)^2 \text{ where}$$

t_S = solidification time, total, (s)
V_i = casting section volume, individual, (m^3)
A_i = casting surface area, individual, (m^2)
B = constant for alloy and mould.

'B' includes the alloy density, mould specific heat, and thermal conduc-

92 • Design for Castings

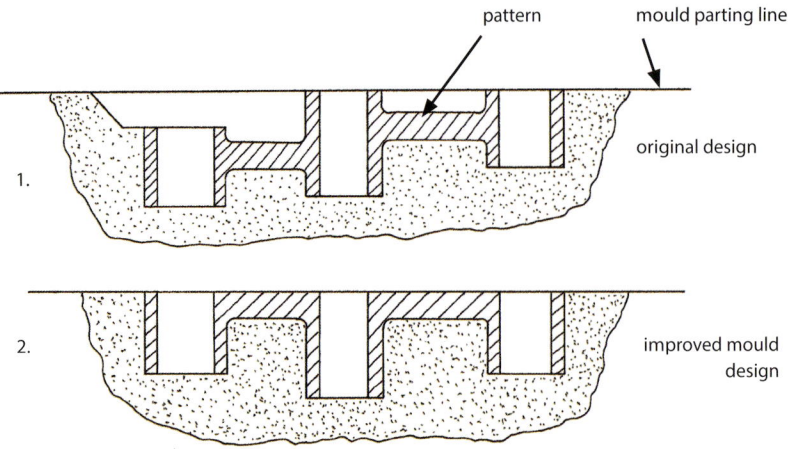

Figure 48 Mould parting line designs.

tivities – normally arrived at by experimentation. This provides a workable equation for prediction of cooling time, by summation of all individual sections of the casting or pattern.

The Five Basic Rules of Casting Design

Consideration of the above sections and behaviour has led to the following rules as adopted by the ASM (see Bibliography), for the optimum casting design efficiency. See figures 45 to 47.

Rule 1 Use the largest fillet radii at changes in section.

Rule 2 Determine the last point of solidification and ensure risers can be placed as close as possible.

Rule 3 Design to keep the number of risers to a minimum.

Rule 4 Design to minimize the number of cores required.

Rule 5 Keep parting lines, between drag and cope, straight; always avoiding steps where possible.

Rule 1 applies in a similarly beneficial manner to that for stress concentrations in mechanical engineering, but in a casting this reduces the differential cooling rates as radii increase, and vice versa.

Rule 2 indicates that the ideal position for a riser is on the parting line, connecting to the last solidification point, assessed from analysis of the SM.

Rule 3 As solidification goes along the feeding path, and each feeder needs a riser, then keeping feeders to a minimum is required for efficiency and casting benefit.

Rule 4 Reducing the number of cores simplifies and improves the casting, through reduced gating complexity, but this needs to be balanced by the unique feature of castings as a manufacturing method that can provide inaccessible internal cavities – such as in the elaborate water jackets contained in a typical car cylinder block.

Rule 5 is self-apparent, as using a non-straight parting line can cause problems with the casting process, and it is normally better to modify a design in order to make a straight line for parting, as Figure 48.

ALLOWANCES AND DIMENSIONS OF DESIGN

The ultimate of producing a casting precisely to the required dimensions and geometry, without recourse to any post-casting operations, is most nearly achieved in processes that fall into the category of 'near net shape', a term that has often arisen in previous chapters.

Near net shape castings are indeed a practical goal, but for our purposes they are restricted to the high-precision methods of die casting and investment casting. These processes can produce castings, normally of the smaller sizes, that are sufficiently close, dimensionally and in surface finish, to the finished article to almost completely eliminate the need for any further work, such as machining or dressing.

However, the main thrust of this book is the manufacture of practical artefacts from the more accessible processes, such as sand casting. For the home foundry worker, unlike the Industrial Production Engineer, the cost in time and effort, machining or hand working, post-casting, is not normally a significant obstacle – at least compared to producing a sound casting. For volume production, the choice of casting method can be critical, and savings made by reducing or even eliminating post-casting work can be of great economic advantage, as explored in detail in, for instance, the *ASM Metals Handbook*, *see* Bibliography.

As usual, there are exceptions to prove the rule, such as the highly effective simple die casting shown in Photo 63. This has successfully produced a near net shape aluminium alloy casting requiring minimal machining for a high-precision, low-cost, small batch production product; achieved with relatively low tooling cost – but with consummate metal-working skill and willingness to tackle areas conventionally regarded as the province of the specialist. Similarly, it is widely known that small artefacts can be produced to near net shape and complex geometry, typical of art and decorative work, from the investment casting method, as described in Chapter 3.

For both the above processes, it is often the case that the as-cast surface finish satisfies the requirement for the final article. It may also be possible to produce holes for fastening and even joint faces that require no machining, enabling complex items, such as vehicle carburettors, to be produced with only final machining of key surfaces and fine jet apertures to complete. In contrast, a green sand casting will produce a less fine surface finish, and also requires a generous oversize allowance for subsequent machining of faces required for joints, or where critical dimensions are to be maintained. The amount of material allowance sensibly relates to the size of the item, but a general rule of thumb is 3mm (⅛in) allowance for 100mm (4in); 6mm ¼in) allowance for 300mm (12in).

It is normally preferable to err on the large side, for nothing is more frustrating than being unable to machine an otherwise successful casting face to clean metal throughout. On the other hand, as machining off material, swarf, is normally lost to remelting, it is often best to judge by test-casting the most economical pattern sizes.

These aspects of casting design provide a basis for allowances in casting, the most economical design normally being the most sound metallurgically, with minimal internal defects. This particularly applies to the problem of distortion that, at best, requires correction by excessive machining. The allied problem of internal stresses, where not revealed as distortion, should always be minimized. The consequences of internal stress may sometimes only become apparent after machining relieves some stress, allowing subsequent distortion. If it is not possible to design out excessive internal stresses, then post-casting operations, such as stress relieving by heat treatment, may be necessary.

5 Materials for Castings

This section deals with the actual material that forms the finished casting. It is, therefore wholly concerned with metals. There are a variety of other materials involved in the casting process, for furnaces, moulds, handling equipment and patterns – but these are discussed in Chapter 4, 'Design for Castings'.

Described below is a reasonably complete range of cast metals, the extent of which is surely far beyond that to be encountered in the small-scale operation, but deemed useful for a background understanding of the products either encountered at first-hand, such as motor vehicle engine and structural parts; or of general interest, such as the remarkable casting sophistication of the jet turbine blade.

Alloy	Fluidity (1 - poor, 10 good)	Leak Tightness	Melting Range (°C) Melting Range (°C)	Machinability	Corrosion resistance	Weldability	sand cast	die cast	permanent mould cast
201	6	6	650 - 570	2	8	4	yes	yes	no
222	6	8	625 - 520	2	8	6	yes	yes	no
355	2	2	620 - 550	6	6	4	yes	yes	no
356	2	2	615 - 560	6	4	4	yes	yes	no
360	5	6	590 - 570	7	5	4	no	no	yes
390	6	6	650 - 510	8	4	4	yes	yes	yes
512	8	8	630 - 590	4	3	8	yes	no	no
520	8	10	600 - 450	2	2	8	yes	no	no
535	8	10	620 - 550	2	2	7	yes	no	no
712	6	8	640 - 600	2	6	7	yes	no	no
850	8	8	650	1	6	7	yes	yes	no
852	8	8	635	1	6	8	yes	yes	no

Table 6 Casting Properties (USA aluminium alloys).

ALUMINIUM ALLOYS

Pure aluminium is well known as an extremely soft and ductile material, and as such is seldom of use for the objects likely to perform in a load-bearing environment. Even for non-engineering items such as statues, as for Eros described in Chapter 1, its lack of strength makes for a limited choice of uses.

However, small additions of alloying elements transform pure Al into an extremely important casting material; as well as providing wrought forms, sheet and sections, upon which modern flight structures are universally built. It is immediately apparent that this family of alloys present an opportunity for the small-scale worker in castings, assisted by their low melting point; low density; relatively good strength and ductility; and excellent corrosion resistance. This offers a tantalizing prospect, but for critical work it is necessary to have a sound understanding of the metallurgical theory upon which the foundation is built of a whole family of alloys, with their wide variation in properties – strength, ductility, toughness, fatigue and corrosion resistance, and individual castability (*see* Table 6).

Process Adaptability

The aluminium alloy system, with its extremely wide range of properties provided by its variety of alloys, can be usefully categorized into two process groups for castability. Firstly, those alloys that can be cast by gravity pouring with any process – non-permanent (e.g. sand),

Alloy (USA)	Cu	Mg	Si	Fe	Mn	Ni	Zn	Sn	Ti	Al	stress max. N/mm2	elongation (%)	Hardness H BHardness HB	HT condition	Remarks
201	5	0.2	0.1	0.15	0.25				0.25	Rem	470	1	130	T7	high strength, high ductility, < 1% Ag
222	10	0.25	2	1.5	0.5	0.5	0.8		0.25	Rem	420	4	115	T62	Solution Treat (ST), Age (A)
355	1.2	0.5	5	0.6	0.5		0.35		0.25	Rem	270	1	85	T61	ST, A
356	0.25	0.3	7	0.6	0.35		0.35		0.25	Rem	235	2	75	T7	widely used, popular alloy, sand or die cast
360	0.6	0.5	10	2	0.35	0.5	0.5	0.15		Rem					similar LM6, die cast only
390	4.5	0.5	17	1.3	0.1		0.1		0.2	Rem	280	<1	90	T6	suitable for all casting processes
512	0.35	4	1.8	0.6	0.8		0.35		0.25	Rem	140	2	50	F	HT NA
520	0.25	10	0.25	0.3	0.15		0.15		0.25	Rem	330	15	100	T4	ST only
535	0.1	7	0.2	0.2	0.2				0.25	Rem	250	10	80	F	ST only
712	0.25	0.6	0.3	0.5	0.1		5 - 6.5		0.2	Rem	240	5	75	F	ST, A at RT
850	1	0.1	0.7	0.7	0.1	.7 - 1.3		6	0.2	Rem	140	9	45	T5	ST, A
852	2	0.8	0.4	0.7	0.1	.9 - 1.5		6	0.2	Rem	185	2	65	T5	ST, A

HB - Brinel Hardness; HT - heat treatment; ST - solution treatment (rapid quench from high temp; A - ageing (low temp heating after ST). See later for explanation.

Table 7 Cast Aluminium Alloys (USA), (nominal values).

or permanent (e.g. die casting moulds.). Secondly, those alloys only suitable for permanent-mould casting.

This is known as process adaptability. The most adaptable alloys can be cast by the full range of processes, which generally means from the most forgiving sand processes with expendable moulds and simple gravity pouring; through shell moulding; to die casting. The alloys with the least process adaptability can only be cast by a dedicated process, usually seen in high-pressure die casting (HPDC). In HPDC, alloys can be specifically designed, typically for high-volume production of near net shape (NNS) for complex items including carburettor bodies in motor vehicles. These alloys require high fluidity, hot strength, resistance to die soldering (adhering to die after cast), and so conform to NNS demands.

Alloy Grouping

This diversity of alloys within the Al family presents the common problem of grouping similar alloys together, in order to simplify a large number of alloys into a more manageable arrangement from which to sort or pick one appropriate for the job. The task is made no easier by the almost complete lack of co-ordination of knowledgeable parties – from industry, to national and international organizations – a familiar lament of workers in the field. One way or another, things need some simplification, otherwise one is unable to readily handle the individual detail of chemical composition, microstructure, heat treatment, castability, mechanical properties, availability, and more.

In the western world the major influences for categorizing metals, including aluminium, originate from the USA and Western Europe and occasionally, for instance in stainless steels, these obtain some congruity. Sadly, however, for the Al alloys there is a particular divergence from what we shall take as outlines from both sources. Firstly, from the USA, the American Society of Metals (ASM) provides the basis for the range of alloys shown in Table 7. This table presents the range of alloys based on the chemical composition. However, there are many further details required in order to find the best choice for the task. These are to be found in the reference works shown in the Bibliography, and include castability index; heat treatment, (if applicable); mechanical properties; and example of applications. Note, for example, that many of the Al alloys, particularly the higher strength varieties, are heat treatable. The effect of this, post-casting heat treatment, is often dramatic with regard to greatly increased strength, or effect on ductility; and the alloy details and processing are, therefore, vital to success.

Alloy Goups USA System

The grouping system of the American system is based on a nine-category arrangement defined by the chemical composition, thus:

1 xx.x	Unalloyed system (pure Al)
2 xx.x	Al-Cu (Cu as main addition)
3 xx.x	Al-Si (can also contain Mg and Cu)
4 xx.x	Al-Si (only)
5 xx.x	Al-Mg (Mg as main addition)
6 xx.x	–
7 xx.x	Al-Zn (can also contain Cu, Mg, Cr, Mn)
8 xx.x	Al-Sn (Sn as main addition)
9 xx.x	–

Note that these are the categories for cast product, not be confused with the comparable system for wrought product, familiar in sheet or tabular forms (e.g. wrought 6061, used widely for bicycle frames).

This is a representative sample of the alloys listed in this system, an example being the commonly used alloy from gravity casting, 356 which can be preceded by letter A, B or C, denoting detailed restrictions within the single alloy specification. Alloy 356 is a popular choice of a heat-treatable alloy of medium-to-high strength with adequate toughness and high process adaptability for good castability, making it a safe choice for casting or structural vehicle parts, from small batch to high-volume production (*see* Tables 6 and 7).

Alloying Elements

At this point, and before exploring in some detail the range of alloys established in the previous UK system for a more practical guide to selection, it is worth touching on some metallurgical aspects to understand the principles of these alloy developments.

Firstly, a listing of the major alloying elements allows a general indication of their effect on the casting.

Beryllium (Be)

At very low levels, just a few ppm, (parts per million), Be is powerful in reducing oxidation and inclusions, for Al-Mg compositions. At > 0.04% it has a significant benefit for the microstructure in Fe-containing alloys, such as Al-Fe-Si, improving strength and ductility. However, Be compounds are carcinogenic and strictly controlled handling in the casting and welding process is required.

Bismuth (Bi)

At > 0.1%, Bi is beneficial to machinability of Al alloys.

Boron (B)

The most apparent effect of B is forming borides, such as, $Al_2 B_2$ and $Al_2 Ti_2$, the latter providing nucleation sites for grain-refining treatments with $Ti Al_3$. Borides are generally detrimental in forming inclusions and machinability.

Cadmium (Cd)

Improves machinability at > 0.1% Cd, but volatilizes (boils) at 767°C, so precautions are very important.

Chromium (Cr)

Used at low concentrations, such as in the form of $Cr Al_7$ phase, with low solid state solubility. Useful in suppressing grain growth in low-temperature ageing of heat treatable alloys. Can improve corrosion resistance, at higher concentrations, in specific alloys.

Copper (Cu)

The addition of around 4–10% Cu produced the first high-strength, heat-treatable alloys (durals), in the early twentieth century. These remain an important class of alloys, the optimum strength obtained around 4–6% Cu. However, Cu reduces general corrosion resistance; stress-corrosion resistance; and castability.

Iron (Fe)

Whilst improving resistance to hot-tearing and die-soldering, increased amounts seriously reduce ductility. Fe can form many phases, such as $Fe Al_3$ and

Fe Mn Al$_6$, serving to improve strength at room and elevated temperatures. At high levels it has detrimental effects on casting fluidity characteristics.

Lead (Pb)

Used for improving machinability, at > 0.1% Pb.

Magnesium (Mg)

Widely used up to its solubility limit of 0.7% Mg. In aluminium silicon alloys, it forms a hardening phase Mg$_2$ Si. Hardenable alloys take the form Al-Si-Mg, with 0.4–0.7% Mg. The other form is Al-Mg alloys using 4–10% Mg; with > 7% Mg providing heat treatable alloys, with ageing possible at conveniently low temperatures.

Manganese (Mn)

Although an important element in wrought alloys, Mn is generally regarded as an impurity, to be controlled in casting alloys.

Mercury (Hg)

Although originally used in Al sacrificial anodes, for corrosion protection of steel structures, it is an element to be avoided in casting.

Nickel (Ni)

Found in alloys, combined with Cu, for improving elevated temperature properties; also for reducing the coefficient of thermal expansion.

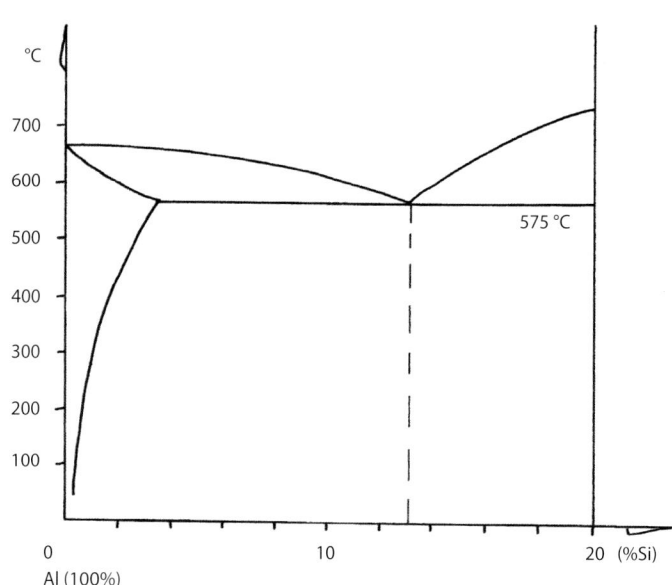

Figure 49 Al-Si equilibrium diagram, cast alloys.

Phosphorus (P)

Used to improve hyper-eutectic Al-Si alloys, (see Figure 50). It forms Al P$_3$ to refine the microstructure. For hypo-eutectic Al-Si, even at low ppm concentrations, P is detrimental, coarsening the microstructure and reducing the effects of well-known Al-Si modifiers (improvers), sodium and strontium.

Silicon (Si)

The addition of Si to Al provides the most common form of Al casting alloy. It greatly improves castability with regard to fluidity, flow and hot-tearing resistance. All processes can be accommodated, with the following general guide: Al – 5 to 7% Si for sand, plaster and investment (non-permanent moulds); 7–9% Si for permanent mould; and 8–12% Si for die casting. Alloys can use up to 25% Si, depending on preferences in fluidity, cooling rate, density and thermal expansion.

Silver (Ag)

Used at concentrations of 0.5–1%, Ag is valuable in alloys for precipitation hardening and corrosion resistance, but in commercial foundries the use of precious metals could be regarded as one more potential difficulty added to the myriad already in train . . . (see alloy 201).

Sodium (Na)

Used in Al-Si alloys as a mhodifier for eutectic alloys and reacts detrimentally with P in this regard, as noted above for P.

Strontium (Sr)

The principal element used (sometimes with Na) for modification of Al-Si alloys, enabling greatly improved properties with additions of Sr around only 0.008–0.04%. Increased levels of Sr can increase porosity and reduce degassing treatment effects. *See* later for further details of the important Al-Si modification process.

Tin (Sn)

Whilst being sometimes added as a minor element in precipitation hardening alloys, Sn is used in amounts up to 25 per cent in casting of bearing alloys, due to its low friction characteristics.

Titanium (Ti)

Used commonly as a grain refining agent, combining with small amounts of B, Ti B_2 is used for effective grain refinement. Also, in greater concentrations to improve 'hot shortness' in susceptible alloys.

Zinc (Zn)

Zn can be combined with Cu and Mg, providing heat treatable alloys, although not used in the binary (Al-Zn) form. Also used in specialized die casting alloys, in lower concentrations as Al-Si-Zn, high concentrations being Zn-based alloys, *see* this chapter, 'Zinc').

Gas Porosity

Hydrogen (H)

Unlike oxygen (O_2), hydrogen is soluble in aluminium and its alloys. Althoug the solubility of O_2 in Al is effectively zero, it plays a significant role in surface oxidation.

Hydrogen has a solubility in aluminium far greater in the liquid state than solid, as shown in Figure 14, with the sudden change at the liquidus around 660°C, shown at 1 atmosphere of H pressure. The solubility also varies directly as temperature and the square root of pressure – although 1 atmos. is appropriate for casting.

The consequences of this high solubility ($\geq$ 0.7mL/100g) in the liquid state means that, given the commonly occurring sources of H in foundry conditions, excess H will be trapped on solidification of the melt. However, for H to produce porosity, it requires an excess, a super saturation, over that which exists in equilibrium conditions during the process of solidification. As for metal solidification, for H porosity to occur, nucleation is required. This can be suppressed, relatively easily, up to ~0.3mL/100g, for instance in the absence of nucleating oxides.

As O_2 does not dissolve in Al, the volumetric oxides arise from entrained surface-oxidation films, as described previously in bifilm theory. H bubbles, as porosity, are resisted by the Al – H liquid surface tension, but with sufficient concentration hydrogen evolution can take the form of interdentric porosity, or secondary porosity. The latter is less damaging to mechanical properties, as it has dimensions of only microns (m x 10^{-6}).

Hydrogen sources, especially at free surfaces, can be difficult to avoid. They can be readily entrained into the melt, as noted above, from lack of cleanliness and moisture-retaining surfaces. Further sources, including alloying elements such as Mg, may also alter the H solubility. Tools, the mould (e.g. green sand), turbulence during pouring, and flow through the gating system are all potential sources of H evolution and entrainment in the melt. The elimination of these sources and the search for high-quality microstructures, free from the interdenritic porosity that significantly reduces mechanical properties, requires avoidance of gravity and ladle pouring, and so lead towards methods such as counter-gravity and submerged-pump feeding (as in the Cosworth process).

It should be noted that, despite the need to generally avoid porosity in the form of H pores, this is still less damaging than the effects of shrinkage, some of which can sometimes be alleviated with moderate porosity. Care is needed, however, as not all porosity is produced as simple spheres, as might be anticipated, but often as long trails, thereby rendering the cast less leak-tight than might be hoped.

There exist methods for removing H either dissolved in the matrix or evolved as porosity, such as by fluxing through the melt with pure, dry gasses such as nitrogen, argon or freon. Alternatively, the melt can be held at high temperature for a prolonged period.

Clearly prevention, wherever possible, is better than cure.

Oxidation

As is self-apparent, Al oxidizes energetically both in the solid and liquid states, and at a significantly higher rate in the latter, forming a continuous and distinct layer in the presence of air, water, vapour, or other reactions with alloying elements.

The structure of the aluminium oxide, on the solid base metal, is polymorphic but becomes crystalline at the liquidus, with a variety of oxides according to the particular reactions. The presence of Mg in the alloy produces a spinel structure, seen as a black deposit occurring at ≥ 750°C, to contaminate all with which contact is made. Although well above general holding temperatures, local hot spots can readily produce this effect.

Separation and removal of these oxides is assisted with gaseous fluxes, or a covering of chemical fluxes, especially with Mg additions; the former based on chlorine and fluorine, the latter on salts, carbon and graphite. The oxides may be skimmed off mechanically, but ceramic filters are now in widespread use to both mechanically trap oxides and provide non-turbulent flow in gating systems (*see* Chapter 6).

Similarly to porosity, the inclusions around oxides entrained in the liquid are detrimental to mechanical properties, resulting in appreciable reduction in strength and ductility.

Microstructure Control

As noted in Chapter 3, 'Methods of Casting', the microstructure controlling the final mechanical properties of the cast is determined by factors such as cooling rate, with the objective to provide the finest dendrite arm spacing from the initial nucleation sequence, see Figure 57. Aluminium castings provide an example of the general need for a fine, equiaxed, randomly orientated, grain structure for the best properties. Grain refinement, mentioned in the listing of elements, is possible in aluminiums with the addition of such as Al-3 to 10% Ti, and Al-Ti-B, as well as compacted salts for Ti Al$_3$ compounds. The detailed mechanism explaining the manner of grain refinement is complex and still controversial, so only briefly pursued further here! (See Bibliography, *ASM Metals Handbook*, Campbell.

Modifications of Ai Si Alloys

As noted earlier in the section on alloying elements, the Al Si system is the most widely used in the field of Al castings, and this is made possible largely because this binary system (simply comprising the two elements, Al and Si up to Al-25% Si) with its highly practical castability characteristics, solidifies as a structure with poor mechanical properties – that can be modified into a significantly improved condition.

The eutectic in Figure 49 is around 12% Si, with greater Si being 'hyper-eutectic', and less Si being 'hypo-eutectic'. These conditions require different treatments, with the 5–12% hypo eutectic, alloys deriving most benefit from modification. This can result in a dramatic factor-of-two improvement in strength and ductility, rendering the alloys suitable for a wide range of engineering tasks – although not to the highest level obtainable with the precipitation hardening alloys, described shortly.

The simplicity of adding small amounts of sodium and strontium (often used in combination), belies the complex and highly specific mechanisms responsible for this transformation. A simplistic explanation concerns the suppression of the Si nucleation to increase the undercooling and subsequently the number and rate of sites for growth, with finer lamellae to the eutectic phase growth. The effects are readily seen in micrographs of the structure, showing a change from the acicular plates to the finer eutectic, in a matrix of the fully modified alloy.

In hyper-eutectic alloys, the primary Si platelets are particularly pronounced, and these are modified with small traces of phosphorus (< 0.03% P). This can be highly effective when preceded by treatment of the alloy before modification, such as by chlorine fluxing to remove P-scavenging impurities, Figure 50.

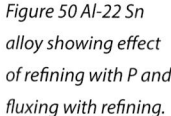

Figure 50 Al-22 Sn alloy showing effect of refining with P and fluxing with refining.

unrefined

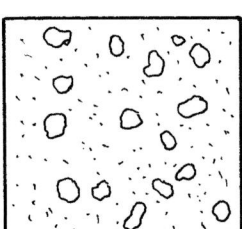

phosphorus refined

refined and fluxed

Al Alloy Heat Treatment

Although heat treatment covers the full range of post-casting thermal processing, for general purposes this is normally taken to imply solution treatment (ST) and ageing (A) by precipitation, in the applicable alloys. However, occasionally use is made of an annealing treatment in order to stress relieve aluminium castings, typically involving holding for a moderate period (≤ 4 hr) at ~350°C, improving ductility by relieving the internal stresses of the casting.

In the USA-based system, a designation for heat treatments is applied as an addendum to the alloy reference, as follows:

O   annealed condition
T4 solution treated (ST) and quenched (Q)
T5 artificially aged (A)
T6 ST, Qu and A
T7 ST, Qu and over-aged
T8 bearing treatment – cold worked and A

For example, alloy 356-T6 would be fully heat-treated for optimum properties.

Precipitation hardening in Al alloys was first discovered with the addition of around 4% Cu (durals), noted previously. In Figure 51, the equilibrium diagram shows that rapid quenching (into water) from ~530°C, arrests the alloy in a metastable, frozen, state on reaching room temperature. Subsequent heating, in the range of RT to 200°C depending on the alloy, enables the process of precipitation hardening to create sub-microscopic particles, platelets, that form throughout the matrix. These are allowed to grow to an optimum size, thereby, causing dislocation pinning – effectively halting the progress of these sub-microscopic crystallographic imperfections – dislocations that otherwise allow the microstructure to slip and slide, resulting in a far lower strength than predicted from structural bonding theory.

As a behaviour of great practical importance, especially in Al alloys, this remarkable mechanism has been well understood since the mid-twentieth century with the advent of direct observation of sub-microscopic structures, by electron microscopy. Beyond the fully aged conditions (T6), continued holding at temperature results in over-ageing (T7) where the particles coarsen, beyond optimum dislocation pinning size, resulting in a reduced strength (Figure 52).

The ability to adjust alloy composition to provide the most convenient ageing temperature can be very useful, for instance with ageing at RT permitting hardening after insertion of pegs or rivets into structures without further heating, albeit allowing no delay in the fitting operation! This mechanism of precipitation hardening also occurs in a number of other alloy systems, includ-

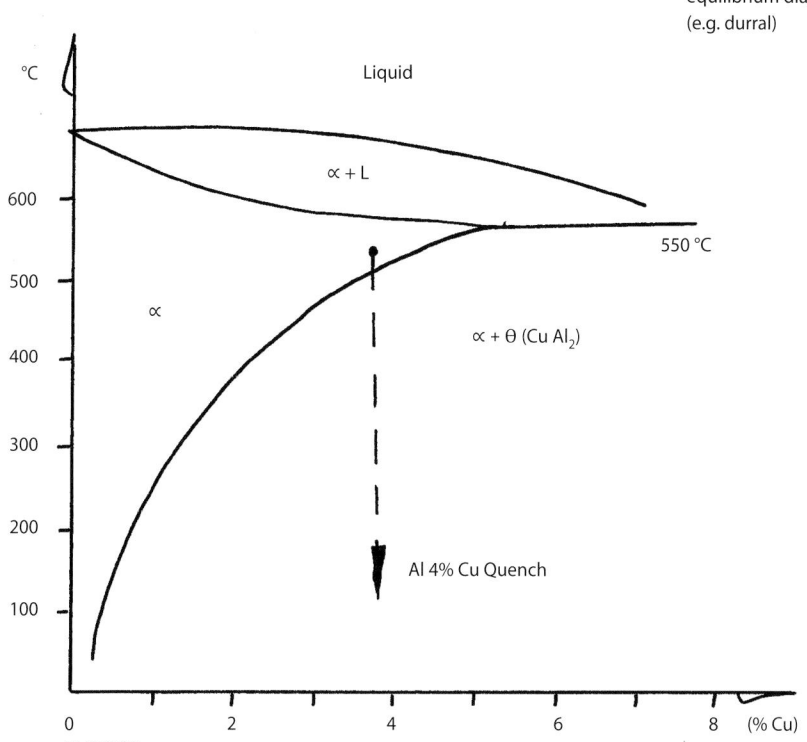

Figure 51 Al–Cu equilibrium diagram (e.g. durral)

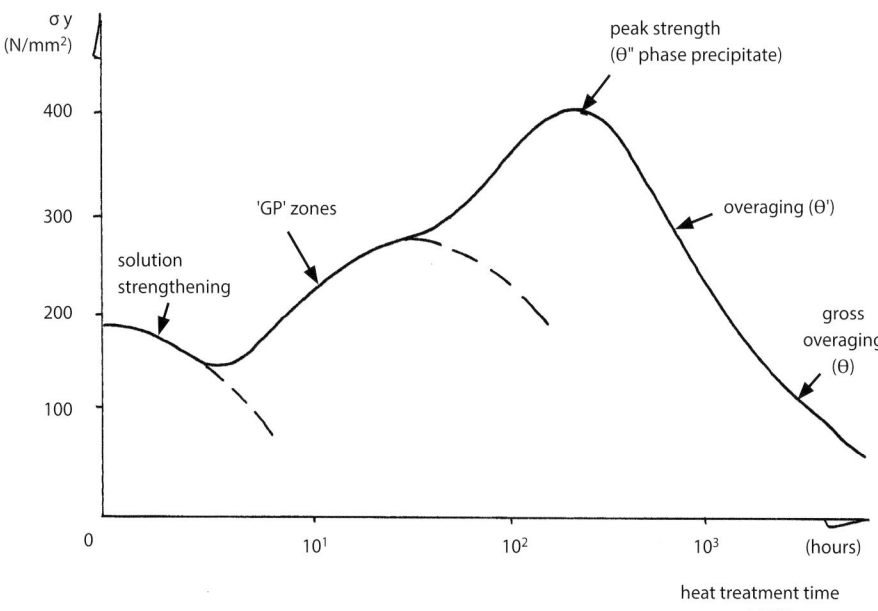

Figure 52 Precipitation hardening diagram.

ing Mg, Ti and particular stainless steels. However, it must not be confused with the, entirely different, heat treatment of higher-carbon and low-alloy steels. In steels, similar quenching treatment procedures produce a different state, that of the Martensitic, ultra-hard, structure that is normally then reheated to temper, soften and toughen the steel before use. This is a subject beyond the scope of a simple casting book, but useful to know about as an area of 'known unknowns', for future reference – see Bibliography, *Tindell, 2013*.

Handling and Post-Processing

The successful production of a load-bearing Al casting requires great attention to be paid to best practice in the handling and transfer of the liquid metal, described in more detail in the Design of Castings section. The gating system, and various liquid metal transfer methods such as counter-gravity, contrast with the simplicity of the gravity method. The latter's simplicity, however, belies the ever-present danger of entrained oxides, as demonstrated in bifilm theory. This is especially vital in the casting of high-quality aluminiums.

Apart from mechanical cutting operations, local repair of the casting can often save the job from an unnecessary remelt, *see* welding repair Chapter 6, 'Post-Casting Processes'.

Practical Alloys – UK Use

Having examined perhaps the most universally adopted system, we now turn to a classification that, although nominally out of date, is still in wide-

Alloy (UK), based BS 1400	Cu	Mg	Si	Fe	Mn	Ni	Zn	Pb	Sn	Ti	Al	other	stress, max (N/mm2)	elongation (%)	hardness (HB)	HT condition	HT process	Remarks
LM 0	0.03	0.03	0.3	0.4	0.03	0.03	0.07	0.03	0.03		99.5	0.5	80	30	25	M	NA	CP - commercial purity, low strenth cast Al
LM 2	.7 - 2.5	0.3	9 - 11.5	1	0.5	0.5	2	0.3	0.2		Rem	0.5	300	1 - 3.0	65 - 90	M	NA	can be die cast
LM 4	2 - 4.0	0.2	4 - 6.0	0.8	.2 -.6	0.3	0.5	0.1	0.1	0.2	Rem	0.25	230 - 390	0 - 2.0	70 - 120	TF	510°C WQ	TF - Solution Treat (ST) and Age (A)
LM 5	0.1	3 - 6.0	0.3	0.6	.3 -.7	0.1	0.1	0.05	0.05	0.2	Rem	0.15	140 - 170	3	50 - 70	M	NA	use for marine application, corrosion resist.
LM 6	0.1	0.1	10 - 13.0	0.6	0.5	0.1	0.1	0.1	0.05	0.2	Rem	0.15	190 - 230	7	55 - 60	M	NA	can be die cast
LM 9	0.2	.2 -.6	10 - 13.0	0.6	.3 -.7	0.1	0.1	0.1	0.05	0.2	Rem	0.15	240	0 - 1.0	95 - 110	TF	530°C WQ	modify with Na, strength better than LM6, poor wear
LM 12	9 - 11.0	.2 -.4	2.5	1	0.6	0.5	0.8	0.1	0.1	0.2	Rem	0.15	170*	.5 - 1.5*	80 - 95	M	NA	prcipitation hardening possible
LM 13	.7 - 1.5	.8 - 1.5	10 - 13.0	1	0.5	1.5	0.1	0.1	0.1	0.2	Rem	0.15	170 - 200	1	100 - 150	TF	520°C WQ	alt HT possible, used elev. Temp., eg. i.c. pistons
LM 16	1 - 1.5	.4 -.6	4.5 - 5.5	0.6	0.5	0.25	0.1	0.1	0.1	0.2	Rem	0.15	230 - 290	1 - 2.0	100 - 110	TF	525°C WQ	
LM 20	0.4	0.2	10 - 13.0	1	0.5	0.1	0.2	0.1	0.1	0.2	Rem	0.2	190 - 230	1 - 3.0	55 - 75	M	NA	good corrosion resist, near LM6, can enhance by anodise
LM 21	3 - 5.0	.1 -.3	5 - 7.0	1	.2 -.6	0.3	0.2	0.1	0.1	0.2	Rem	0.35	150 - 200	1 - 4.0	70 - 100	M	NA	poss HT but results v composition sensative
LM 22	2.8 - 3.8	0.05	4 - 6.0	0.6	.2 -.5	0.15	0.15	0.1	0.05	0.2	Rem	0.15	245*	8	70 - 80	TB	520°C WQ	ST only, pouring temp depends on mould design
LM 24	3 - 4.0	3	7.5 - 9.5	1.3	0.5	0.5	3	0.3	0.2	0.2	Rem	0.5	320	1 - 3.0	85	M	NA	can be die cast, sim to popular USA die cast alloy
LM 25	0.2	.2 -.6	6.5 - 7.5	0.5	0.3	0.1	0.1	0.1	0.05	0.2	Rem	0.15	230 - 280	2*	90 - 110	TF	535°C WQ	strength loss at > 135 C, prolonged temp
LM 26	2 - 4.0	.5 - 1.5	8.5 - 10.5	1.2	0.5	1	1	0.2	0.1	0.2	Rem	0.15	210*	1*	90 - 120	TE		alt for pistons LM 13, sim to SAE 332, USA alloy
LM 28	1.3 - 1.8	.8 - 1.5	17 - 20	0.7	0.5	.8 - 1.5	0.2	0.1	0.1	0.2	Rem	0.3	120	0.5	100 - 140	TF	500°C Air Q	refine with P, avoid Na influxing
LM 29	.5 - 1.3	.8 - 1.3	22 - 25	0.7	0.6	.8 - 1.5	0.2	0.1	0.1	0.2	Rem	0.3	120	0.5	100 - 140	TF	500°C Air Q	remarks as LM 28
LM 30	4 - 5.0	.4 -.7	16 - 18	1.1	0.3	0.1	0.2	0.1	0.1	0.2	Rem	0.3	230	1	110	TS	T 175°C 8hr	can be die cast. TS - stress relieved after HT
LM 31	0.1	.5 -.75	0.25	0.5	0.1	0.1	4.8 - 5.7	0.05	0.05	0.25	Rem	0.15	215	4		TE	T 160°C 8hr	

Table 8 Cast Aluminium alloys (Mechanical Properties). Long-established UK system.

spread use and well understood in industry. For this reason it is useful for the small-scale worker; and also provides the foundation for the current European standards. Despite the logical efforts at harmonization, long-established, apparently superseded standards still have a value for the practitioner who needs to know as much as possible about the relevant alloys that are available – rather than the many appearing in standards, but not generally available.

Tables 8, 9 and 10 summarize the alloys from the LM series from LM 0 to 31, a sufficient range from which to select a suitable casting alloy.

THE COPPER-BASE ALLOYS

Perhaps only second to aluminium alloys for our purposes, the copper-base alloys provide a wide range of casting alloys that have retained an important role in the canon of metal castings in a direct and uninterrupted line, from the Bronze Age to the present day. However, not all of these alloys are easily cast, including the important aluminium bronzes, so that a reasonably detailed review is worthwhile:

These may be grouped as:

◆ High conductivity (Cu)
◆ Brasses (Cu-Sn)
◆ Phosphor bronzes (Cu-Sn-P, with P from 0.4 to 1%)
◆ Lead bronzes (Cu-Sn-Pb)
◆ Gunmetals (Cu-Sn-Zn-Pb)
◆ Aluminium bronzes (Cu-Al)
◆ Copper nickels (Cu-Ni)

See Table 11.

Alloy (UK)	Class	Applications	Machinability	Remarks
LM 0	Al	Limited use as low strength, high elec conductivity, use elec industry. Ductility used in cable fixings.	Soft, build-up on tool, long swarf, coolant used.	Non-heat treatable, too soft for structural work.
LM 2	Al Si10	Die castingalloy, generally interchangable with LM24, lower density. Corrosion resist OK, but inferior to LM6 or 20.	Si makes moderate M/Cing, better than LM6 or 20.	Can improve corrosion props by anodising.
LM 4	Al Si5 Cu3 Mn.5	General purpose, incl cylinder heads, structural, good weldability, section thickness and process tolerant.	OK, between Al Si & Al Cu alloys. Liberal coolant used.	Various HTs can be used, before or after processing. ST for max ductility.
LM 5	Al Si12	Mainly sand cast, other process poss. High corrosion resist, use marine applications, retains high surface finish.	v. good M/Cing, good surface finish.	Also used domestic food handling, cooking.
LM 6	Al Si12	Widely used, genral purpose alloy. Can be used as non- HT.	High Si, difficult M/Cing, use carbide tools and lubricant	Excellent corrosion resist, enhance with anodising.
LM 9	Al Si12 Mg.5 Mn.5	Sand or Low Press die cast. Used where fluidity & corrosion resist of LM6 reqd but extra strength reqd.	Simiar LM6, tool wear, low speeds.	Poor weldability.
LM 12	Al Cu10 Mg.3	Originally used I.C. pistons, now use LM13 or 26, low expansion rate. High pressure parts, brake systems.	Good M/Cing and surface finish.	Used hydraulic systems, good machinability.
LM 13	Al Si12 Cu1 Mg1	Good wear resist, bearing props, low expansion coeff, used IC engines, incl pistons & elevated temps.	Better than LM6 tool wear, use carbide tools and lubricant.	Anodise sulphuric acid, lube retention, dark grey finish.
LM 16	Al Si5 Cu1 Mg.5	Widely used, structural and IC engine, eg. complex cyl heads, good leak tightness. Cast sand & permanent moulds	M/Cing fair, use sharp HSS tools.	Good weldability, care with HT condition.
LM 20	Al Si12	Good corrosion resist, used marine, water jackets, street furature. LM2 & 24 preferredfor die cast, unless LM20 corr resist.	M/Cing difficult, but better than LM6.	Corrosion resist almost as good as LM6, can anodise.
LM 21	Al Si6 Cu4 Mn.4 Mg.2	Similar use as LM4, where no HT. Structural IC engine parts, moderate section OK, general domestic uses.Sand or die cast.	Fair M/Cing, better than LM4, use W-C tools, lube.	Poss HT, not as std. Age hardens at RT, deform before age, if reqd.
LM 22	Al Si5 Cu3 Mn.4	Good castability, high shock resist and strength, use heavy section structural vehicle parts. Chill moulds, min Mg >shock res. resist	Good M/Cing as chill cast, Si limits as above.	Used in ST condition, corrosion resist fair, better than LM4.
LM 24	Al Si8 Cu3.5	Preferred as die cast, better castability than LM6, used unless LM6 corrosion resist reqd. Most popular LM die cast, as SAE 333.0.	Similar to other Si alloys, use W-C or HSS tools and lube.	Poor weldability, corrosion resist sim LM4, for severe use paint protect.
LM 25	Al Si7.5	High strength, good crrosion resist, good castability, use marine, structural, food process. As cast or HT, elev temp OK, < 30 mins.	Fair M/Cing, better than LM6, use sharp HSS tools, lube.	Good weldability. Looses HT strength if longer time at elev temp, (> A T)
LM 26	Al Si10 Cu3 Mg1	Low coeff thermal exp, wear resist, elev temp strength, alt to LM13 for piston & engine parts, sim to USA use as SAE 332.0	Better than LM6 & 13, use W-C tools, lube, but tool wear.	Principal use engine parts, OK corrosion resist, oil absrbing anodise useful.
LM 28	Al Si10 Cu1.5 Mg1 Ni1	HT, properties sim LM26, high strength for high performance engine, eg. Pistons. Refined with P, (hyper-eutectic alloy).	Poorest M/cing of LM alloys, W-C or diamond tools for piston mfe.	Full modification to re-structure large Si platelets, or bad M/Cing, incl. tearing of Si.
LM 29	Al Si18 Cu1.5 Mg1 Ni1	Lower coeff thermal exp than LM28. Alt to LM 28. Control of Si particle size vital to satisfactory M/Cing.	As LM28, v. high Si.	As LM28, refine with P.
LM 30	Al Si17 Cu4.5 Mg.5	Designed as die cast alloy for special IC engine parts, eg cyl blocks without cast Iron liners, structural, pumps, brake shoes.	Usual precautions with hyper-eutectic Si, W-C tools & lube.	Modification of Si reqd for M/Cing as LM28, 29, etc.
LM 31	Al Zn5 Mg.7 Cr.5 Ti	Good shock resist, used large sand castings, general structural parts, generally sand cast. Elev temp relatively good properties.	good M/Cing, (low Si).	HT - TE condition. For M condition, needs 3 weeks aging at RT before use.

Table 9 Cast Aluminium alloys, applications and manufacturing. IC = internal combustion (engines), M/cing machining; W-C = tungsten carbide (tools); SAE = Society of American/Auto Engineers.

Alloy	Fluidity (1 – poor, 5 – good)	Leak Tightness	Pouring Temp. °C
LM 0	3	3	730 - 760
LM 2	5	5	615 - 700
LM 4	4	5	720
LM 5	3	1	700
LM 9	4	4	710
LM 12	3	4	710
LM 13	5	4	670 - 780
LM 16	4	4	710
LM 20	5	5	
LM 21	4	4	720
LM 22	4	4	
LM 24	5	5	700
LM 25	4	5	710
LM 26	4	3	700
LM 28	3	3	735
LM 29	3	3	830
LM 30	4	3	760
LM 31	3	3	620 - 650

Table 10 Al Cast Properties UK.

Equilibrium Diagrams – Copper-Base Alloys

An insight into the characteristics of these different alloys is provided by using equilibrium diagrams. These show how the mixture of two elements provide a range of melting points and different phases across a specified range of compositions, possibly from 0 to 100%, but sometimes for only a very restricted range relating to practical applications. These are most simply seen as two-dimensional charts, although often there are several other elements, and therefore dimensions. With multi-element alloys, it is usual to have a series of 'slices' across a three, or greater, dimensional chart by keeping the third/other element(s) constant. For instance, a lead bronze alloy (Cu Sn Pb) could have a series of graphs of Cu-Sn at slices of constant Pb. This is normally more practical than trying to grasp the complexities of a 3D structure, although modern computing can now facilitate this with appropriate software.

The other principal limitation of equilibrium/phase diagrams is that the details shown are those that exist at equilibrium, which may take a significant time to achieve; it pays no heed to the rate of reactions. Notwithstanding this limitation, equilibrium diagrams can still provide an invaluable guide to the mixing of copper-base alloys, such as in melting points, freezing ranges and intermediate phases. Examples include the complexity of the brasses (Cu Zn) system, where intermediate phases can exist at elevated temperature, but not in equilibrium (slow cooled), at RT. These high-temperature phases can however be captured by rapid quenching to RT, producing an arrested, metastable phase that will remain intact until reheated.

Thus, equilibrium diagrams provide a certain amount of information about the resulting copper-base (and all other) alloys as-cast, but are most useful when used in conjunction with various other analytical tools, such as microstructure examination and mechanical testing, to establish the properties and efficiency of a casting destined for critical application. However, for many, low-stressed jobs it is not necessary to understand these aspects – as is generally the case for much domestic work and statuary, successfully cast over the centuries.

Figures 53 to 55 show examples of simple equilibrium/phase diagrams for Cu-Zn (brass), Cu-Sn (tin bronze) and Cu-Al (aluminium bronze). A full range of data can be found via the Bibliography, such as the ASM metals reference volumes.

Applications of Copper-Base Alloys – Grouping

This section provides a general description of the categories described in Table 11, while the following section indicates the application of the various alloys for specific service conditions.

High Conductivity Copper

These are specialist applications using, effectively, pure Cu for its excellent electrical and thermal conductivity, but not requiring load-bearing strength. An expensive material, it has rather poor castability, and is not generally of immediate concern for casting in the small-scale workshop. It surely caused the ancients some grief until bronze was discovered (see Introduction). A range of alloys containing Cr and other small additions permit use at elevated temperatures, and provide specialist welding electrodes.

Brasses (Cu Zn)

Notable alloys for sand and die casting are SCB3 and DCB3 for a wide range of applications in small to medium castings. These offer good castability, machinability, strength and corrosion

Materials for Castings

categoury	BS:1400	ISO	Cu %	Sn %	Zn %	Pb %	Ni %	Fe %	Al %	Mn %	Si %	P %	cast process	stress yield N/mm2	stress max N/mm2	elongation %	hardness HB	density g/cm3	
high-conductivity Cu	HCC 1	Cu											sand	40	150	25	40	8.9	elec. equipment - connectors, fasteners
	CC1-TF	Cu Cr 1											sand	250	350	10	95	8.9	as HHC1, but where greater strength required
brasses	SCB 3	CuZn 33 Pb 2	63 - 67	1.5	Rem	1.3		0.8	0.1	0.2	0.05	0.05	sand	70	180	12	45	8.5	general, gas, water fittings, good m/c ability
	DCB 3	CuZn 39 Pb 1 Al	58 - 63	1	Rem	0.5 - 2.5	1	0.7	.1 - .8	0.5	0.05	0.02	die	120	280	10	70	8.4	wide use plumbing, greater strength than SCB3
	DCB 3	CuZn 39 Pb 1 Al	58 - 63	1	Rem	0.5 - 2.5	1	0.7	.1 - .8	0.5	0.05	0.02	HP die	250	350	4	110	8.4	improved strength & finish to die cast alloy
	DCB a	CuZn39Pb1Al B	59 - 61	0.35	Rem	1.2 - 1.7	0.2	0.2	.4 - .7	0.05	0.05		die	130	380	30	75	8.5	fine grain, improves SCB 3
	DZR 1	CuZn35Pb2AlAs	61 - 65	0.4	Rem	1.5 - 2.5	0.25	0.35	.3 - .5	0.15	0.01		die	120	280	10	70	8.5	wide use engineering, gravity cast, good brazing
	DZR 1	CuZn35Pb2AlAs	61 - 65	0.4	Rem	1.5 - 2.5	0.25	0.35	.3 - .5	0.15	0.01		HP die	215	370	5	110	8.5	good corrosion resist, use to avoid de-zinkificn.
	DZR 2	CuZn33Pb2Si	64 - 66	0.8	Rem	1.3 - 2.2	0.8	0.5	0.1	0.15	0.6 - 1		HP die	280	400	5	110	8.4	improved strength, surface finish
	HTB1	CuZn35Mn2AlFe	57 - 65	1	Rem	0.5	6	.5 - 2	.5 - 2.5	.5 - 3	0.1	0.03	sand	170	450	20	110	8.5	general eng, corrosion resist, marine, propellor
	HTB1	CuZn35Mn2AlFe	57 - 65	1	Rem	0.5	6	.5 - 2	.5 - 2.5	.5 - 3	0.1	0.03	die	200	475	18	110	8.5	ditto, die cast
	HTB1 Pb	CuZn35Mn2AlFe	59 - 67	1	Rem	1.5	2.5	.5 - 2	1 - 2.5	1 - 3.5	1		sand	150	430	10	100	8.6	sim to HTB1, used ton reduce wear, eg. Spindles
	HTB1 Pb	CuZn35Mn2AlFe	59 - 67	1	Rem	1.5	2.5	.5 - 2	1 - 2.5	1 - 3.5	1		HP die	330	440	3	130	8.6	ditto, die cast
	HTB3	CuZn25Al5Mn4Fe	60 - 67	0.2	Rem	0.2	3	1.5 - 4	3.0 - 7	2.5 - 5	0.1	0.05	sand	450	750	8	180	8	wear resistant, v. high strength, not marine useswear resistant, v. high strength, not marine uses
	HTB3	CuZn25Al5Mn4Fe	60 - 67	0.2	Rem	0.2	3	1.5 - 4	3.0 - 7	2.5 - 5	0.1	0.05	die	480	750	8	180	8	ditto, die cast
high-tensile brass	Si brass	CuZn15O6si.4	78 - 83	0.3	Rem	0.8	1	0.6	0.1	0.2	3.0 - 5	0.3	sand	230	400	10	100	8.6	low Pb, water fittings, valves
	Si brass	CuZn15O6si.4	78 - 83	0.3	Rem	0.8	1	0.6	0.1	0.2	3.0 - 5	0.3	die	300	500	8	130	8.6	ditto, die cast
	Si brass	CuZn15O6si.4	78 - 83	0.3	Rem	0.8	1	0.6	0.1	0.2	3.0 - 5	0.3	HP die	370	530	5	150	8.6	ditto, die cast, v high strength

Table 11 Cast Copper Alloys (UK system) part 1 of 2.

category	BS:1400	ISO	Cu %	Sn %	Zn %	Pb %	Ni %	Fe %	Al %	Mn %	Si %	P %	cast process	stress yield N/mm2	stress max N/mm2	elongation %	hardness HB	density g/cm3	Applications / Remarks
Sn and Phosphor bronze	PB1	CuSn11P	87-89	11	0.05	0.25	0.1	0.1	0.01	0.05	0.01	1	sand	130	250	5	60	8.8	high duty brgs on hard shafts, use lube
	PB1	CuSn11P	87-89	11	0.05	0.25	0.1	0.1	0.01	0.05	0.01	1	die	170	310	2	85	8.8	ditto die cast
	CT1	CuSn11	87-89	11	0.05	0.25	0.1	0.1	0.01	0.05	0.01		sand	130	250	5	60	8.8	corrosion resist in alkaline, acidic, pollute water
	PB2	CuSn12	85-89	12	0.5	0.7	2	0.2	0.01	0.2	0.01	0.6	sand	140	260	7	80	8.7	use gears, bevel gears, worm wheels, couplings
	PB2	CuSn12	85-89	12	0.5	0.7	2	0.2	0.01	0.2	0.01	0.6	die	150	270	5	80	8.7	ditto die cast
	PB4	CuSn11Pb2	84-87	11	2	1-2.5	2	0.2	0.01	0.2	0.01	0.4	sand	130	240	5	80	8.7	high load brgs. Medium speed, less lube PB1 OK
leaded bearings	LB4	CuSn5Pb9	80-87	5	2	10	2	0.25	0.01	0.2	0.01	0.1	sand	60	160	7	55	8.9	moderate load brgs. Less lube than PB4 OK
	LB2	CuSN10Pb10	78-80	10	2	10	2	0.25	0.01	0.2	0.01	0.1	sand	80	180	8	60	9	eg. Heavy machinery, plain brgs, greased
	LB2	CuSN10Pb10	78-80	10	2	10	2	0.25	0.01	0.2	0.01	0.1	die	110	220	3	65	9	ditto die cast
	LB1	CuSn7Pb15	74-80	8	2	15	.5-2	0.25	0.01	0.2	0.01	0.1	sand	80	170	8	60	9.1	moderate load brgs. Less lube than LB2 OK
	LB5	CuSn5Pb20	70-78	5	2	20	.5-2	0.25	0.01	0.2	0.01	0.1	sand	70	150	5	45	9.3	moderate load brgs. Less lube than LB1 OK
Gunmetals	LG1	CuSn3Pb5Zn8	81-86	3	8	5	2	0.5	0.01		0.01	0.05	sand	85	180	15	60	8.8	lower duty brgs, water service, below 250 deg C
	LG2	CuSn5Pb5Zn5	81-87	5	5	5	2	0.3	0.01		0.01	0.1	sand	90	200	13	60	8.8	general purpose, good corrosion resist, marine
	LG2	CuSn5Pb5Zn5	81-87	5	5	5	2	0.3	0.01		0.01	0.1	die	110	220	6	65	8.8	ditto die cast
	LG4	CuSn7Pb3Zn2	85-89	7	2	3	2	0.2	0.01		0.01	0.1	sand	130	230	14	65	8.7	structural, marine, pumps, couplings, pipes
	LG4	CuSn7Pb3Zn2	85-89	7	2	3	2	0.2	0.01		0.01	0.1	die	130	230	12	70	8.7	ditto die cast
Aluminium bronze	AB1	CuAl10Fe2	83-90	0.2	0.3	0.3	1.5	2	10	1	0.2		sand	180	500	18	100	7.5	high strength, good wear resist, structural use
	AB1	CuAl10Fe2	83-90	0.2	0.3	0.3	1.5	2	10	1	0.2		die	250	600	20	130	7.5	ditto die cast
	AB2	CuAl10Fe5Ni5	76-83	0.1	0.5	0.03	5	5	10	3	0.1		sand	250	600	13	140	7.6	ultra high strength, corrosion resist, marine duty
	AB2	CuAl10Fe5Ni5	76-83	0.1	0.5	0.03	5	5	10	3	0.1		die	280	650	7	150	7.6	ditto die cast
	CMA1	CuMn11Al8Fe3Ni3	68-77	0.5	1	0.05	3	3	8.0	11	0.15	0.05	sand	275	630	18	150	7.5	seawater critical parts, pumps, impellors
Cu-Ni alloys	CN1	CuNi30Cr2FeMnSi	Rem		0.7	0.005	30	1	0.01	1	0.50	0.01	sand	230	440	18	115	8.8	high strength, good corr resist, critical use
	CN2	CuNi30Fe1Mn1Nb	Rem		0.5	0.01	30	1	0.01	1	0.60	0.01	sand	230	440	18	115	8.8	as CN1, also good weldability

Table 11 Cast Copper Alloys (UK system) part 2 of 2.

Materials for Castings • 107

resistance, including in fresh water. *See Table 11.*

Familiar applications are common plumbing fittings and domestic items where a high surface finish (polish) is preferred, also suitable for electro-plating. Si can be substituted for Pb additions where required, and this family of alloys can provide relatively low-cost casting for valves and fittings exposed to fresh water.

Alloys HTB1 and HTB3 are of significantly higher strength, the former with good corrosion resistance in marine applications, and more general use. The latter alloy is particularly hard, used for its wear resistance properties at slow sliding velocities, but not advised for marine or similar corrosion environments.

Tin Bronzes (Cu Sn)

These are usually chosen for their very good corrosion resistance in harsh waters such as acidic, polluted in-shore, boiler-feed, and those contaminated with particles of sand or silt. As expensive alloys, those with greater Sn can be deployed in wear-resistant applications, as an alternative to phosphor bronze.

Phosphor Bronzes (Cu Sn P)

These are critically dependent on the P content ($0.4 \leq P \leq 1.0\%$), harder and less ductile than tin bronzes, and used where bearings are required to sustain high loads and surface speeds. They may also be used in wear-critical gears such as worm wheels. Use is often made of high production methods such as centrifugal- and continuous-casting,

category	BS:1400	ISO	Cu %	Sn %	Zn %	Pb %	Ni %	Fe %	Al %	Mn %	Si %	P %	cast process	stress yield N/mm2	stress max N/mm2	elonga-tion %	hard-ness HB	density g/cm3	Applications / Remarks
high- conduc- tivity Cu	HCC 1	Cu											sand	40	150	25	40	8.9	elec. equipment - connectors, fasteners
	CC1-TF	Cu Cr 1											sand	250	350	10	95	8.9	as HHC1, but where greater strength required
brasses	SCB 3	CuZn 33 Pb 2	63 - 67	1.5	Rem	1.3				0.2	0.05	0.05	sand	70	180	12	45	8.5	general, gas, water fittings, good m/c ability
	DCB 3	CuZn 39 Pb 1 Al	58 - 63	1	Rem	0.5 - 2.5	1	0.7	.1 - .8	0.5	0.05	0.02	die	120	280	10	70	8.4	wide use plumbing, greater strength than SCB3
	DCB 3	CuZn 39 Pb 1 Al	58 - 63	1	Rem	0.5 - 2.5	1	0.7	.1 - .8	0.5	0.05	0.02	HP die	250	350	4	110	8.4	improved strength & finish to die cast alloy
	DCB a	CuZn39Pb1Al B	59 - 61	0.35	Rem	1.2 - 1.7	0.2	0.2	.4 - .7	0.05			die	130	380	30	75	8.5	fine grain, improves SCB 3
	DZR 1	CuZn35Pb2AlAs	61 - 65	0.4	Rem	1.5 - 2.5	0.25	0.35	.3 - .5	0.15	0.01		die	120	280	10	70	8.5	wide use engineering, gravity cast, good brazing
	DZR 1	CuZn35Pb2AlAs	61 - 65	0.4	Rem	1.5 - 2.5	0.25	0.35	.3 - .5	0.15	0.01		HP die	215	370	5	110	8.5	good corrosion resist, use to avoid de-zinkificn.
	DZR 2	CuZn35Pb2Si	64 - 66	0.8	Rem	1.3 - 2.2	0.8	0.5	0.1	0.15	0.6 - 1		HP die	280	400	5	110	8.4	improved strength, surface finish
high-tensile brass	HTB1	CuZn35Mn2AlFe	57 - 65	1	Rem	0.5	6	.5 - 2	.5 - 2.5	.5 - 3	0.1	0.03	sand	170	450	20	110	8.5	general eng, corrosion resist, marine, propellor
	HTB1	CuZn35Mn2AlFe	57 - 65	1	Rem	0.5	6	.5 - 2	.5 - 2.5	.5 - 3	0.1	0.03	die	200	475	18	110	8.5	ditto, die cast
	HTB1 Pb	CuZn35Mn2AlFe	59 - 67	1	Rem	1.5	2.5	.5 - 2	1 - 2.5	1 - 3.5	1		sand	150	430	10	100	8.6	sim to HTB1, used ton reduce wear, eg. Spindles
	HTB1 Pb	CuZn35Mn2AlFe	59 - 67	1	Rem	1.5	2.5	.5 - 2	1 - 2.5	1 - 3.5	1		HP die	330	440	3	130	8.6	ditto, die cast
	HTB3	CuZn25Al5Mn4Fe	60 - 67	0.2	Rem	0.2	3	1.5 - 4	3.0 - 7	2.5 - 5	0.1	0.05	sand	450	750	8	180	8	wear resistant, v. high strength, not marine uses
	HTB3	CuZn25Al5Mn4Fe	60 - 67	0.2	Rem	0.2	3	1.5 - 4	3.0 - 7	2.5 - 5	0.1	0.05	die	480	750	8	180	8	ditto, die cast
	Si brass	CuZn15O6si.4	78 - 83	0.3	Rem	0.8	1	0.6	0.1	0.2	3.0 - 5	0.3	sand	230	400	10	100	8.6	low Pb, water fittings, valves
	Si brass	CuZn15O6si.4	78 - 83	0.3	Rem	0.8	1	0.6	0.1	0.2	3.0 - 5	0.3	die	300	500	8	130	8.6	ditto, die cast
	Si brass	CuZn15O6si.4	78 - 83	0.3	Rem	0.8	1	0.6	0.1	0.2	3.0 - 5	0.3	HP die	370	530	5	150	8.6	ditto, die cast, v high strength

Table 12 Cast Copper Alloys (UK system) based on superceded BS 1400 part 1 of 2.

or chill casting, for optimum as-cast properties.

Lead Bronzes (Cu Sn Pb)

Predominantly used for less rigorous conditions of load and speed than phosphor-bronze bearing applications. Increasing Pb content improves tolerance of intermittent lubrication, harmlessly embedding any stray abrasive particles retained by the lubrication system, operating with water or oil lubrication.

Gunmetals (Cu Sn Zn Pb)

These provide useful, general purpose, low-cost alloys – known for all-round good castability, strength, and machinability. Corrosion resistance is very good in most environments, and superior to the brasses. Used for intricate castings and those requiring leak-resistance such as valve bodies, pumps and associated fittings. Bearings for moderate loads and speeds and backing material for high-duty white metal bearing shells are common applications, and it is recognized from familiar dark gunmetal patina of public statuary.

Aluminium Bronze (Cu Al)

The Al confers a thin alumina oxide film, further enhancing the extremely good corrosion resistance in marine environments, with resistance to tarnishing and elevated temperature oxidation. Applications range from architectural products and critical engineering parts to high-duty marine propellers and shafts, operating at high velocities.

category	BS:1400	ISO	Cu %	Sn %	Zn %	Pb %	Ni %	Fe %	Al %	Mn %	Si %	P %	cast process	stress yield N/mm2	stress max N/mm2	elongation %	hardness HB	density g/cm3	Applications / Remarks
Sn and Phosphor bronze	PB1	CuSn11P	87-89	11	0.05	0.25	0.1	0.1	0.01	0.05	0.01	1	sand	130	250	5	60	8.8	high duty brgs on hard shafts, use lube
	PB1	CuSn11P	87-89	11	0.05	0.25	0.1	0.1	0.01	0.05	0.01	1	die	170	310	2	85	8.8	ditto die cast
	CT1	CuSn11	87-89	11	0.05	0.25	0.1	0.1	0.01	0.05	0.01		sand	130	250	5	60	8.8	corrosion resist in alkaline, acidic, pollute water
	PB2	CuSn12	85-89	12	0.5	0.7	2	0.2	0.01	0.2	0.01	0.6	sand	140	260	7	80	8.7	use gears, bevel gears, worm wheels, couplings
	PB2	CuSn12	85-89	12	0.5	0.7	2	0.2	0.01	0.2	0.01	0.6	die	150	270	5	80	8.7	ditto die cast
	PB4	CuSn11Pb2	84-87	11	2	1-2.5	2	0.2	0.01	0.2	0.01	0.4	sand	130	240	5	80	8.7	high load brgs. Medium speed, less lube PB1 OK
leaded bearings	LB4	CuSn5Pb9	80-87	5	2	10	2	0.25	0.01	0.2	0.01	0.1	sand	60	160	7	55	8.9	moderate load brgs. Less lube than PB4 OK
	LB2	CuSN10Pb10	78-80	10	2	10	2	0.25	0.01	0.2	0.01	0.1	sand	80	180	8	60	9	eg. Heavy machinery, plain brgs, greased
	LB2	CuSN10Pb10	78-80	10	2	10	2	0.25	0.01	0.2	0.01	0.1	die	110	220	3	65	9	ditto die cast
	LB1	CuSn7Pb15	74-80	8	2	15	.5-2	0.25	0.01	0.2	0.01	0.1	sand	80	170	8	60	9.1	moderate load brgs. Less lube than LB2 OK
	LB5	CuSn5Pb20	70-78	5	2	20	.5-2	0.5	0.01	0.2	0.01	0.1	sand	70	150	5	45	9.3	moderate load brgs. Less lube than LB1 OK
Gunmetals	LG1	CuSn3Pb5Zn8	81-86	3	8	5	2	0.3	0.01		0.01	0.05	sand	85	180	15	60	8.8	lower duty brgs, water service, below 250 deg C
	LG2	CuSn5Pb5Zn5	81-87	5	5	5	2	0.3	0.01		0.01	0.1	sand	90	200	13	60	8.8	general purpose, good corrosion resist, marine
	LG2	CuSn5Pb5Zn5	81-87	5	5	5	2	0.3	0.01		0.01	0.1	die	110	220	6	65	8.8	ditto die cast
	LG4	CuSn7Pb3Zn2	85-89	7	2	3	2	0.2	0.01		0.01	0.1	sand	130	230	14	65	8.7	structural, marine, pumps, couplings, pipes
	LG4	CuSn7Pb3Zn2	85-89	7	2	3	2	0.2	0.01		0.01	0.1	die	130	230	12	70	8.7	ditto die cast
Aluminium bronze	AB1	CuAl10Fe2	83-90	0.2	0.3	0.3	1.5	2	10	1	0.2		sand	180	500	18	100	7.5	high strength, good wear resist, structural use
	AB1	CuAl10Fe2	83-90	0.2	0.3	0.3	1.5	2	10	1	0.2		die	250	600	20	130	7.5	ditto die cast
	AB2	CuAl10Fe5Ni5	76-83	0.1	0.5	0.03	5	5	10	3	0.1		sand	250	600	13	140	7.6	ultra high strength, corrosion resist, marine duty
	AB2	CuAl10Fe5Ni5	76-83	0.1	0.5	0.03	5	5	10	3	0.1		die	280	650	7	150	7.6	ditto die cast
	CMA1	CuMn11Al8Fe3Ni3	68-77	0.5	1	0.05	3	3	8.0	11	0.15	0.05	sand	275	630	18	150	7.5	seawater critical parts, pumps, impellors
Cu-Ni alloys	CN1	CuNi30Cr2FeMnSi	Rem		0.7	0.005	30	1	0.01	1	0.50	0.01	sand	230	440	18	115	8.8	high strength, good corr resist, critical use
	CN2	CuNi30Fe1Mn1Nb	Rem		0.5	0.01	30	1	0.01	1	0.60	0.01	sand	230	440	18	115	8.8	as CN1, also good weldability

Table 12 Cast Copper Alloys (UK system) based on superceded BS 1400 part 2 of 2.

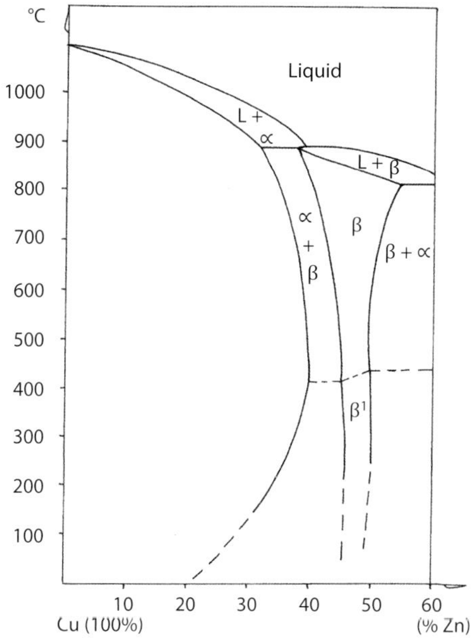

Figure 53 Cu–Zn (brass) equilibrium diagram.

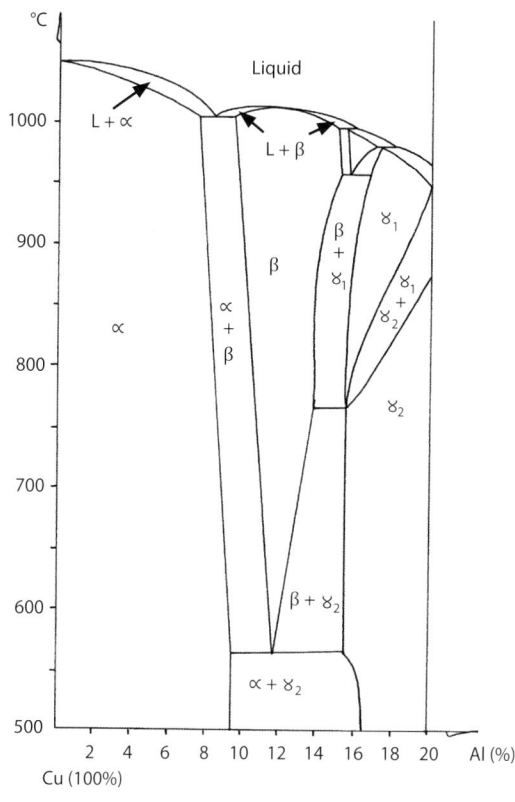

Figure 55 Cu–Al (aluminium bronze) equilibrium diagram.

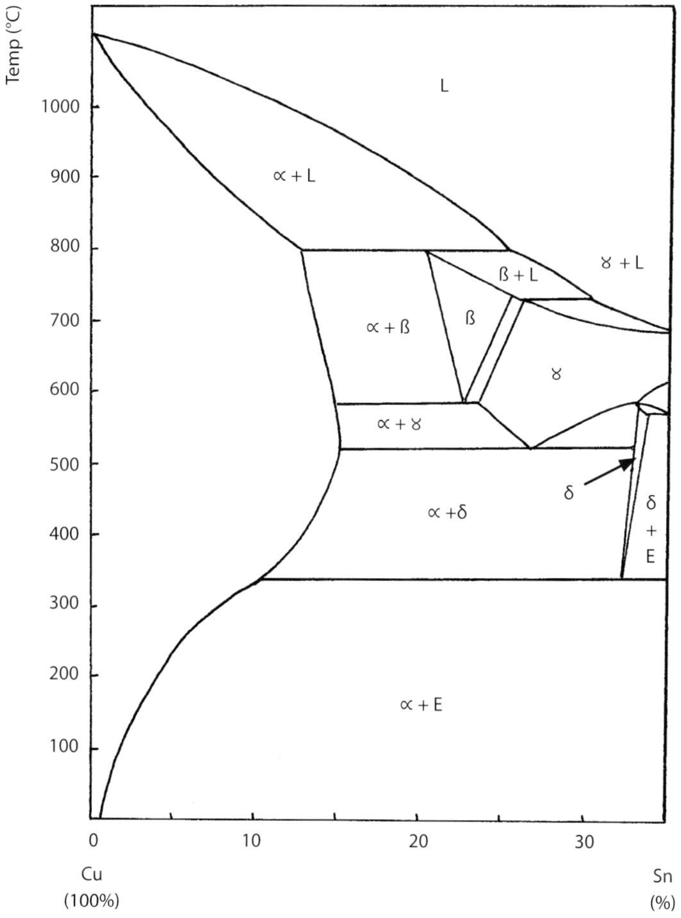

Good wear-resistance and non-sparking are also features. While castability is relatively poor, processes have been successfully developed to overcome this difficulty, see Bibliography, Meigh, 2000.

Copper Nickel (Cu Ni)

These alloys tend to be used where particularly difficult and aggressive marine applications involve high velocities, loading, and corrosion, in preference to aluminium bronze. They are typically employed for pumps and valve bodies, pipes and fittings. Cu-Ni alloys are generally expensive, and tend to be used for low-volume production items.

Figure 54 Cu-Sn (tin bronze) quilibrium diagram.

Choice of Alloy by Application

Corrosion Resistance

Wherever corrosion is of concern, then the copper-base alloys are likely candidates. A large body of experience is of great assistance in alloy selection, as outlined below. In common usage, the alloys compare favourably with stainless steel and can present a viable choice for the amateur foundry, in contrast to the practical difficulty in producing steel castings without industrial-scale equipment and facilities.

Copper-base alloys do slowly tarnish on exposure to normal internal and external conditions, but the rate of general corrosion is usually negligible – unlike the ferrous alloys, except the stainless steels. Carbon- and low-alloy steels suffer badly from general oxidation – rusting – due to their porous oxide film, which fails to offer compete protection in the damp climates familiar in many locations, causing an acceleration in corrosion rate. Some copper-base alloys are even resistant to tarnishing, as for the aluminium bronzes, with Cu-9Al, or die cast DCB3, known for retaining a bright finish, desirable for indoor decorative items. Even for external use these alloys perform well, and the gunmetal patina is often the finish desired for statuary.

In marine environments the copper-base alloys often develop a familiar green patina, and remain resistant to general corrosion with a penetration rate of < 0.003mm per year, virtually nil. Polluted urban environments generally have little effect, beyond typically developing a darker tarnish and penetration < 0.007mm per year. Again, Cu-9Al retains its brightness well. For heavy concentrations of sulphur dioxide (SO_2), such as chimneys, the aluminium bronzes AB1 and AB2 are recommended.

Where significant loading and aggressive environments are encountered, the brasses can suffer from stress corrosion cracking (SCC); although arsenical brass is less affected. The aluminium bronzes, AB1 and AB2, are noted for their strength and resistance to SCC, AB2 is used in high SO_2 exposure fittings. Gunmetals, such as Cu-10Sn, are also resistant, although of lower strength than the aluminium bronzes.

Fresh Water Service

Plumbing fittings for domestic application often use brasses SCB3 and DCB3. Alternatively, DZR1 or DZR2, if de-zincification is a concern, such as sub-soil with possible acidic water attack. Where Pb additions need to be avoided, silicon brass can be used, albeit at increased cost.

For large industrial pumps the choice of alloy requires great care, as impellers can be subject to erosion and cavitation damage if particular operating conditions are not avoided. In aqueous liquids, the impeller can be made more noble than the body, for sacrificial corrosion of the heavier-section body. LG2 and LG4 can be used for impellers (to 25m/sec), until more serious conditions dictate AB2, for impeller velocities to 45m/sec.

Boiler feed-waters can be handled satisfactorily with tin bronzes although, once again, aluminium bronze, AB2, is the alloy of choice.

Sea Water Service

Generally, the use of the brasses is not recommended for serious marine sub-surface use. The gunmetals and aluminium bronzes with their higher strength, typically AB2, are preferred. This applies also to bearings for rudders, and structural items subject to heavy loading. Where avoidance of crevice corrosion and impingement attack is vital, then the Cu-Ni alloys CN1 and CN2 are the choice for naval use, but are normally considered too expensive for general application. For propellers, AB2 is preferred for its high resistance to corrosion fatigue, around a factor of two better than the brass HTB1, which can be used for less onerous work or smaller vessels. CMA1 is a possible alternative, although not as good for corrosion fatigue as AB2. The good weldability and castability of the latter alloy is also beneficial.

Chemical Handling

In the chemical industry, many fittings and valves are selected from the copper-base alloys of gunmetals, tin bronzes and aluminium bronzes. These find use in handling non-oxidizing acids: acetic; citric; carbolic; oxalic; paper making; sulphite liquids; leather industry; tannic acid; and soap industry fatty acids. See the Bibliography for further details and corrosion rates, as this is an area where general assumptions can be disastrously misleading, with experimental data and experience of processes being of paramount importance. Generally, the brasses are not used for these applications.

For sulphuric acids, aluminium bronze is preferred, although gunmetal and tin bronze may be suitable. Hydrochloric acid is normally avoided in copper-base alloys, and nitric acid promotes rapid attack.

Superheated steam and dry industrial gasses, O_2, N_2, CO_2 and natural gas can be handled with brass, gunmetal, tin bronze, and aluminium bronze castings. Similarly, dry SO_2 and the halogen gasses, with some corrosion in moisture; aluminium bronze pumps and associated parts have proven satisfactory in moist sulphur dioxide (SO_2) up to 100°C. Hydrogen sulphide and ammonia are unsuitable for copper-base alloys; and for acetylene, only brasses with < 65% Cu are useable.

For food handling, copper-base alloys are in theory suitable, with low rates of attack and non-toxic action. However, copper traces can affect taste, well before toxicity concerns, and normally these castings are provided with an impermeable coating of tin or nickel. If uncoated, the best choice is aluminium bronze.

Bearings

Copper-base alloys are widely used for plain bearings, where the lowest coefficient of friction of white metal bearings is not necessary. Phosphor bronze is the most popular alloy, with high resistance to wear; and the leaded brasses, SCB3 and DCB3 are used for their ability to handle imperfect lubrication conditions. Copper-base alloys are also widely employed in critical heavy duty steel roller- and ball- races for rolling-element cages.

The design of bearings relies not only on the yield strength, but critically on the fatigue strength of the material. For instance, AB2 sand cast has a fatigue limit ~220N/mm^2 (at 10^8 cycles), appropriate for the high-cycle service of bearings that can fail in the unusual mode of compression fatigue.

Thermal expansion of copper-base alloys should be considered in design, being some 50 per cent greater (at ~18 x 10^{-6}m/m), than the popular plain and low-alloy steels. This expansion is important in bearing-to-shaft fit.

For optimum wear service, the shaft:bearing hardness should be ~3:1, possible with a high-strength, low-alloy steel shaft, running in a relatively low-strength copper alloy bearing. Where high-impact loading and sliding velocities are encountered, a high-tin phosphor bronze alloy, e.g. PB1 or Cu-12Sn -2 Ni, can be employed. Proper lubrication is necessary in these circumstances, with a shaft hardness > 300 H_B, appropriate with a heat-treated, low-alloy steel, such as EN19 (AISI 4140).

For medium loading conditions, alloy LB2 with shaft hardness ≥ 250 H_B, or the less costly LG4, with shaft ≥ 280 H_B, can be used. These are more tolerant of fit and lubrication than the high-performance phosphor bronze combinations, but still require a reasonable system. Where lubrication is less efficient and wear product present, the higher lead content of LB4 or LB5, from 9–20% Pb respectively, is acceptable in water-lubricated bearings. Shaft hardness of 200 to 150 H_B, respectively, are suitable.

Low-load bearings can use LG2 or LG1, with small bearings possible in brass SCB3, although lubrication is still important. Shaft hardness of 250 H_B is advised with these selections.

Aluminium bronzes are not usually employed for bearings, although the good corrosion resistance of AB2, combined with shaft > 300 H_B, is a useful combination for marine use, where heavy loads and corrosion resistance are important.

Copper Alloys for Gears

Important parameters in the design of gears are the bending fatigue strength of the teeth, and surface stresses arising from the frictional resistance of mating teeth sliding over one another. These are aspects of copper-base alloys that can be favouhrably compared to other alternative materials, with the additional benefit of corrosion resistance and castability. However, the case integrity is very important, requiring low levels of porosity and inclusions. Larger gears are therefore often centrifugally cast, the chill effect also promoting a fine grain structure.

For high-duty worm wheels, the preference is PB2, PB1 and Cu -12Sn -2 Ni alloys. For lower surface velocities, brasses HTB1, HTB3, or aluminium bronze AB2, can be considered. Where less critical, lower loads, speeds, and gear sizes, SCB3 or LG2, can be employed.

Other Applications

Copper alloys are often chosen for severe service requiring wear-resistant capabilities, such as gear selector forks in motor vehicles, where aluminium bronze AB1, or leaded high-tensile brass HTB1, is often used. In high load conditions, subject to sliding wear, high-strength brass HTB1 and HTB3, aluminium bronze AB1 and AB2, or even the harder Cu -11Al -5Fe -5Ni, are likely candidates. Valve spindles can be produced from continuously cast gunmetal, phosphor bronze, or aluminium bronze, in order of increasing strength requirements. Valve seats in internal combustion engines can be produced from the same range of alloys, either sand cast or centrifugally cast, and machined to size.

Non-sparking tools are an important application where working in potentially explosive environments. Originally, copper-beryllium alloys were cast, but difficulty in foundry hazards means that AB1 and AB2 are normally chosen.

Pressure-tightness or freedom from leak-paths can be an important feature for pressure-retaining castings, and this is a function of process, control, and alloy selection. SCB1, SCB2, LG2, and LG4, provide best choice for these castings.

CAST IRONS

After aluminiums and copper base alloys, the next important casting alloy system is undoubtedly the cast irons. While there are a number of other metals of vital importance in the modern world, namely zinc, magnesium, cobalt and nickel-based, plus titanium and the many steels – these are unlikely to fall within the remit of any but the most advanced small-scale foundry worker – and so are described later in less detail. They deserve some attention as they have important applications in many familiar commercial products, from domestic machines to critical aerospace engines – rather than as practical prospects for processing in the amateur foundry.

Considering casting metals of direct processing relevance, we are interested in the long-established **grey cast irons**. There are, of course, many other varieties of cast iron that have been developed, largely in the nineteenth and twentieth centuries, touched upon as important commercial iron castings, but more appropriate to larger scale operations, namely: malleable, Blackheart, Whiteheart, ductile (spheroidal graphite), high alloy (Ni-resist, Ni-hard), and heat-treated irons. While for practical purposes we are principally concerned with grey cast iron, it is useful to know about its close derivatives; white cast iron, and ductile iron. The former, white CI, derives its name from the fracture face appearance, in contrast to the grey fracture face of its eponymous relative. Ductile iron is based on a similar chemical composition to grey CI, and relies on a remarkable process involving the late addition, 'inoculation', of small additions, including cerium and magnesium that spheroidize the grey iron graphite flakes. This transforms the notoriously brittle grey CI into a remarkable ductility – thereby opening up a whole range of applications previously considered far beyond such castings.

Grey Cast Iron

First produced in China in the fourth century BC, cast iron came to the West with the Iron Age, following the copper alloy development that led to the Bronze Age. But cast iron was not of universal importance until the Middle Ages, such as for the cannons cast during the reign of Henry VIII. This was a precursor to the eighteenth century Industrial Revolution in England, which demanded a stronger and more adaptable material than wood, to power the fast-developing machinery that was ushering in the Machine Age.

The development of blast furnaces at Coalbrookdale in Shropshire, England, saw an explosion in the applications of (grey) cast iron, from the famous iron bridge, built in 1779 (see Introduction, Photos 3 and 4), to many others across the UK. This progressed until the understanding of engineering structures identified the limitations of these cast irons. With their extremely low ductility, it led to unexpected failures – many disastrous – when structural members were placed in tension and subjected to unexpected overloading. The immediate response, in the late Victorian period, was to substitute the recently developed low-carbon stehel, wrought-iron or latterly, mild steel, throughout such structures. The long-established practice of using cast iron in compression, as for Ironbridge, remained sound and continues to this day, where products excel when designed appropriately. It was not until the 1940s that ductile iron was developed, to subsequently provide a low-cost ferrous metal casting alterna-

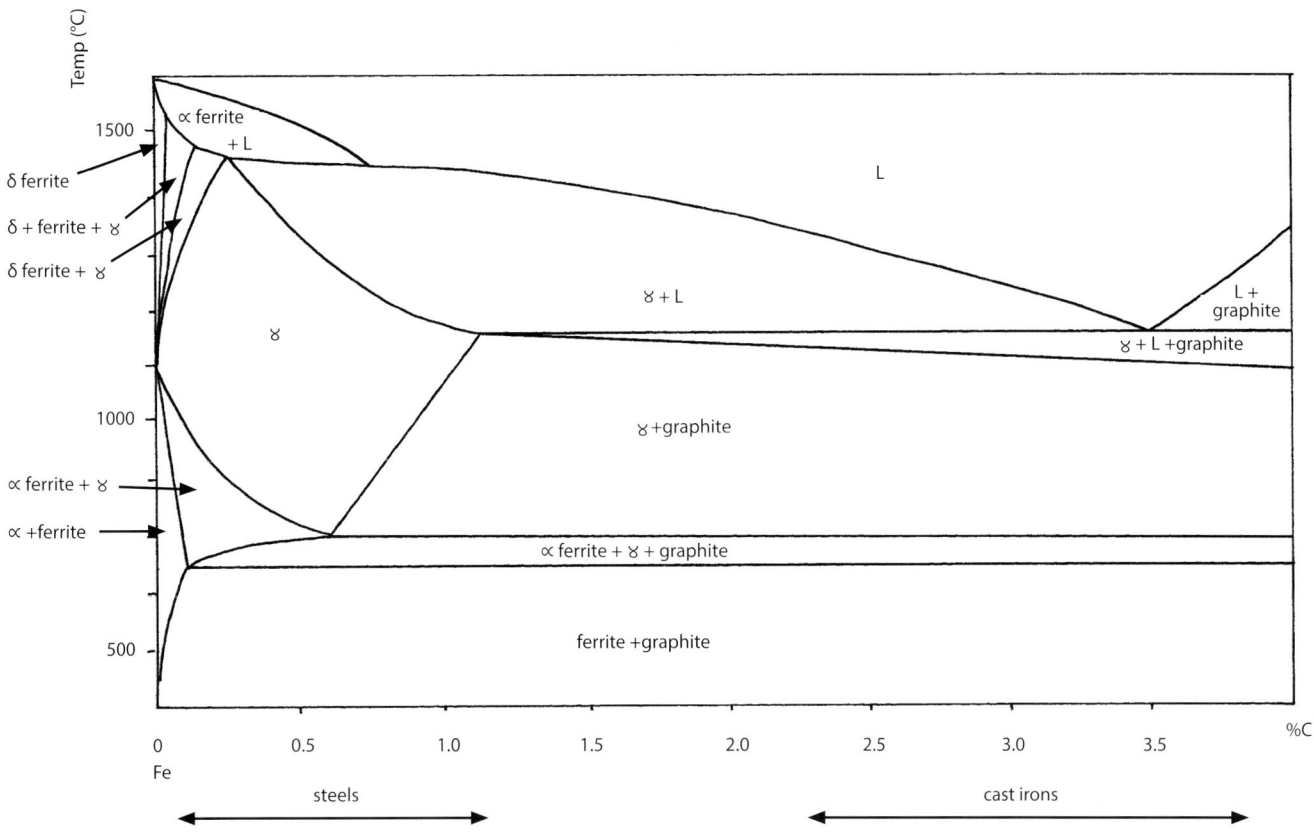

Figure 56 Fe-C equilibrium diagram (at 2% Si).

tive to parts and structures fabricated from steel.

Grey Cast Iron Composition

It is useful to consider cast iron composition with the assistance of the equilibrium diagram (Figure 56). The effect of the primary elements of Fe, C, Si, and P, can be simplified by considering the familiar Fe-C diagram at particular values of Si, in Figure 60, at 2% Si. There is a substitution effect with C and Si that enables a carbon equivalent (CE) to be used as: $CE = (C + Si + P)/3$.

The important feature of grey CI concerns the graphite flake, type, and distribution. Characterized in the USA system by the ASTM as in Figures 58 and 59, and known as 'Graphite morphology'. Also usefully, the ASTM system classifies grey CI into categories based on tensile strength and composition, (C + Si), as Table 12. These cast irons generally comprise 3–3.5% C and 1.8–2.4% Si, as major elements in the Fe (iron).

This contrasts dramatically with the C in steels, which ranges from ~0.1% for mild steel to ~1.0% for high C steel. The effect of this increased C in CI is profound, and results in the C forming long graphite flakes emanating from rosettes, perhaps more like the heart of a cabbage and sprouting leaves than a rose. This structure determines the lack of ductility, due to the pronounced stress-raiser effects of the discontinuous interruptions to the Fe-based matrix. However, these graphite flakes also provide for ready machinability, a high 'damping capacity'; and inherent surface lubrication – all features of great value in, for instance, machine-tool beds such as lathe slideways. Bear in mind that all these features apply to

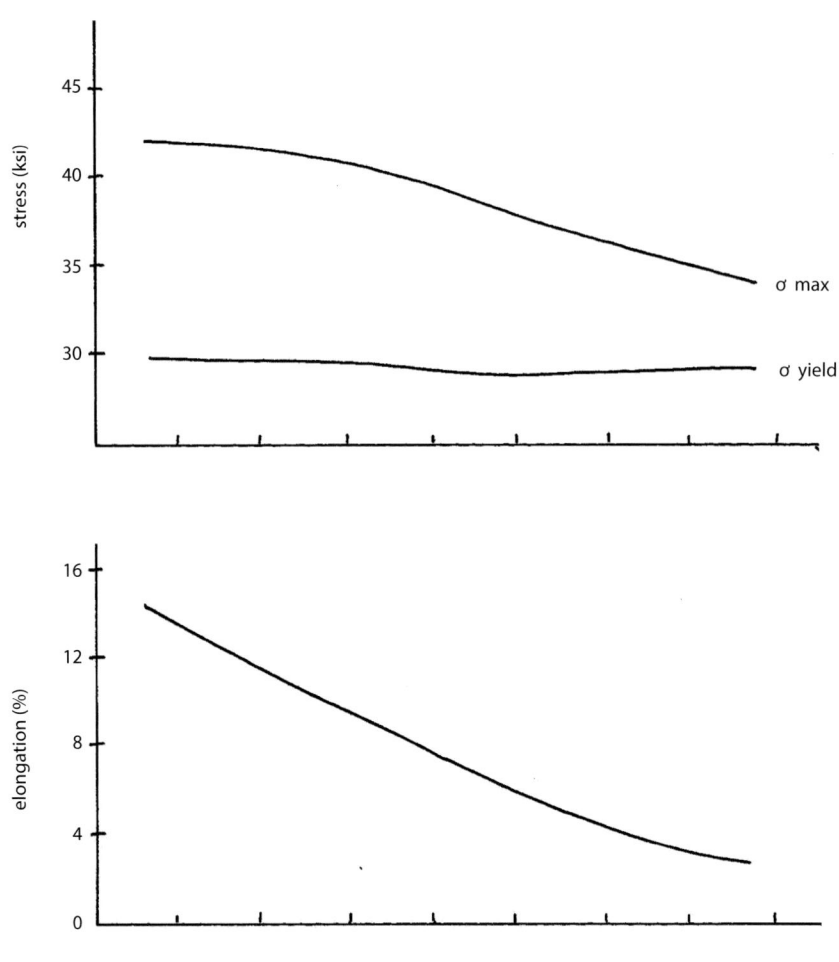

Figure 57 Effect of dendrite cell size on mechanical properties of an Al-Si alloy (A356).

a microscopic scale, although clearly visible when prepared for the optical microscope, at magnifications above ~100 x.

Returning to the Fe C equilibrium diagram, compositions for grey CI are chosen as hypo-eutectic with C < 4.3, this being the eutectoid point on the diagram. The cooling melt undergoes structural changes as a consequence of this near-eutectic profile, as shown in Figure 61. The general effects of omni-present minor elements, **phosphorus** (P) and **sulphur** (S), are important. Phosphorus, present to some extent, is not normally a deliberate addition, but arises from the scrap charge or pig iron. Forming a low melting point phosphide, it can produce a phase known as steadite. Phosphorus promotes fluidity, but too much can produce shrinkage porosity, and usually 0.02–0.1% P is sought. Sulphur is important in CI, normally in the range 0.05–0.12% S content must be balanced with manganese (Mn) additions, in order to produce non-harmful Mn sulphides, MnS, according to the simple relationship:

% Mn ≥ 1.7S + 0.3%. (≥ 1.7S + 0.3%)

Note that, as with many aspects of cast iron theory and practice, there remains scope for refinement and development of detailed mechanisms and optimizations, despite the long-term usage and research into this remarkably common, familiar, and important material.

A particular feature relevant to casting of grey CI, is the balance between shrinkage due to solidification and expansion due to the growth of the graphite flakes, resulting in a near-zero overall shrinkage, and resultant as-cast shape near that of the pattern, for compositions around the eutectoid, C ≥ 4.3. Combined with its relatively low melting point (around 1,150°C), and fluidity enabling it to virtually run like water, it has been seen as 'Nature's gift to the foundryman. . . .' (see Bibliography, Campbell 2011).

Among the many and varied minor alloying elements in various CI, are nickel (Ni) and chromium (Cr). Ni is used to refine the pearlitic and graphite structures, thereby potentially improving toughness, as resistance to low-energy fracture; and reducing the section sensitivity, where different thickness of the cast form structures severely affected by cooling rates. Cr can be added, with Ni, as a carbide stabilizer, reducing free graphite and acting as a chilling medium.

Copper (Cu) and molybedenium

Materials for Castings • 115

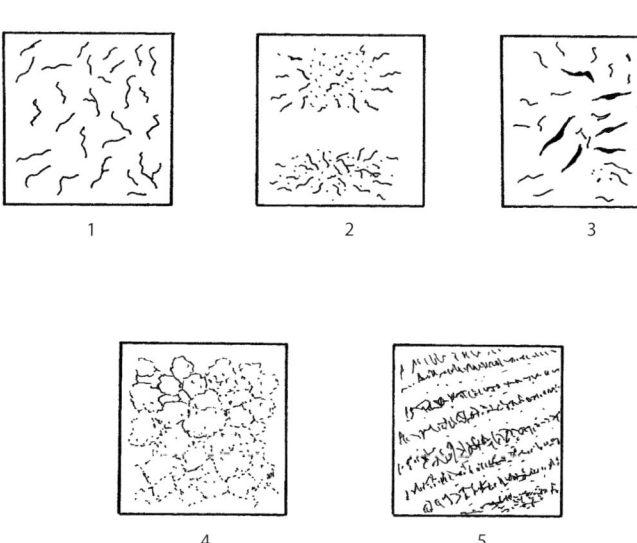

1. Random flake orientation
2. Flake rosettes
3. Variation in flake sizes
4. Interdendritic segregation – random
5. Interdendritic segregation – preferred orientation

Figure 58 Cast iron graphite flake characterization, based on ASTM, A247.

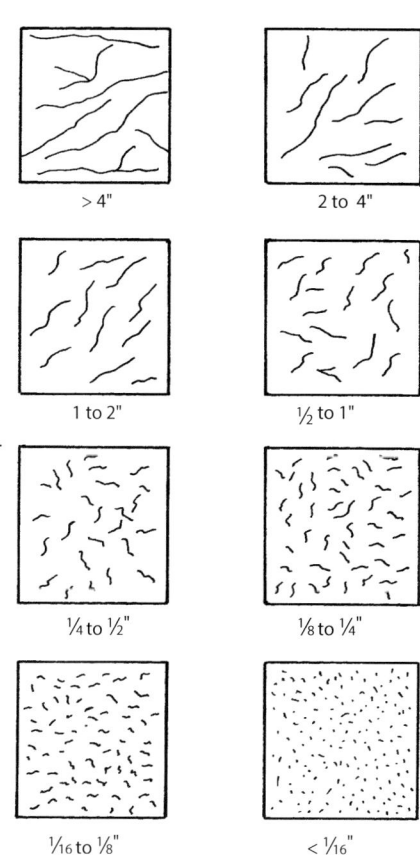

Figure 59 Cast iron graphite flake size, length, based on A247.

Cast Iron ASTM A48 Class	carbon (%)	silicon (%)	tensile strength (ksi)	modulus of elasticity, E (x 10³ ksi)
20	3.4 - 4.6	2.3 - 2.5	22	10
30	3.1 - 3.3	2.1 - 2.3	31	14
40	3.0 - 3.2	1.7 - 2.0	57	18
60	2.5 - 2.9	1.9 - 2.1	63	21

Table 13 Grey Cast Iron

(Mo), around 1%, can be added; the former to improve fluidity and decrease chilling; the latter to increase chill and as a graphite- and pearlite-refiner.

Vanadium (V), in small amounts, is added as a cementite-stabilizer, also for increasing hardness, wear, and heat resistance. Titanium (Ti) and zirconium (Zr), are added – the former as a degassing agent, and for assisting fluidity; both as deoxidizers; and the latter as a graphite-former.

Grey Cast Iron – Structures

The critical feature of grey CI is the graphite flakes – emanating from rosettes, three-dimensional structures through which micro sections are cut to reveal the two-dimensional flakes as shown on micrographs, as in Photos 78 and 79. The low density of these rosettes balances the freezing contraction of the melt, thereby providing a greater probability of avoiding shrinkage porosity in the final casting.

The graphite flake morphology is damaging to the matrix, clearly providing severe, albeit often small-scale,

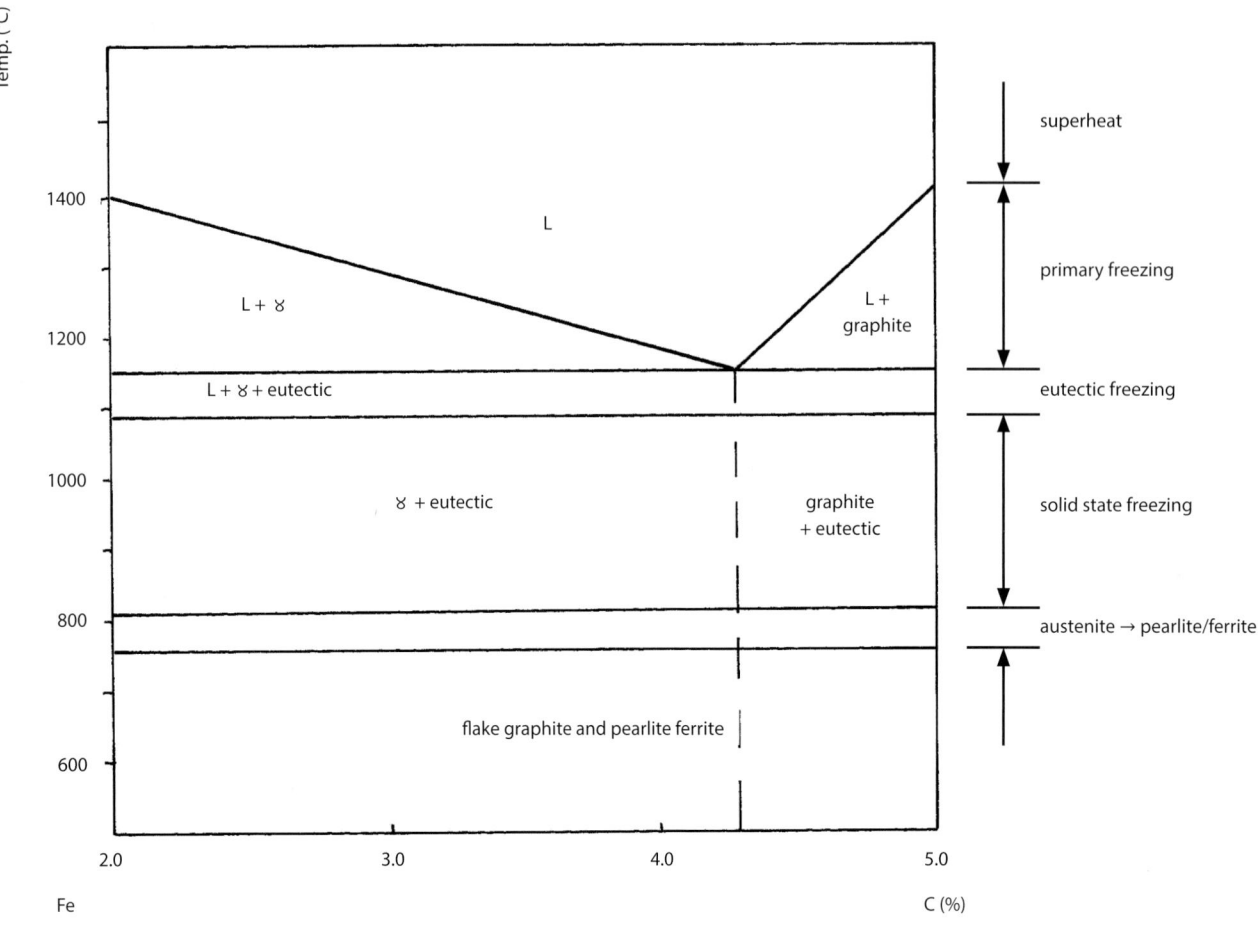

Figure 60 Fe-C equilibrium diagram at 2% Si (schematic).

stress-raisers. This leads inevitably to the poor ductility – near zero elongation beyond yield, to fracture – and toughness, rendering grey CI unsuitable for sustaining tensile loads beyond around 25 per cent of yield, in order to safeguard against sudden overload failure. Note, however, that compressive strength is comparable to that of the structural steels. This discontinuous structure has benefits to the matrix where shock and vibration resistance is required, measured as damping capacity; and where lubrication and chip-breaking characteristics, due to free graphite flakes, benefit dry-running bearings and machining operations.

Grey CI is a softer material where the graphite is formed in a matrix of transformed austenite and cementite. Where a low-strength CI is required, for instance in non-weight-sensitive parts, such as casings where discontinuous machining damages cutting tool tips – then the matrix can often be softened with heat treatment by annealing. Where strength is not critical, this can lead to dramatic improvements in machining operations, especially where machining power is limited, as with multi-purpose or machining-centre equipment, rather than earlier generations of high-powered centre lathes and capstans.

Although all cast metals are to some degree section sensitive, with increasing size reducing the cooling rate, grey CI is particularly sensitive, with regard to strength and hardness. In hypo-eutectic irons (C < 4.3), the initial phase that is affected on cooling is the austenite-forming dendrites at the liquidus. With

Photo 78 Micrograph of grey (or flake) cast iron, showing graphite flakes in ferrite matrix. (Photo: Thomas Dudley Foundry)

further cooling the growing austenite dendrites are enriched with C until the eutectic composition (C = 4.3 per cent) is found, at ~1,130°C, depending on the Si content. At this stage, eutectic austenite and graphite flakes form simultaneously. These deposition centres form according to the number of nucleation sites appearing throughout the melt, growing until all the liquid is consumed, thus forming a cellular structure.

As the cells grow, the phosphorus is displaced to the boundaries of the cells, freezing at ~980°C, as a eutectic. Study of microstructures, arrested at this point, demonstrate that the graphite flake growth is restrained by the cell size, which in turn is determined by the number and disposition of nucleation sites, and the freezing rate of the casting. Cell size has been found to range from ~1 to 40 per mm^2.

Ductile (Spheroid Graphite SG) Iron

The starting point for producing SG iron is the composition of a grey CI, with the treatment through inoculation designed to alter the mechanically damaging flake structure of the graphite. (See photos 80 and 81).

The formation of graphite rosettes and flakes is promoted by sulphur, so that a spherical structure can be imposed on the graphite if the S can be deleted. This can be assisted by addition of small amounts of cerium and magnesium, following a treatment with calcium carbide. The effect is to upset the preference for the graphite to grow along preferential planes and instead extend isotropically, in all directions, resulting in spherical structures, free from the gross stress-raisers of the graphite flakes. Care with the treatment is required as the calcium carbide is used initially to deplete the S, with the introduction of traces of Mg, which also has an attraction to S and O_2. The Mg is required to reach solution in the liquid iron in order to precipitate the spherical growth-mode of the graphite. In order to assist this process, the Mg is often provided as an inoculant, in the form of a Fe-Si-Mg compound.

While this appears a deceptively simple route to producing perfectly spherical graphite nodules, the mechanisms involved at a structural level are complex, and controversies about formation and growth remain some way from resolution, despite considerable research effort on a topic that has been utilized to great effect for well over half a century. However, as noted above, the result is that SG iron can complete

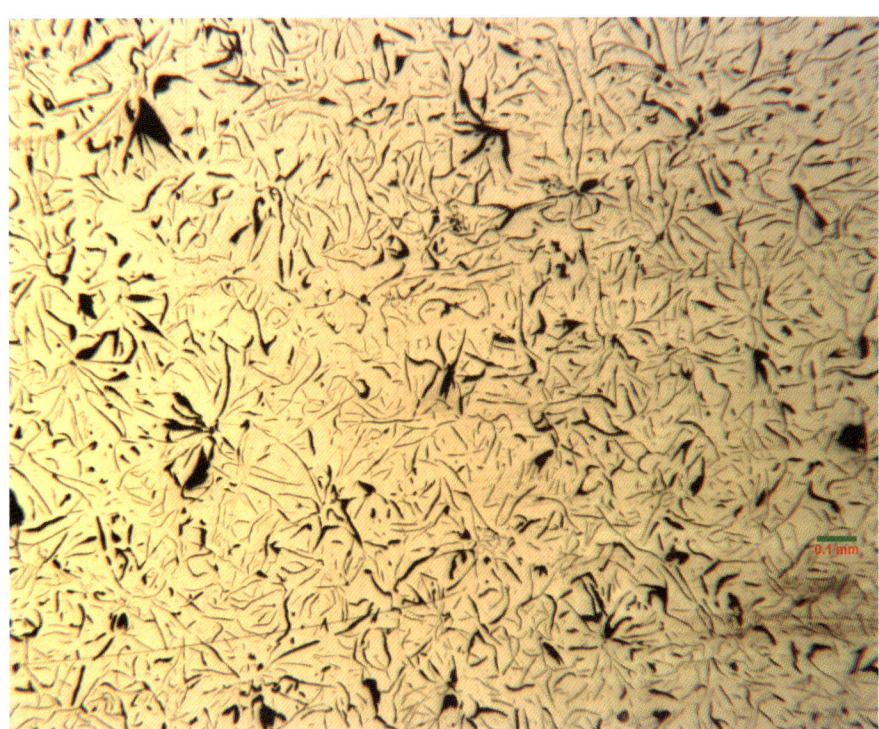

Photo 79 The same micrograph at higher magnification. (Photo: Thomas Dudley Foundry)

in terms of ductility and toughness, as well as strength – with structural steels. This provides the designer with an alternative route to fabrication in the production of critical and complex components familiar in the modern world, as discussed in Chapter 4, 'Design for Castings'.

The usual structure of SG iron as graphite spheroids embedded in a pearlitic matrix, provides a strong and tough material. Where increased ductility is sought, the casting may be heat-treated, by annealing. This causes the carbon from the pearlite matrix to either precipitate on to the graphite spheroids; or to produce smaller spheroids, thus depleting the matrix towards becoming fully ferritic. This provides even greater ductility, albeit naturally at a lower strength.

An important development of SG iron is austempered SG iron, using a multi-stage heat-treatment as an austenitizing treatment at ~950°C, followed by austempering at ~350°C for one hour. This provides a Bainitic structure, analogous to that produced by the multi-stage heat treatments of high-strength, low-alloy steels used for the most exacting tasks requiring strength and toughness, such as in high-performance internal combustion engines. The Bainitic matrix of the austempered SG iron is reported to have mechanical properties of strength, toughness, and fatigue resistance that has enabled these castings to successfully replace expensive fabrications; for instance, high-performance car suspension components.

White Cast Iron

In contrast to the grey fracture face of grey CI, white CI displays a white fracture face, a consequence of its matrix of cementite (Fe_3C) phase, and whereas grey CI is a relatively soft alloy with minimal ductility (< 1% elongation), white CI is extremely hard with virtually zero ductility (~0% elongation).

The composition difference is relatively small, but the lower Si content and faster cooling – for instance, in thin sections – means that the Fe_3C phase is precipitated as a metastable, non-equilibrium phase as seen on the FeC phase diagram (Figure 61). During cooling the cementite is precipitated as fairly coarse particles, part of a eutectic mixture with the austenite phase. The latter can then undergo a transformation to a martensitic phase, as encountered in high C steels. Thus, a eutectic carbide structure is formed, creating a matrix of considerable hardness and strength. This is not the precipitation hardening mechanism that operates in other alloy systems to pin dislocations – but simply as a consequence of the bulk effect of its large volume-fraction of intrinsically very hard constituents. The predominance of hard carbide could constitute classification as a cermet, providing a material harder than most metals. It is therefore employed for cutting tools, including hand files, and wear-resistant products such as in abrasive fluid handling pumps and crushing mills. As a relatively low-cost material, it finds many beneficial applications, where deliberately chosen. By way of warning, where encountered unintentionally in section-sensitive parts of a casting, it can provide a nasty shock when attempting machining by the usual methods!

Malleable Cast Iron

An earlier development than SG CI, malleable CI begins as a white CI, then is heat treated at ~900°C for an extended period (days). This produces graphite that precipitates at a lower rate than the rosette formation of grey CI, the action of increased surface tension serving to encourage spheroids, rather than flakes. Although tending to be a less controlled process than for SG CI, the effect is similarly to reduce the stress-raising problems associated with flake graphite, thereby greatly improving ductility. Apart from being a slow process, an inherent problem with this route to less brittle castings is the need for a white CI casting, which normally restricts it to thinner section components.

Blackheart Cast Iron

The terms Blackheart and Whiteheart relate to forms of malleable iron, all attempting to convert the flake graphite to spheroids through heat treatment, as described above, the names deriving from the fracture-face appearances. They have largely been superseded by the considerably more efficient and practical approach of in-process inoculation, as a route to providing ductile CI, although specialist variants are still being developed.

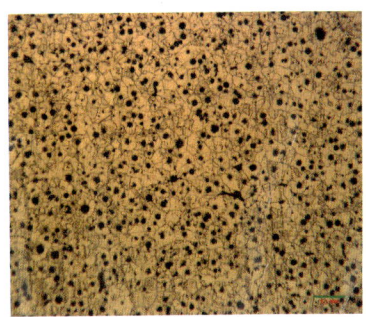

Photo 80 Ductile (or nodular/spheroidal graphite) cast iron, graphite forming spheroids in second phase matrix. (Photo: Thomas Dudley Foundry)

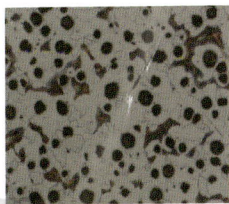

Photo 81 The same micrograph showing graphite nodules within mainly ferrite matrix. (Photo: Thomas Dudley Foundry)

High Alloy CI (Ni-Resit, Ni Hard)

There are a number of high alloy specialist cast irons developed for specific applications, usually for larger industrial products, such as petro-chemical power plant pump casings. High-Si grey CI was developed in the 1930s, in the UK by the British Cast Iron Research Association (BCIRA), and was known as Silal. These include 2% Cr or Ni, for their wear resistance in pumps and equipment for use above ~250°C, proving successful until generally being superseded by the high-Ni alloys.

Ni-resist and Ni-Hard are typical of the high-Ni (up to 36 per cent Ni) Fe-alloys, with spherodized graphite structures, designed for exacting duty in high temperature or corrosion-resistant service. This can include food handling and internal combustion engine components, such as exhaust manifolds, cylinder liners and valve guides. Naturally, these are expensive items and the province of extensive R&D, for volume production or industrial prototype work.

Steels

The range of steel castings is so extensive – from the low C, mild steels, to high C; tungsten carbides (WC); low-alloy, heat-treatable; to high-alloy, stainless steels – to be beyond the scope of this review. In practice, the casting of steels is effectively beyond the practical aspiration of the small-scale operator, for whom by far the most common application of these materials is in the wrought form, either as discrete components, such as forged suspension link or valve spring; or fabricated, as in structural steel welded framework – so these alloys are not considered here.

FURTHER NON-FERROUS ALLOYS

Zinc

Zinc alloys are primarily of interest as a high-pressure die casting (HPDC) material, some 80 per cent of zinc-based castings being produced in this manner; one that is considered the province of high-volume production due to the cost and complexity of the equipment involved in the whole process.

Nevertheless, Zn-based castings abound in everyday life, especially for smaller domestic and commercial components, including computer-based equipment and high-precision components in vehicles, such as carburettors and electrical systems.

These materials were first cast around 1914 using HPDC methods, but early problems with their practical application caused a loss of confidence until the restriction in impurities of Bi, Pb, Cd, and Sn, in the Zn, led to a purity level of 99.99% Zn. This reduces the problem of migration of these heavy elements to the grain boundaries, with consequent loss of mechanical properties when in the presence of heat or moisture.

All practical Zn alloys for die casting include Al. The first to be developed, in the 1920s, were the alloys ZAMAK 3 and 5, zamak from 'Z' for Zn, 'A' as Al, 'MA' as Mg and 'K' for Cu, (in German). Both alloys contain 4% Al and correspond closely with the USA alloys A and B respectively.

These alloy compositions were developed to provide reliable thin-wall sections down to 0.75mm (0.030in); but recent alloy developments, increasing the Al content to 4.5 per cent, nearer to the 5 per cent eutectic of Zn-Al, are anticipated to render wall thicknesses of 0.3mm (0.012in) possible. The use of these hypo-eutectic, < 5% Al alloys also confers temperature advantages, reducing the melting point from ~420 to ~380°C. *See* Figure 62.

There are also a series of hypereutectic alloys, containing 8, 12 and 27% Al, known as ZA8, ZA12, and ZA27. These were developed in the 1960s, and provide quite remarkable properties, as used in HPDC applications – with strength, toughness, and bearing capability, superior to the other competing low-cost alloys. As-cast A27 has a strength of 440N/mm^2 (~60ksi), higher than almost all comparable Al and Mg cast alloys. Note, however, the higher melting point of these alloys, ~500°C for A27, as Figure 61.

There is also the interesting property of 'superplasticity' exhibited by certain Zn alloys. At particular (slow) deformation rates, combined with fine grain size and heat treatment, it is possible to obtain a remarkable 1,000 per cent deformation at room temperature, approaching two orders of magnitude greater than that normally obtained! Limited by microscopic cavitation, it promises even greater capability with improved casting technique, and attention to bifilm theory, noted in Chapter 1. While such possibilities may be of futuristic interest, an existing occasional problem with Zn casting has been limited creep resistance, defined as a dimensional relaxation at temperature, over the long term. Not usually an engineering problem, there are instances where this failure mode is critical, such as in high-temperature turbine blades, where it is the defining characteristic requiring special high-Ni alloys to cope. Fortunately, the normal Zn-alloy casting applications can avoid such problems.

Finally, Zn alloys can be developed to provide an improved 'damping capacity', a feature previously encountered in cast irons. Although, not as significant, alloys have been developed for vehicle use by Mitsubishi R&D, using 40–80% Al – making them more Al-Zn alloys than Zn-based.

Magnesium (Mg)

Whilst Mg is actually the lightest of the common metals and possesses the highest specific stiffness combined with a high specific strength, it unfortunately presents an insurmountable obstacle to the amateur casting worker in that it is too dangerous to handle in the molten state. Experience and considerable expertise is essential in casting Mg and its alloys.

Despite the tempting properties provided by its low specific weight, it is also difficult to machine, join, and form, plus it has an inherently poor corrosion resistance. Alloy development, such as alloy AZ91 (Mg-9% Al-1 Zn), has overcome these problems to a degree, but this remains a highly specialist area. However, the potential benefits of production from an even lighter product than the aluminium alloys is so appealing – for highly weight-sensitive consumer items such as a mobile phones and cameras, and structural parts for aircraft and high-performance vehicles – that it has driven manufacturers to employ Mg alloys wherever possible.

The oxide film MgO is of prime importance when considering the processing of Mg, especially in the molten state. Its density is greater than the base metal, thereby failing to fully cover the solid and protect from the atmosphere. Foundry practice was originally to protect the melt by the fluxes of chloride and fluoride, but this has been superseded by the adoption of dry melting methods using gases protection. Initial use of the ozone-depleting SF_6 has been replaced with less damaging chlorine- and fluorine-based gases, or SO_2 and CO_2. It should be noted that among the highly reactive behaviour of Mg is its affinity with argon (Ar), and nasty accidents have occurred where Ar has been present in contact with the melt and the atmosphere.

From the above, Mg is clearly not a material to be cast without due consideration, but nevertheless it is found in quite widespread applications that benefit from its unique physical properties, almost exclusively where weight is of critical importance.

Cobalt (Co), Nickel (Ni) and Titanium (Ti)

Cobalt-based alloys were developed in the 1930s, particularly for aircraft turbochargers, as the Vitallium series, from the dental alloy of Co -27Cr-5Mo-0.5C. Produced with properties superior to the Fe-based alloys, they are used in high-temperature applications, with the capability of operating up to 800°C.

Although to some extent overtaken by the high-Ni alloys, Co-alloys are still produced to fulfil important applications. These are split three ways, between high temperature aerospace engine components; industrial cutting tools and valve parts; and medical prosthesis. The latter form part of the small group of metals authorized for implantation in the human body. All of these applications arise from the Co-alloy characteristics of resistance to heat, corrosion, and wear; combined with high strength – albeit where its high density dictates the less weight-critical applications.

These are not alloys of direct workshop application for the home foundry

Materials for Castings • 121

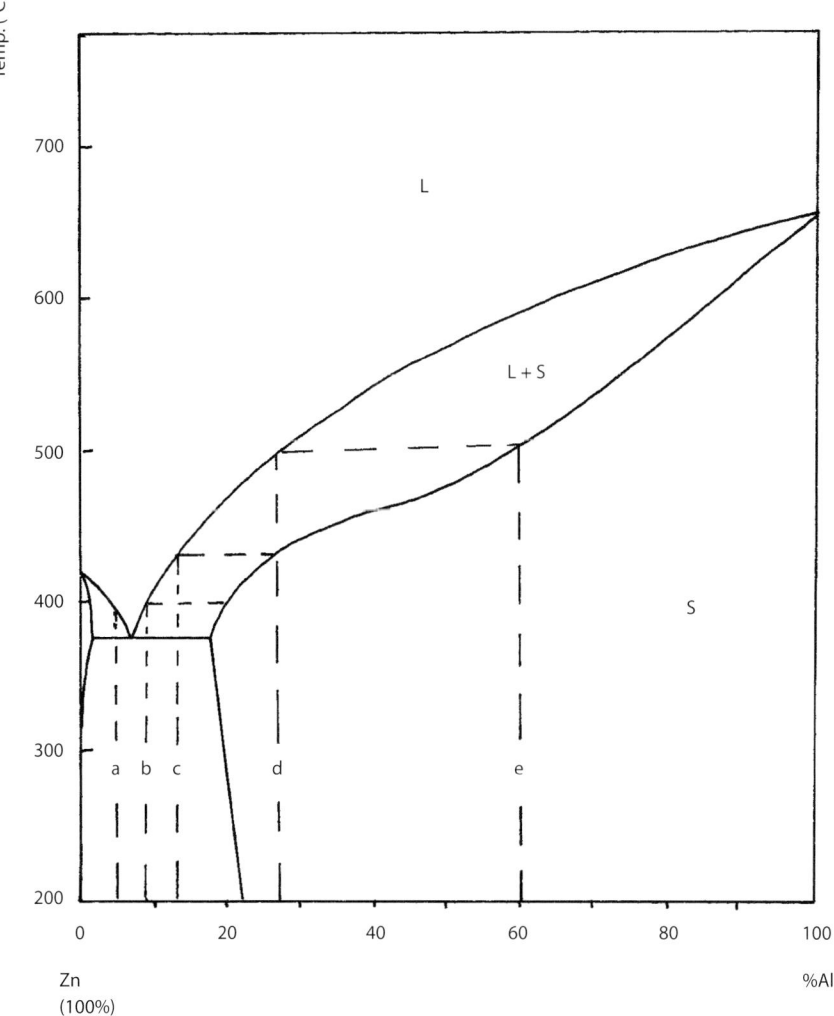

Alloy		
a	ZA 4	(Zn–4Al)
b	ZA 8	(Zn–8Al)
c	ZA 12	(Zn–12Al)
d	ZA 27	(Zn–27Al)
e	ZA 27	(composition – range d to e)

Figure 61 Zn-Al equilibrium diagram (ZAMAK die-cast alloys), after Campbell, 2011.

due to their high raw material cost and specialist applications, but for a background knowledge of cast alloys.

High Ni alloys have been highly developed during the latter half of the twentieth century, particularly as the need for creep resistant turbine blades in jet engines became the performance-limiting factor, see Figure 62. This has led to a series of alloys, typically containing > 50% Ni, with Cr, Co, and Mo, as major alloying elements. In conjunction with this compositional development it has been found that, in marked contrast to the normal pursuit of fine-grained material, the production of single crystal turbine blades provides the highest creep resistance. This is a measure of extensive testing under load at high temperature, as measured in a 10,000 hour rupture test, (as Figures 62 and 63).

High Ni alloys have been developed for a very wide range of industrial applications, and can now be found in almost every application requiring high strength, with corrosion-, heat-, and wear-resistance, albeit at a relatively high cost. The cost of raw materials processing, and specialized application, make this another sector beyond practical consideration of the small-scale worker.

Titanium is the final element in this review, and is likewise of interest more for its important applications than practical consideration as a material for the home foundry.

The serious development of Ti alloys only began in the 1950s, but rapid growth has seen it become a mainstay of the aerospace industry, particularly in the jet engine sectors where the temperature is less than that sustained by the front end, High -Ni alloys. The great advantage of Ti alloys lies in their low density, and relatively high resistance to temperature, plus a renowned corrosion resistance in a wide variety of media.

These properties have seen important applications for human body implants, taking advantage of the lower density than Co-based and stainless steel alloys, with excellent corrosion resistance and bio-compatibility. Industrial applications include use in marine

122 • Materials for Castings

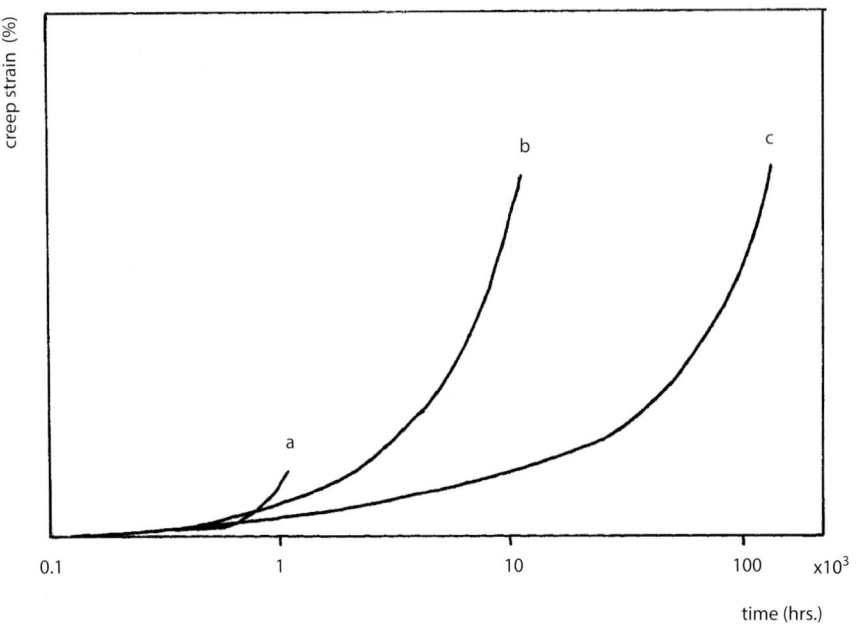

a – conventional cast (equiaxed structure)
b – long grains (columnar growth)
c – single crystal

Figure 62 Creep curve comparisons for Ni-base superalloy (schematic).

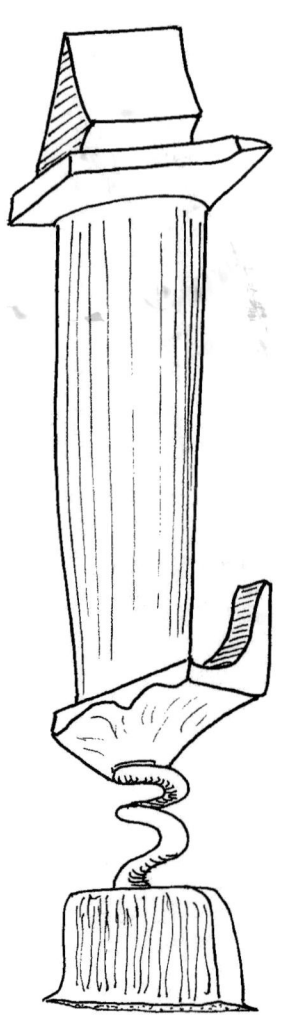

Figure 64 Single crystal turbine blace, as-cast.

environments, such as in offshore heat exchangers for the petro-chemical industries.

Ti is a surprisingly common element, being the fourth most abundant structural metal in the earth's surface, but its extraction is vastly more expensive than Fe, and near twice that of Al. As with many of the 'exotic' metals discussed, reprocessing is limited, compared with Al where the extensive reprocessing of Al scrap has greatly enhanced the economics of its supply as raw material for the casting charge.

The high level of Ti reactivity with O_2, in the liquid state, is most important in Ti- processing. It has been found that Investment casting is often the best method for casting. This has made the casting of Ti a practical proposition for complex and critical products, over a wide range, from small- to large-batch manufacture.

There are now many alloys available to meet a wide range of applications, beginning with the almost pure Ti, as Ti-1, -3, and -5, containing only the additions of 0.1 to 0.5% O_2 respectively. The long-established á+β phase alloys, such as 318, Ti-6Al-4V, are a useful benchmark. These provide strengths, as annealed, of ~930 N/mm^2 (135ksi), with 12% elongation; thus, potentially ultra-high specific strengths, ductility, formability, and even weldability. The principal drawback of these alloys is cost, of raw material and processing, partly due to high reactivity, and the constant control needed for handling and melting.

6 Post-Casting Processes

FETTLING

Fettling is the general term applied to the making good of the raw casting after removal from the mould, known as, for obvious reasons, knocking out. Simply done for sand castings, it requires basically brushing off the sand from the fully disposable mould. There may well be places where sand is trapped, or even entrained in the casting surface. This may require mechanical abrasion for complete removal, hence the reference to other methods such as shot-blasting, described later.

The different disposable mould processes, described in detail in Chapter 3, have similar requirements for knock-out to the green sand process. For the home workshop operator, some increase in time to knock-out a casting is not significant, but for industrial purposes it can be important with regard to casting cycle-times in production. For permanent moulds, as in die casting, the removal of the casting is normally a simple process of ejection cleanly from the mould. However, the casting material and mould preparation can be vital if problems are encountered with adhesion between mould and casting, known as die wetting, *see* Chapter 3.

Removal of Runners and Risers

The first stage of fettling, after producing a clean casting free from any mould debris, concerns the removal of the runners, risers and any extraneous flash produced by slight leakage along the jointing line, or similar. There may also be the need to remove additional material, such as that introduced to balance cooling rates, from casting design considerations, as Chapter 4.

These are not usually too difficult tasks, but depend on the placement and sizes of the various extraneous items to be removed, as well as the cast material. For relatively small items in the familiar alloys – aluminium, bronze and cast iron – these can usually be tackled with the normal hand metalworking tools of hacksaw and file, or small angle grinders such as can be readily found in the tool shop and DIY store.

Care needs to be exercised in handling grinders, observing proper safety precautions (see Appendix 1), and noting that it is easy when removing unwanted material to spoil the casting and so incur a problematic restoration by welding, as described later. For larger sections, especially in the more difficult-to-cut materials, such as bronze and the

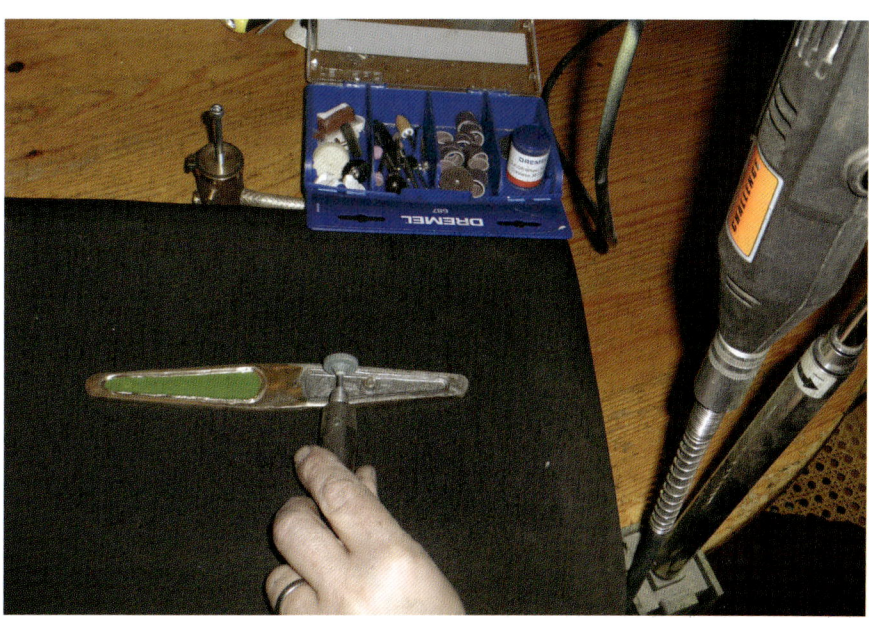

Photo 82 Hand grinding of bronze model beam engine casting.

Photo 83 Machining of beam engine pillar casting.

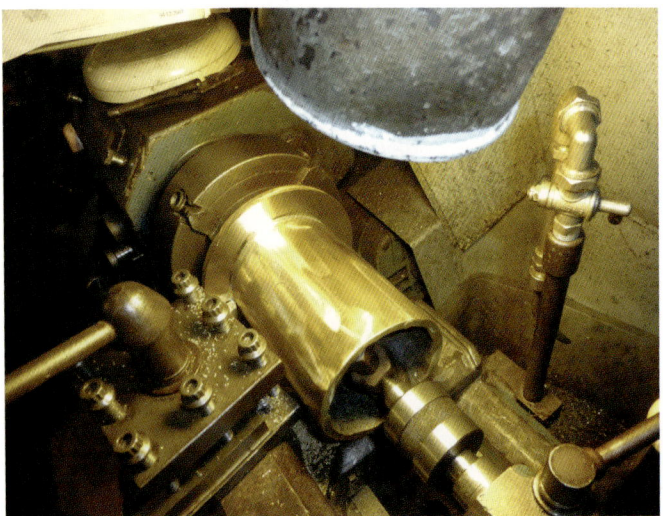

Photo 84 Machining of flask, cast for use during investment casting in the home foundry.

Photo 85 Drilling of casting shown in Photo 84.

ferrous alloys, it can be useful to employ a mechanical saw, such as the low-cost bandsaws available to the amateur worker. Alternatively, the ubiquitous angle-grinder can be used with a thin blade, slitting wheel, or larger abrasive disc, to cut off runners and risers; noting that these are kept for the next similar alloy casting charge.

Removal of material where attachments were made, flash, and other small surface protrusions, can be undertaken with the familiar workshop hand tools such as chisels and files. The grinding marks can be smoothed with a small high-speed hand grinder using grinding stones or burrs, as Photo 82. A range of large and medium hand files, complemented by needle files, will be found extremely useful in the general fettling or castings. Naturally, a good workbench and vice plus an area that can safely accommodate these inevitably dirty and dusty operations is a basic requirement.

Machining of Castings

For parts with structural and engineering applications, a small lathe such as the amateur's workshop favourites of the Myford or Boxford type is of great value in the finishing of some castings. The benefit of appraisal at the design stage soon becomes apparent when attempting to finish-machine a casting, as a means of holding the workpiece is required for grasping in a three- or four-jaw chuck, or on a faceplate – bearing in mind that the work has to be spun rapidly, rigidly and safely, for the cut to be made.

The mechanical properties of the cast will also determine if it can be machined satisfactorily. For instance, a cast envisaged as a low-strength grey

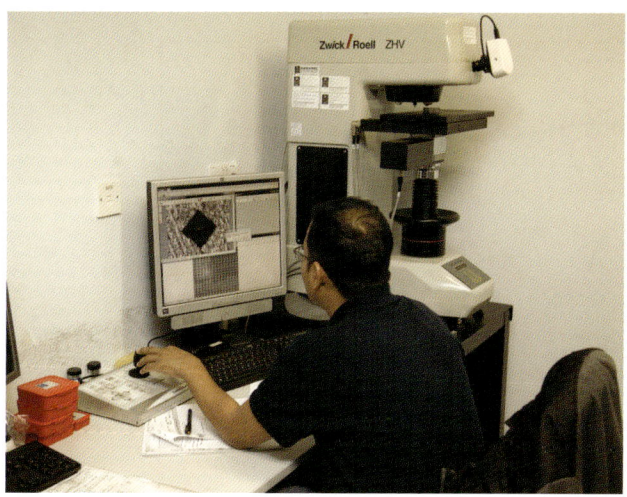

Photo 86 Commercial laboratory hardness testing of prepared sample.

Photo 87 Milling air-draught slots in the furnace burner. (Photo: Colin Mills)

Photo 88 Milling profile in the casting shown in Photo 83. (Photo: Colin Mills)

cast iron that transforms to a white cast iron, or produces a hard surface skin, can prove unmachinable by home workshop standards. Cast irons are particularly susceptible to variations in microstructures, hardness, and machinability, and it is wise to always check. In the absence of hardness testing equipment, *see* Photo 86, a fair guide is a check with a hand file, with a failure to cut readily determining if the surface is too hard for conventional machining.

Combined with the centre lathe, a small milling machine is also valuable in the finishing of castings, for producing flat faces where joints are to be made. This machine tool, unlike the lathe, keeps the workpiece stationary, and employs a rotating cutting tool. It can therefore also perform as a precision drilling machine. It is a common requirement to be able to drill holes in the casting, and use of a handheld power drill is not usually satisfactory for this purpose (see Photos 87 and 88).

Cleaning and polishing the casting can, however, be done with a combination of the tools mentioned above, where the powered hand drill can provide valuable assistance, utilizing a variety of abrasive discs and pads. It should be noted that often the as-cast finish may be preferred for aesthetic reasons, for example in replicating a domestic or vehicle part that is familiar in its original, as-cast, finish. Replication by machining from the solid, even if possible or practical, can never achieve the surface finish of the original, and may look inconsistent as a result.

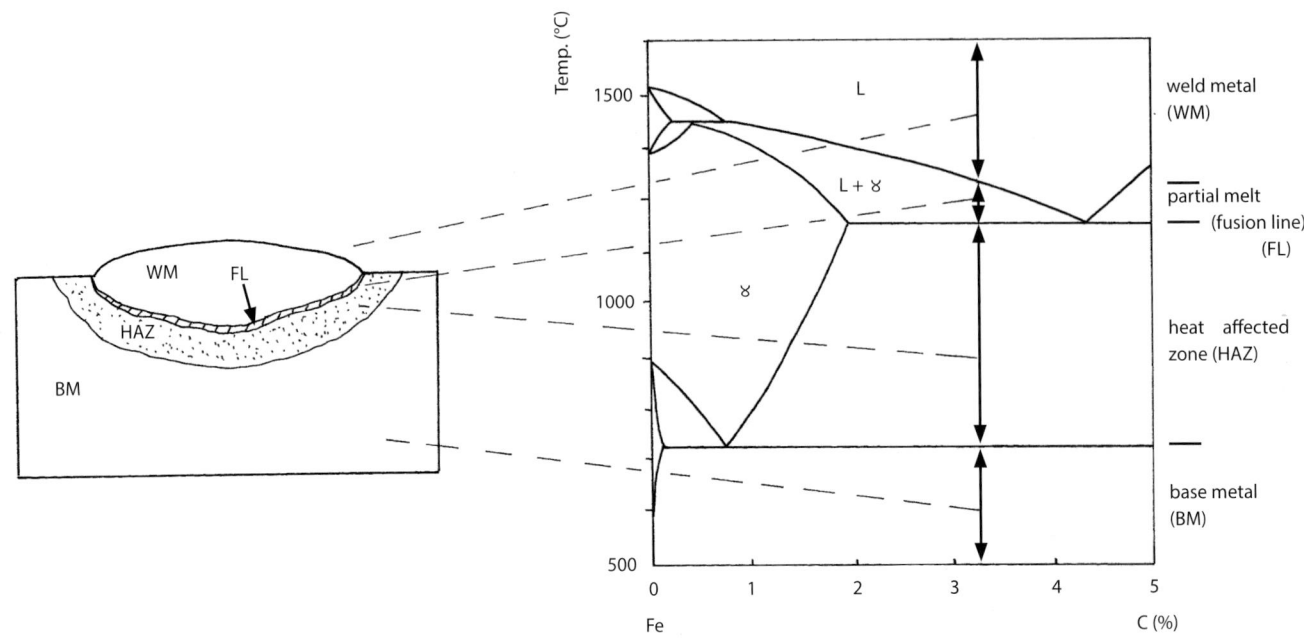

Figure 64 Principal regions of the weld band.

WELDING

While the topic of welding is extensive and complex, for our purposes we can concentrate on the aspects concerning repair of new and used castings, principally to correct defects introduced in the casting process, or wear during extended use. This substantially reduces the scope of the subject, as the usual application of welding and joining processes involve the eponymous business of connecting parts together to make a rigid structure or artefact. Admittedly, there are occasions where welding is invaluable for joining parts of castings, but for the purposes of this book, they are confined to the non-load-bearing castings, such as for thin-wall statuary. For these cases, fusion welding is employed and performed satisfactorily without recourse to the metallurgical concerns that require expertise in the load-bearing item. It is sufficient, therefore, to just select the appropriate process, welding consumables, and attain sufficient practical skills to effect a satisfactory result. *See* Bibliography Tindell, 2012.

Notwithstanding the above, welding repair of castings is an extremely valuable tool in the foundryman's armoury, as will be realized from the importance of the subject in the professional foundry. This recognizes the practicality of producing a fault-free casting, under the constraints of the imperfect conditions that apply in the small foundry. Weld repair enables an otherwise satisfactory cast, with local defects, to be saved from remelting. Also, to a lesser extent, non-fusion processes such as these need to be understood before being safely deployed for making satisfactory casting rework.

Solidification of the Weld

A basic understanding of the weld bead demonstrates how it can affect a casting. Fundamentally, the weld bead bears a number of similarities to a miniature casting, when deposited by one of the welding processes described later.

Figure 65 shows the principal regions of the weld bead, transferred in the plasma-arc, and impacted on to the workpiece to form a fully fused microstructure, as encountered earlier, see Chapter 1, 'Plasma'). This is a dramatically energetic process, as a typical GTAW process (see Figure 71) provides arc temperatures of ~5,000°C. The plasma is sufficient to transfer the droplets of molten alloy from the consumable welding electrode, across the arc, to form the welding pool – in a manner analogous to the transfer of liquid metal from ladle to mould cavity, albeit the latter being at significantly lower temperature. In the metal transfer to the weld pool we have, effectively, a miniature arc furnace harnessing a plasma envelope.

From Figure 64, the regions of concern are: weld metal (WM); fusion zone (FZ); heat-affected zone (HAZ); and base metal (BM). The base metal is metallurgically unaffected by the process, but governs the choice of welding parameters including: welding process, heat input from the process, and welding consumable. The HAZ is the region typically 1 to 5mm wide, depending on process and heat input, that sees a significant part of the intense heat from the weld pool. The FZ is the critical region that interfaces the molten weld pool and the solid metal of the HAZ; and the WM comprises the solidified 'as-cast' metal that has been transferred across the arc, and mixed in the weld pool with melted base metal.

Therefore, it is apparent that as the WM behaves as a miniature casting, its solidification microstructure is produced as a function of the alloy's chemical composition; nucleation growth rate (R); thermal gradient (G); and extent of undercooling (ΔT). The adjacent HAZ remains in a solid state, but the high temperatures conducted from the FZ cause thermal transformations depending on the characteristics of the BM, which can be anticipated from the alloy's unique cooling diagrams, see Bibliography. In general terms, the HAZ tends to have a larger grain size at the FZ boundary, reducing to the BM line, as a consequence of grain-growth due to the high thermal energy gradient. Smaller grain size is normally associated with beneficial mechanical properties, such as strength and toughness.

Solidification of the WM proceeds in a similar manner to a casting, although the former occurs at a far greater rate, due to the relative temperature gradient. In the WM, unlike a true casting, there is no chill zone, with the part-melted grains at the FZ triggering columnar growth, see Chapter 1, 'Solidification – Growth'. Despite the perturbed nature of the liquid flow in the WM, the growth and fragmentation of columnar grains or dendrites is insufficient to produce the equiaxed, randomly arranged, grains desirable in castings. There is, however, convection operating in the weld pool, caused by the stirring action of the liquid buoyancy, surface tension, and varying electro-magnetic forces, derived from the violent power of the arc.

The high rate of solidification of the WM can result in the formation of meta-stable, non-equilibrium, phases – according to the mixture from welding consumable and FZ compositions, effectively diluting the consumable composition. The WM has a free surface, unlike the casting. Growth can behave more freely, with no energy barrier to nucleation, as for the casting. Also, it is possible that layers of growth can occur, each with its own crystallographic orientation, as an alternative to long-range columnar grain growth.

In spite of this apparently unhelpful behaviour, the small size of the weld means that the microstructure is far finer than in the casting. With correspondingly small cells and dendrites, coupled with a high level of mixing in the WM, solid solubility is enhanced, thus providing, almost universally, improved properties in the weld compared to the parent metal.

Unless gross defects, such as centre-line cracking, are produced by poor welding procedures, the weakest point is found in the HAZ, the source of most common problems following welding. The occurrence of HAZ deficiencies is largely determined by the characteristics of the base metal; for instance, in grey cast irons, where the high carbon content, > 2% C, can transform to ultra-hard cementite, and risk cracking. Such problems can often be overcome or alleviated, as outlined later.

Practical Aspects – Welding Processes

The principal processes of interest are: oxy-fuel gas welding (OFW); shielded metal arc welding (SMAW); gas metal arc welding (GMAW); and gas tungsten arc welding (GTAW). This employs the North American, AWS, nomenclature as the most familiar world standard, avoiding the various confusing descriptions from other international sources.

OFW was the original process adopted for fusion welding, and for our purposes uses oxygen and acetylene mixed at the torch in approximately equal parts, to provide a maximum heat of ~3,000°C at the top of the inner cone, see Figures 67 and 68. The equipment is relatively simple, compact, portable, and readily available. It is also extremely versatile, providing a heat source for welding by fusion; brazing/bronze welding for ferrous alloys using a non-fusion, diffusion, process; and

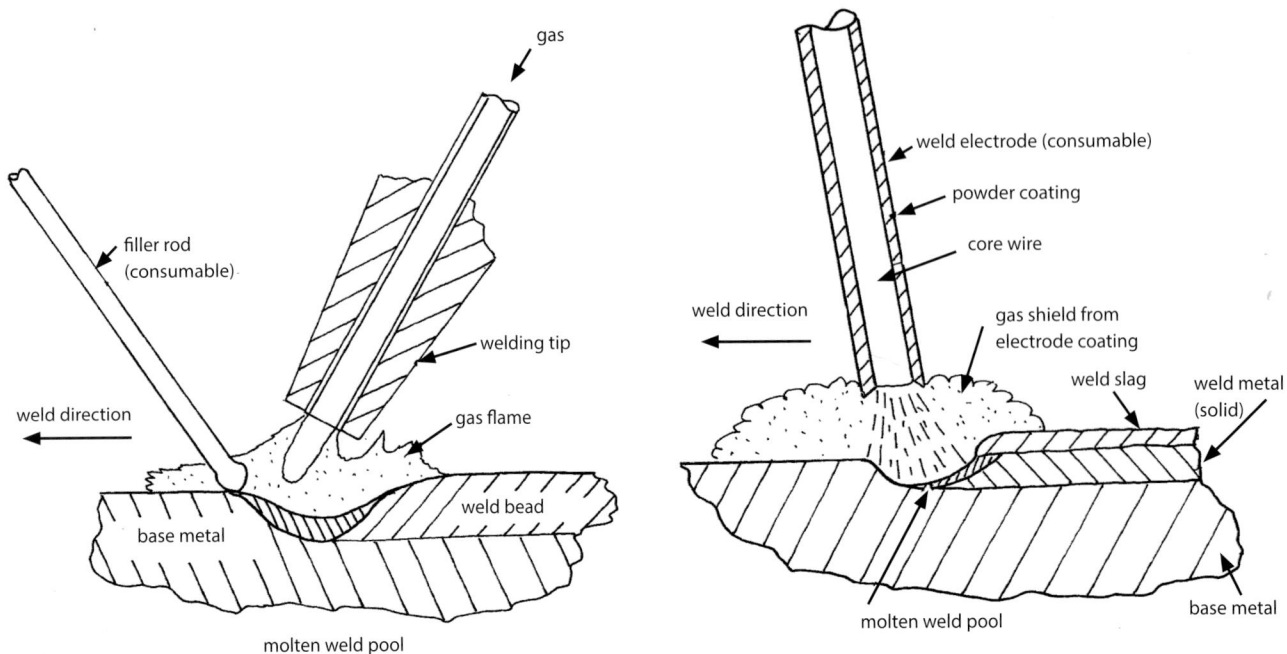

Figure 65 Gas welding (OFW) schematic.

Figure 66 'Stick' welding (SMAW) schematic.

general heating for hot working, particularly for steel fabrications.

The principal disadvantage, compared to the arc processes, is the less intense heat input, some 2,000°C below that of the other methods. Therefore, this makes it a process well adapted to the smaller and thinner section work, where fusion welding is required, essentially limited to a few millimetres thickness. However, by using different torch adaptations, such as the 'pepperpot' type, it can provide an invaluable general heat source for preheating a casting to be welded by the other methods. This is particularly important where the intense thermal shock of local welding can upset the thermal balance of a casting, causing internal stresses or distortion akin to that during the casting process, as related in Chapter 4.

Use of OFW for brazing of ferrous metals, including cast irons, can be a useful alternative to fusion welding, due to the reduced temperatures involved, circa 850°C. This diffusion process avoids much of the danger of distortion of the higher fusion temperatures of these alloys. Brazing/bronze welding is satisfactory, provided the reduced joint strength is accommodated by increasing the load-bearing area of the attachment.

OFW uses a consumable electrode that is presented to the weld pool, and droplets of molten wire are transferred across the small space between heat source and workpiece, in a manner relatively easy to control, Figure 65. With some practice and skill, it can be utilized on very thin material, including worn components. However, for sheet metalwork the relatively large heated region needs to be managed, by tacking, restraining, and planned weld progression, in order to avoid the severe distortion that can occur in thin sections. For this reason, processes such as GTAW and GMAW are often a preferred choice.

SMAW is the original electric-arc process, developed from early bare wire experiments around the start of the twentieth century, to the present day profusion of metal-wire electrodes, coated with a highly developed range of compacted powders. The apparent simplicity of this consumable electrode, through which the electric power is delivered to create the arc between it

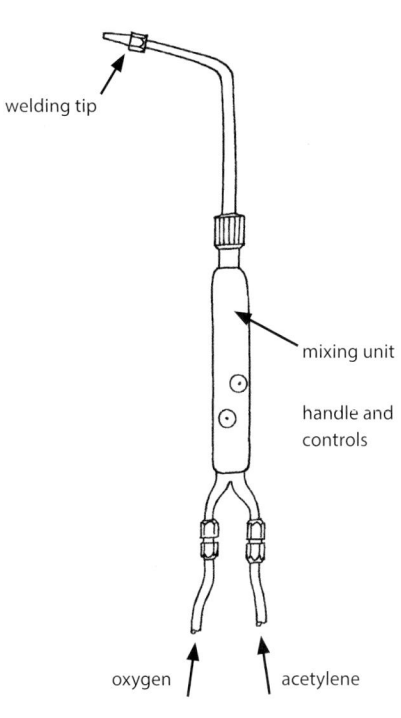

Figure 67 Gas (oxy-acetylene) welding torch.

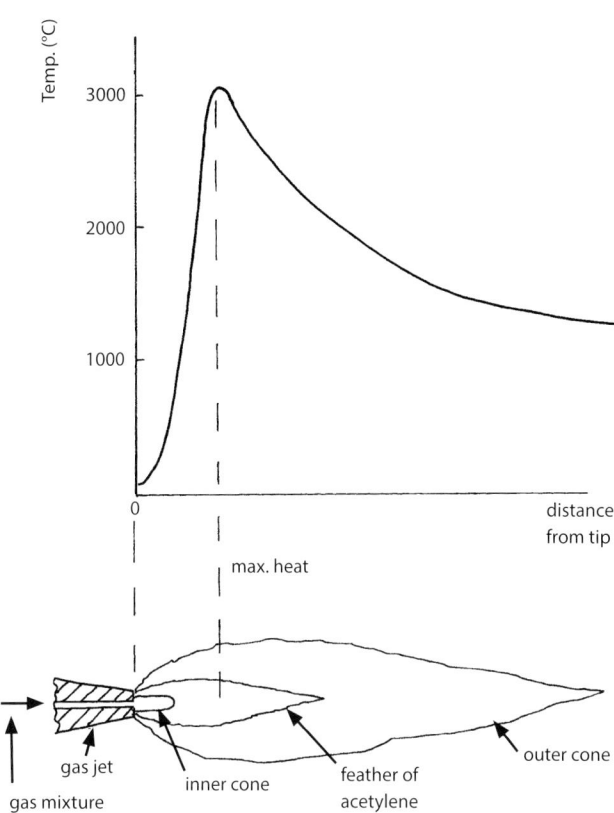

Figure 68 Typical flame and temperature profile, oxy-acetylene welding.

and the work, belies the complexity of the physics of metal transfer across the plasma and into the weld pool, as discussed previously under 'Solidification of the Weld'.

The coated electrode provides the greatest process adaptability, as an extremely wide range of electrode compositions can now be sourced from the major international suppliers. This is particularly valuable for the repair of castings, including the hard-to-weld cast irons. The coating can be produced with almost any combination of metal alloy as a powder, set in a slurry that solidifies to retain a compact coating around the electrode. This decomposes in the intensity of the arc, providing a shield against the atmosphere and adding the required elements, much as miniature arc furnace, see Figure 66.

While equipment is simple and relatively easy to use, electrodes can be expensive if the more exotic alloys are required in quantity. However, it is surely fair to say that the basic SMAW equipment is, or should be, at least as much a staple of the home workshop as the ubiquitous lathe or pedestal drill. No other welding process can match the range of alloys that can be tackled, particularly in the ferrous metals. Perhaps the most significant limitation, besides the need for a certain skill in tackling work such as thin sections, lies in welding of the aluminium alloys. Neither SMAW or OFW is really suitable, and the GTAW process is undoubtedly the first choice (*see* later).

The Gas Metal Arc Welding (GMAW) process is known as 'semi-automatic', as the welding consumable comprises a wire wound on to a large spool, fed through the welding torch nozzle, with the electrical settings and characteristics determining the burn-off rate as it forms a molten metal stream, transferred across the arc and into the weld pool. A particular benefit of the process is the continuous wire feed, as long as the weld run required. This has made it particularly convenient for production work on long-run weld fabrications. The efficient deposition of the weld bead has also proved useful in distortion-prone and sheet metalwork, by reducing the effects of heating and

130 • Post-Casting Processes

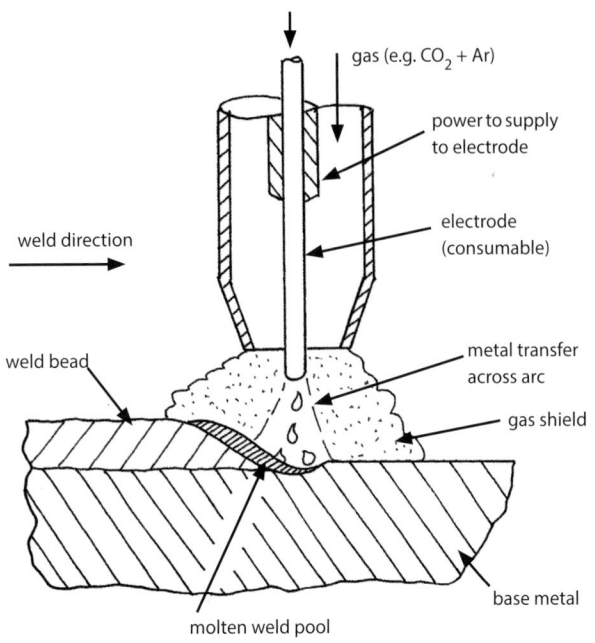

Figure 69 GMAW – Gas Metal Welding (UK – MIG – Metal Inert Gas).

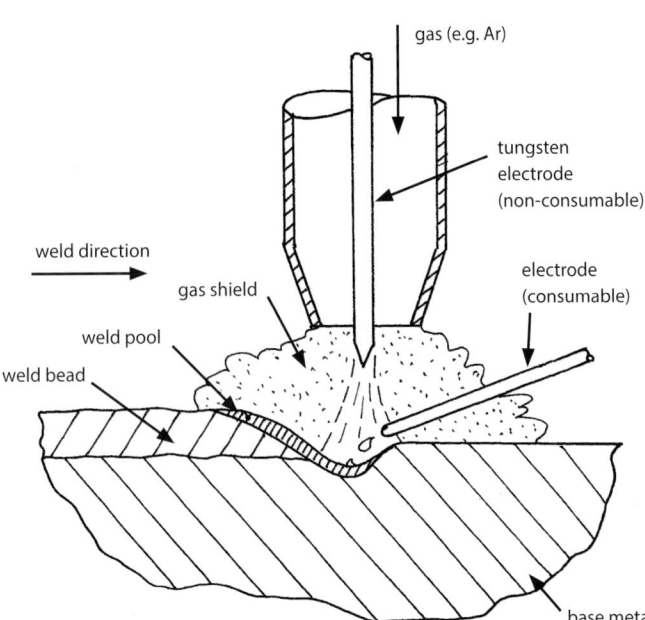

Figure 70 GTAW – Gas Tungsten Arc Welding (UK – TIG – Tungsten Inert Gas).

subsequent internal stresses.

For casting work, these advantages tend to be of less value, and the difficulty with delicate work, coupled with the limitations in consumable metal compositions of the wire reels, makes it less versatile than the other processes. Nevertheless, widespread use in the amateur workshop means that it may be useful for certain jobs, such as in some copper-base alloy castings, *see* Figure 69.

Gas tungsten arc welding (GTAW) is a valuable asset in the repair of castings, especially for Al, as noted earlier. While it does not have the enormous range of alloy compositions available because of its consumable electrode, as straight wire – compared to the SMAW, coated electrode – there are normally sufficient GTAW wires available for most work. This is a process that has a separate heat source, as for OFW, and uncoated wire consumables. However, the arc is generated between the non-consumable tungsten electrode and workpiece. This produces an intense plasma arc and with sophisticated electrical power controllers, suitable for a wide range of jobs. From small, delicate work, to large castings – albeit heavier work progresses at a relatively slow rate – seldom a problem outside of professional work cycles, (Figure 70).

For Al work, however, it is essential to have the significantly more expensive AC, rather than DC, power unit. This enables a disruption of the tenacious and high melting point oxide film, which thwarts attempts at welding with the other processes described here. Although OFW can be used for Al-alloy welding, it requires a highly aggressive flux to overcome the oxide film. Also, the manipulation of the OFW heat input requires considerable skill as the low melting point of Al-alloys means that they lie below easily visible effects. This is unlike, for instance, ferrous alloys, which show dramatic colour changes at temperature. Combined with a high heat conductivity, many a worker has experienced the sudden and sad collapse of their fine Al casting during an apparently minor repair!

Cast Iron Weld Repair

The welding of cast irons is one of the most daunting tasks for the welder with knowledge to understand the potential pitfalls, while those jolly souls without sufficient understanding of the metallurgy of these alloys can gaily proceed on the basis of 'ignorance is bliss'! But trusting to luck is neither necessary nor advisable.

A principal difficulty with these alloys is their wide range, from those weldable with appropriate procedures – to the truly unweldable. In the former camp are many grey and ductile (SG) cast irons; the latter include the white cast irons, with their extremely hard microstructures of martensite and cementite (Fe_3C), as described earlier (*see* Chapter 5, 'Cast Irons').

Cast Iron Structures

As a brief recap of the metallurgy of the grey and ductile cast irons, these contain > 2% C and > 0.5% Si that, on solidification, causes the excess C to form rosettes and long flakes of graphite, assisted by the Si and slow cooling rates. The poor ductility of this structure is not actually the direct result of these solidification products, rather the mechanical effect of the long graphite flakes interrupting the continuity of the ductile matrix. Hence, ductile cast iron is essentially a grey cast iron treated to transform the graphite flakes into spheres – providing the spheroidal graphite appellation. This transformation renders a structure of such ductility and strength as to compete with mild steel structures; and despite the potentially even better weldability than grey cast iron, the welding of ductile cast iron may degrade some of its improved properties, as will be seen shortly.

As noted before, where composition and increased cooling rates do not favour the formation of grey cast iron, the ultra-hard white cast iron forms from the transformation of the C into the inter-metallic phase of Fe_3C, cementite. Thus, white cast iron generally comprises a matrix of pearlite and eutectic carbide, with the hyper-eutectics (> 4% C) providing the hardest structures. Hypo-eutectic white cast irons are the most common, still very hard, typically > 400 H_B. Welding of such zero-ductility cast irons is therefore normally avoided, for obvious reasons.

The Cast Iron Weldment

With reference to Figure 65, it can be seen that the equilibrium diagram can provide a guide to the behaviour of the weldment, bearing in mind that the structures formed are also dependent on phase reaction times, not shown on the equilibrium diagram.

However, we can examine the key parts of the weldment, which also have general application in welding metallurgy, as described earlier (*see* Chapter 5, 'Cast Irons'). The base metal, BM, is essentially unaffected by the intense local heat from the weld, but the heat-affected zone, HAZ, does undergo significant effects due to this heating, while still remaining below the liquidus temperature. Also as noted earlier, the HAZ is often the region of most concern after welding, where the heating can cause phase changes, or grain growth, and structural stresses – rendering it a zone of weakness. Therefore, considerable effort is devoted to the understanding of this, largely hidden, region for critical work. Telltale signs of danger include; raised hardness, detectable in the band of the few millimetres where the HAZ breaks the surface, as Figure 65. In severe cases of HAZ degradation, a loss of ductility can lead to micro-cracks; either at the surface or, more insidiously, as under-bead cracking.

In the fusion zone, FZ, this small region comprises an area of mixed composition of the WM/HAZ, which has experienced localized melting. Subjected to the extremes of cooling rate from being sandwiched between the HAZ and molten weld metal, WM, its structure forms as discussed in Chapter 5. The FZ can suffer from the same shortcomings as the HAZ, and may require non-destructive examination, NDE, to provide confidence of a sound weld.

The weld metal is a mixture of weld consumable with some base metal, but this dilution should be minimized. Therefore, the composition and properties of the WM are largely determined by the welding consumable, with structure as described in Chapter 5, 'Cast Irons'. Typically, in these ferrous alloys, it has a hardness < 300 H_B, compared to the HAZ which can range from 200–600 H_B, depending on the control during welding, and BM composition.

Welding Consumables and Processes

The vast majority of cast iron is welded by SMAW, as this provides the greatest process adaptability, with its extensive choice of welding electrodes. The most popular approach is based on the AWS class E Ni Fe – CI electrodes. These use a pure nickel core wire, with iron additions in the coating, to provide a predominantly Ni-weld deposit. This allows the weld pool to solidify at the FZ and eject the carbon, which has a low solubility in nickel, and is precipitated as graphite. This is also associated with an increase in volume, as for casting, countering the contraction stresses from the rapidly cooling weld pool.

An alternative to E-Ni Fe CI electrodes are the E-Ni CI type, but unlike the former they do not have the benefit of producing the superior ductility, tolerance of phosphorus, and reduction in tendency for FZ cracking. Either way, the Ni-based electrodes are normally preferred to using the familiar steel electrodes, such as E6018 or E7018 types, which can produce crack-sensitive first layers as deposited on to the cast iron BM. Another approach is to use matching electrodes, designated E-CI, but this requires very careful procedures to avoid problems with cracking.

Control of HAZ hardness can be achieved with application of preheat, using oxy-acetylene torches, as shown in Table 13. This shows that, with a 5mm E Ni-Fe Ci SMAW electrode, a weld can be made with no preheat – but at the expense of high HAZ hardness, and thus increased crack sensitivity. The figure shows how the use of 300°C preheat has reduced the HAZ hardness, almost to that of the BM.

OFW Welding of Cast Irons

The lower heat input provided by the OFW process has significant implications for the welding of cast irons, making it considerably slower and requiring a very high preheat of > 600°C for larger castings, but even > 400°C for smaller work. This also greatly increases the HAZ width and time at temperature, both of which are generally undesirable.

Nevertheless, OFW is used extensively as a convenient and adaptable process. Reduced HAZ hardness can be of benefit in post-process machining of grey cast irons.

Porosity can be a problem, alleviated by using a marginally reducing flame. Minor work can often be tackled successfully, such as surface defects, and building up worn castings. Finally, the use of bronze welding/brazing – as a diffusion, non-fusion, process requiring working temperature of c. 850°C, far below the liquidus – can be used for joining castings, or making dissimilar base-metal joints, for low-stress work, see earlier in this chapter, 'Practical Aspects – Welding Processes'.

TESTING

Whilst the testing of castings deserves a substantial book in its own right, a short summary and reference to the *Bibliography* should satisfy the needs of the small-scale worker, especially as most professional foundries now outsource destructive testing to specialists.

Testing encompasses: in-process sampling; destructive testing; and non-destructive testing (NDT).

Sampling can take the form of an in-process chemical analysis and microstructure examination of sample test pieces, taken from the melt around the time of actual casting. With high-value equipment, it is possible to get a good indication of the chemical composition of the casting, before committing to an expensive casting.

However, for the small-scale operation this is not normally an option and such testing has to be done post-casting, obviously too late to make changes other than a remelt.

Preparation of a microstructure sample takes some time to effect, the small test piece being cut, mounted in a plastic mould, polished and etched to reveal features in the optical microscope, *see* Photo 89. This is naturally a retrospective examination, and may be sensibly taken at a variety of sections in the casting, subjected to different cooling rates. Local testhouse/laboratories can provide a service that is invaluable in critical work and the study of microstructures of, for instance, grey and ductile iron. This is the normal route used to establish the effect of inoculation treatments, or the modification of Al Si alloys.

Destructive Testing

Where once the professional foundry would have a full range of testing facilities, these can now be found in specialist test houses, providing the familiar range of mechanical testing such as tensile, bend, and impact testing. This generates data from separately cast sample test bars, for analysis of strength, ductility, and toughness, from the standards referred to earlier, Chapter 5, Table 7, 8 and 11. When combined with chemical analysis and microstructure examination, these tests establish conformance to material specification of the base metal – a necessary, but not necessarily sufficient, evaluation of the casting. The final regime of non-destructive testing aims to provide confidence that the casting's integrity, and freedom from internal flaws, is up to the tasks and standards specified.

Non-Destructive Testing

This has always been a highly specialized topic, and for the most critical work is an exacting discipline, with many practitioners working to rigorous national and international standards.

For our purposes, however, it is sufficient to be aware of the types of testing readily available.

The most important, and simple test, is a visual examination of the casting. This can reveal important details of surface finish, dimensional accuracy, and surface defects such as laps, scabs, tears, porosity, and adherence of foreign matter, such as sand residue. Such an examination can often be sufficient to consign the labour of many hours to the remelt bin!

Surface examination can be progressed by using dye penetrant inspection (DPI); and, for ferrous alloys, magnetic particle inspection (MPI) and their derivatives. The former technique uses surface sprays; and the latter magnetic flux equipment. Both methods highlight surface breaking defects, particularly cracks, not readily visible to the naked eye.

The Holy Grail of NDT is the search for sub-surface, buried defects such as cracks, voids or cavities. It is important, at the outset, to be clear about what is constituted by an unacceptable defect, as the search for an *entirely* defect-free casting – or metallic material, come to that – is likely to be a long and fruitless one.

Where component stresses are low, which is common in many familiar castings, volumetric NDT is unnecessary, expensive, and best avoided. For more critical work, such NDT is of fundamental importance, and the theory of castings as espoused (see Chapter 1, 'Casting Defects') should help in the understanding the common buried defects, as found by volumetric NDT.

The principal methods used in volumetric NDT are based on radiography, RT; and ultrasonic testing, UT. **RT** has many similarities to the processes used in medicine, basically exposing the casting to a radiographic source, from the gamma rays of an isotope, or X-rays generated from an RT power unit. These rays, having passed through the workpiece, are traditionally captured on photo-sensitive films which are subsequently processed to provide a hard copy negative, analogous to a medical X-ray film of a bone structure. Essentially, a significant local variation in density provides an indication – voids showing as darker – of a defect. Interpretation, as with medical RT films, is of paramount importance, requiring skill and experience to form a sound judgement about the *apparent* defect compared to *actuality*. The potential for misinterpretation – or loss in confidence of the workpiece – can be enormous. Examples of consequences include the ripping up of hundreds of miles of suspect gas pipelines, in North America and another in the North Sea based on contentious NDT data, or problematic interpretations.

The final process involves the use of ultrasound waves sent from a probe, reflected through the casting back-surface and received as a signal displayed, traditionally, on a CRT screen. This is **UT** (ultrasonic testing), a very powerful and sensitive method used to detect cracks and discontinuities from deep within a casting. While many variants have been developed, the basic method relies on the operator's skill and experience in covering the job and interpreting the transient signal on a viewing screen. One limitation is that the signal is unreliable at the near surface depth, say from 0–10mm; but some materials, such as stainless steel, are difficult to interpret. However, it is easier to obtain a nearer-to-3D view than with RT, and arguably UT is more sensitive to finding buried cracks, while being less able to detect internal microporosity (*see* Photo 103).

The conclusion is that a thorough examination of castings is difficult and probably best accomplished by a combined approach, plus sectioning of sample castings to check results before embarking on critical work or extended production – but a sensible engineering judgement of defect tolerance is pre-eminent!

Surface Finishing of Castings

This concluding section briefly registers the final touches that can be applied to castings, drawn from a list that stretches back hundreds, if not thousands, of years – according to the tastes,

Photo 89 Thermoplastic mounts for micrograph specimens used in laboratory preparation. (Photo: Colin Mills)

Photo 90 Commercial test house, Exova, Salford, UK; tensile specimen test piece. (Photo: Colin Mills)

Photo 91 Bend test pieces for ductility test. (Photo: Colin Mills)

and the demands of the ages. For our purposes these are: patination; electroplating; diffusion coating; hardfacing; hot-dip coating; porcelain enamelling; and painting.

Patination

It is common, for the non-ferrous castings of the aluminiums and bronzes, to rely entirely on their indigenous oxide film for corrosion resistance in general use, *see* Chapter 5, 'Oxidation'. Nevertheless, the patination process has been employed since antiquity to enhance the appearance of bronze statuary. The process is highly sensitive to the variables of surface cleanliness, heating and chemicals applied, but it can afford most attractive and elegant surface finishes on bronze art work. Detailed procedures are available, *see* Bibliography, *Caske, 2012*.

Electroplating

This is a coating well suited for castings, such as where wear or corrosion resistance is required at the casting surface. It is often chosen for purely cosmetic reasons, and it should be emphasized that a smooth finish, as-plated, is only as good as the surface finish of the casting on to which it is deposited. This, relatively thin, coating, is typically of Cr, Ni Cu, Au or Ag. Electrodeposition is a particularly environmentally onerous business, so that it is usually best left to specialists. However, completing the surface finishing/polishing will often greatly reduce the work, and cost, of the plating process.

Plating thicknesses range from

Photo 92 Tensile test machine. (Photo: Colin Mills)

Photo 93 Commercial NDT, Nortest, Salford, UK; DPI preparation for crack testing of large machine shaft. (Photo: Colin Mills)

Photo 94 Fluorescent DPI of aluminium casting. (Photo: Colin Mills)

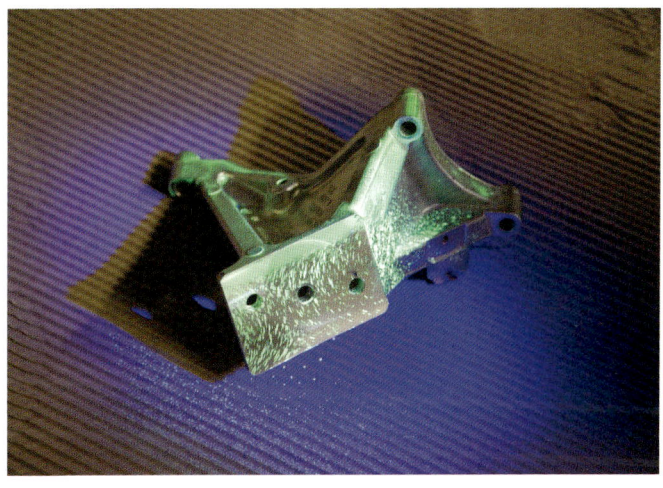

Photo 95 Under controlled lighting. (Photo: Colin Mills)

microns, upwards. For fine work such as the Cr-plating of internal combustion engine piston rings, made from spun cast iron, thicknesses of microns are the norm. Far greater thicknesses are employed in larger wear-condition plating, such as the Cr-plating of exposed hydraulic rams. Note, that where the greater thickness of deposited hard metals, such as Cr, requires final machining to close tolerances, this can normally only be done with expensive machine tools such as centre grinders.

Diffusion Coatings

This is a particularly specialized process, albeit widely used in industrial manufacture. It requires special heat treatment facilities with atmosphere control, for the impregnation, to a depth of microns, of a diffused layer. This does not affect the original dimensions of a finish-machined part, while rendering a significant increase in surface hardness and wear resistance. Carbonitriding and nitriding are common processes, akin to the case-hardening widely used in certain steel products. As such, this is unlikely to be required for items from the home foundry.

Hardfacing

A treatment normally achieved by welding with a high hardness electrode, this forms part of the discussion on welding of castings, this chapter. The SMAW process is often favoured, as there exists an extensive range of hardfacing alloys, for buttering of wear-prone faces. The risks and benefits of this approach can be assessed from the discussion earlier in this chapter, 'Welding Consumables and Processes'.

Hot Dip Coatings

Familiar examples of hot dip coatings are based on dipping into a vat of Zn, as in galvanizing. This process is equally applicable to cast iron, and is the common method for corrosion resistance of mild steel exposed to damp environments. It is widely employed for cast pipe fittings that would otherwise suffer surface corrosion. Once again, the temperatures involved with baths of molten Zn mean that this is a treatment best tackled by the specialist, of which there is seldom a shortage as it is a well-proven method, especially where function precedes cosmetic considerations.

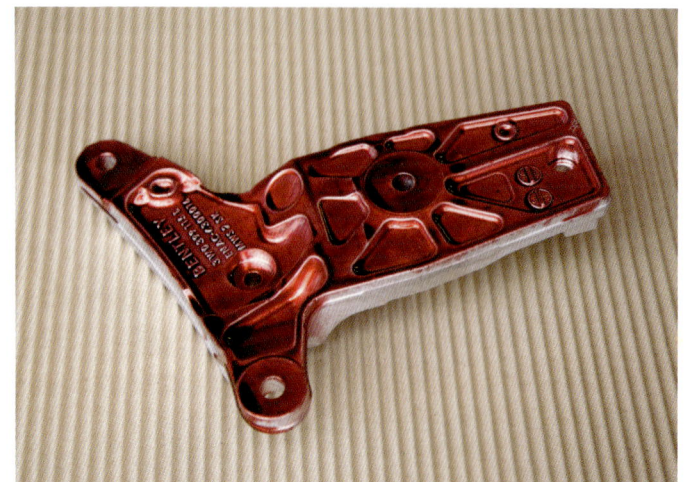

Photo 96 Die casting, developer applied by spray. (Photo: Colin Mills)

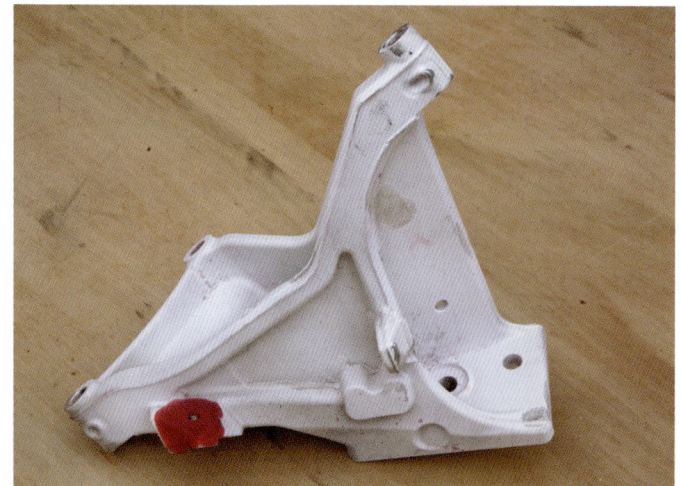

Photo 97 Different casting, red bleed-out shows potential defect, requires careful interpretation. (Photo: Colin Mills)

Photo 98 MPI testing of steel welded plate, at Nortest. (Photo: Colin Mills)

Post-Casting Processes • 137

Photo 99 RT set-up for X-ray of aluminium casting at Nortest. (Photo: Colin Mills)

Porcelain Enamelling

This is worthy of inclusion, as an industrial process of widespread application, familiar in domestic use in the coating of cast iron utensils and large vessels. The porcelain enamels are vitreous coatings, cured by heat, forming an extremely tenacious bond to a cast iron substrate and thus providing unfailing resistance to a wide range of chemicals, proving virtually indestructible in domestic use.

Photo 100 Radiograph of casting defect, for specialist interpretation. (Photo: Colin Mills)

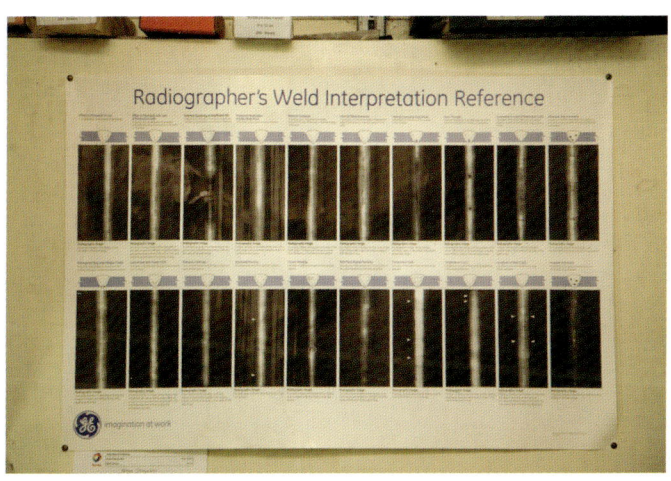

Photo 101 Reference radiographs, aid for comparative interpretation. (Photo: Colin Mills)

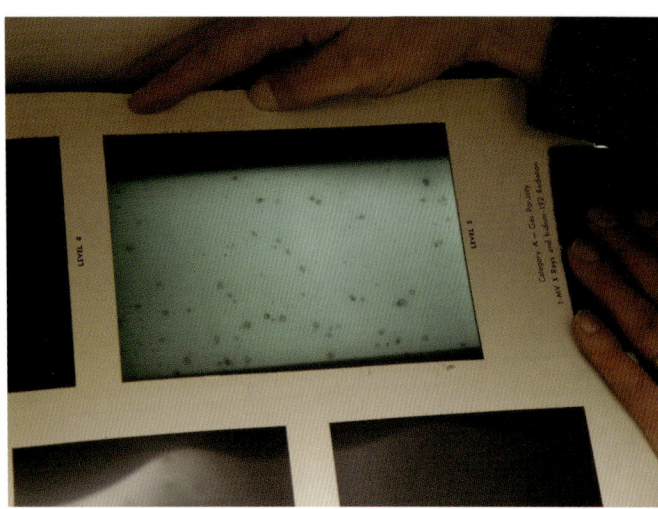

Photo 102 Radiograph showing porosity in casting. (Photo: Colin Mills)
HI-RES VERSION REQUIRED

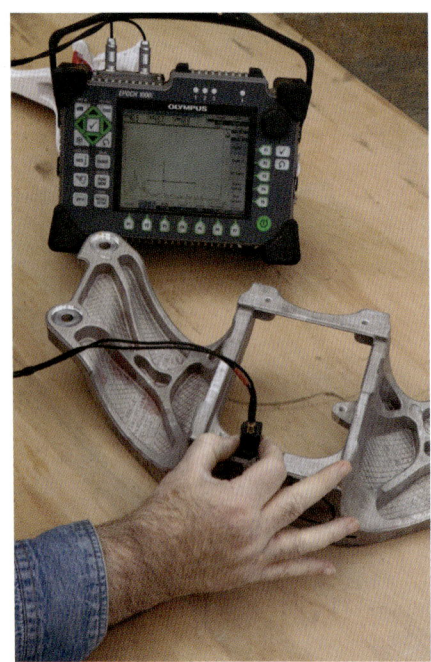

Photo 103 UT NDT, showing manual probe and CRT screen display of UT signal trace. (Photo: Colin Mills)

Painting

Whilst the non-ferrous castings can be readily painted, after appropriate cleaning and degreasing, they can often be used with no surface coating, or perhaps just a simple domestic clear varnish to retain bright, polished surfaces, typically for polished brass artefacts. The cast irons can also often be used with little or no coating, unless subjected to damp atmospheres. Even then, for heavy wall items, a general surface corrosion can sometimes be acceptable, provided that prolonged damp conditions do not prevail.

Where such difficult conditions or cosmetic conditions occur, it is normally sufficient to use a selection from the widely available range of domestic or industrial paints, applied according to the particular product instructions. These simply, but effectively, operate on the barrier theory of separating environment from the casting. If the previously described processes are not considered necessary or appropriate, then painting provides a simple and effective means for the preservation of the hard-fought product of one's labours.

7 Case Studies, Processes and Projects

PROCESSES

Sand Casting Sequence

Photos 104 to 154 (Photos: Colin Mills) show the sequence of producing a sand mould, using parts from the model beam engine as patterns to replicate the beam and beam trunnion, as a demonstration of this most versatile of processes.

Photo 106

Photo 104

Photo 107

Photo 105

Photo 108

140 • *Case Studies, Processes and Projects*

Photo 109

Photo 112

Photo 110

Photo 113

Photo 111

Photo 114

Case Studies, Processes and Projects • 141

Photo 115

Photo 118

Photo 116

Photo 119

Photo 117

Photo 120

142 • *Case Studies, Processes and Projects*

Photo 121

Photo 124

Photo 122

Photo 125

Photo 123

Photo 126

Case Studies, Processes and Projects • 143

Photo 127

Photo 130

Photo 128

Photo 131

Photo 129

Photo 132

144 • Case Studies, Processes and Projects

Photo 133

Photo 136

Photo 134

Photo 137

Photo 135

Photo 138

Case Studies, Processes and Projects • 145

Photo 139

Photo 142

Photo 140

Photo 143

Photo 141

Photo 144

146 • *Case Studies, Processes and Projects*

Photo 145

Photo 148

Photo 146

Photo 149

Photo 147

Photo 150

Case Studies, Processes and Projects • 147

Photo 151

Photo 154

Photo 152

Photo 153

Photo 155

148 • Case Studies, Processes and Projects

Investment Casting

An example of a practical investment casting process, undertaken in the home workshop, is illustrated in Photos 156 to 172 (Photos: Colin Mills). The result of the initial trial, shown in Photo 172, demonstrated a problem with feeding, and the feeder system was subsequently modified from the top feeder shown, to a bottom feeder. This resulted in successful, porosity-free castings, as shown later.

Photo 158

Photo 156

Photo 157

Photo 159

Case Studies, Processes and Projects • 149

Photo 160

Photo 161

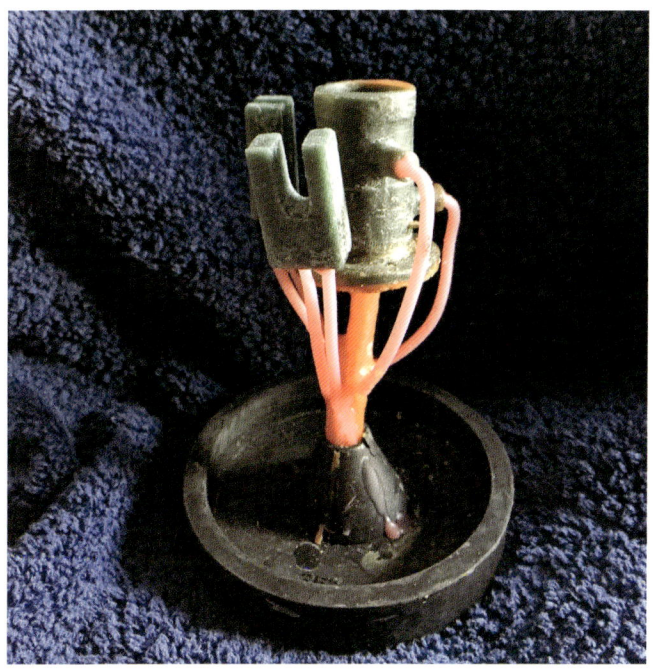

Photo 162

Photo 163

150 • Case Studies, Processes and Projects

Photo 164

Photo 165

Photo 166

Photo 167

Photo 168

Case Studies, Processes and Projects • 151

Photo 169

Photo 171

Photo 172

Photo 170

152 • Case Studies, Processes and Projects

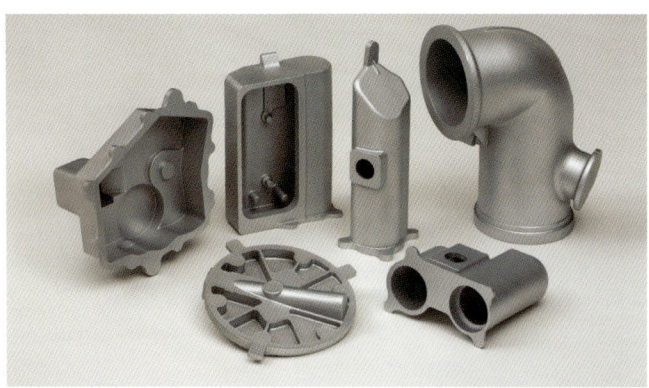

Photo 173 Aluminium for Boeing.

Investment Casting as a Commercial Process

Photos 173 to 182 show some of the product and process from PI Castings, of Altrincham, Cheshire, UK.

These images are courtesy of PI Castings, one of Europe's longest established and experienced investment casting manufacturers of high-integrity product in both ferrous and non-ferrous alloys.

Photo 174 Aluminium, electro-optical.

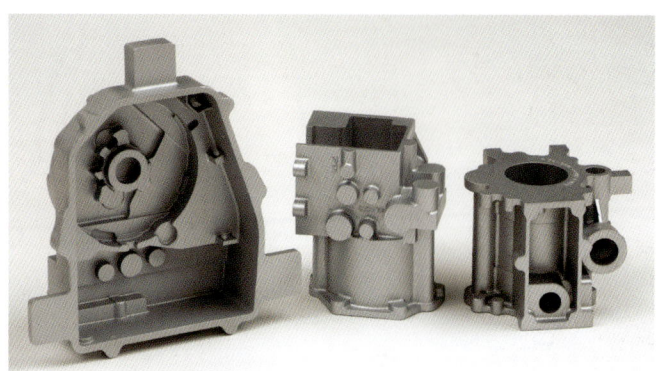

Photo 176 Aluminium, aerospace.

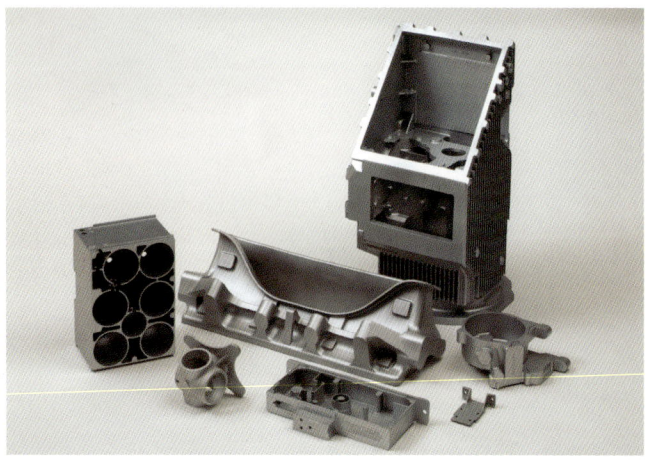

Photo 175 Aluminium, PI castings.

Photo 177 Brass and bronze.

Case Studies, Processes and Projects • 153

Photo 178 Steel structural.

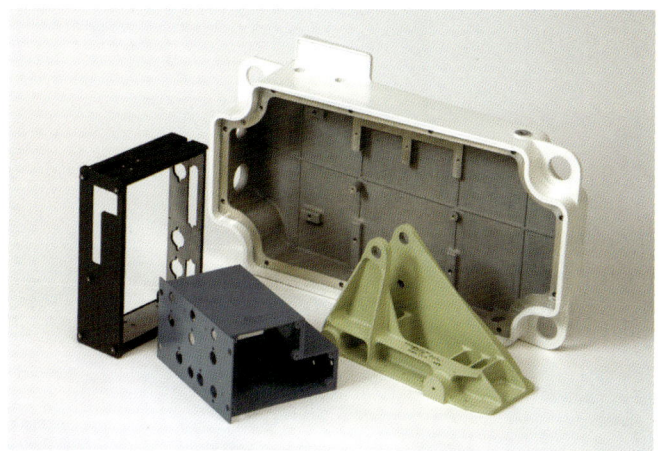

Photo 179 Machined castings.

Photo 180 Steel, commercial.

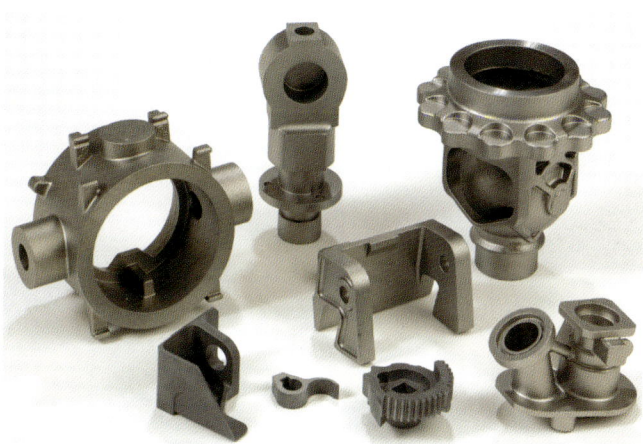

Photo 181 Steel, PI castings.

Photo 182 Threaded investment castings.

154 • Case Studies, Processes and Projects

Projects

Special items were cast for the purpose of making the micro foundry's investment casting equipment, such as those shown in Photos 183 to 188.

Photo 185 Casting boxes, before opening.

Photo 183 Bronze casting for ramming-up tool; as-cast, still hot.

Photo 186 Trial cast of investment flask, showing insufficient charge of bronze to complete casting. Later, successfully recast.

Photo 184 Ramming-up tool, finish machined.

Photo 187 Casting, including feeder, of flange for bronze investment flask.

Case Studies, Processes and Projects • 155

Photo 188 Pouring from ladle into investment casting flask. (Photo: Colin Mills)

Decorative Money Box

Photo 190 Finished casting assembled.

Photo 189 As-cast bronze model, including feeder and riser.

Speedometer Holder

Photo 191 Speedometer holder (see Chapter 3).

156 • Case Studies, Processes and Projects

Velocette 'Carb Tickler' Arm and Bracket

Firegate

Photo 192 Cast bronze 'tickler' from home foundry.

Photos 195 and 196 Firegate, cast iron, as cast.

Photo 193 In situ.

Photo 196

Photo 194 General view.

Photo 197 Sand mould showing cavity.

Case Studies, Processes and Projects • 157

Model Beam Engine Parts

Photo 198 Mould for model flywheel, pattern in situ.

Photo 199 As cast bronze. Including feeder and runners.

Photo 200 Alternative small casting moulds for model flywheel, showing cope, drag and pattern.

Photo 201 As cast model flywheel with feeder, in cast iron.

Photo 202 Feeder removed, ready for machining.

Photo 203 Bronze flywheel, ready for machining.

158 • Case Studies, Processes and Projects

Photo 204 Machining in progress.

Photo 205 Cylindrical mould box, for tall pillar casting (plan view).

Photo 206 As-cast bronze casts for model pillar and guide, feeder still in place.

Independent Commercial Jobbing Foundry

The following photos (207 to 220) represent a small-batch production local foundry, based in Broadheath, Cheshire, UK, dedicated to producing cast iron, copper-base and aluminium alloys by sand casting. Run by generations of highly skilled craftsmen, the superficial appearance of some disorder disguises the great depth of knowledge and experience gained from long-term operation in a tough commercial industry.

Photo 207

Photo 208

Case Studies, Processes and Projects • 159

Photo 209

Photo 212

Photo 210

Photo 213

Photo 211

Photo 214

160 • Case Studies, Processes and Projects

Photo 215

Photo 218

Photo 216

Photo 219

Photo 217

Independent commercial small-jobbing foundry – sequence showing aspects of mould preparation, casting, and typical final product of industrial conveyor sprockets in cast iron. Based in Altrincham, Cheshire, the foundry can make a wide variety of castings, from small to medium weight, with cast iron capacity of 0.5 tonne. Also non-ferrous, aluminium and copper-base alloys, for general engineering applications. (Photos: Colin Mills)

Appendix I Safety Aspects

SAFETY ASPECTS

Safety is naturally the pre-requisite of all casting and related operations. The obvious potential dangers must be handled appropriately so that risks are managed for a level of safety from accidents and surprises that is well-considered and acceptable to all concerned.

In order to manage the risks of casting operations, the following are guidelines for processes such as furnace melting of the charge and pouring into the mould, where the highest level of dangers are present. It is essential to proceed only when satisfied that a proper safety framework for preparation and personnel and process capability has been established. The first golden rule is never to begin these operations without a clear plan and ability to avoid un-expected hazards during the high temperatures involved; in flying terms, 'Take-off is optional – landing mandatory.'

The basic areas of concern are:

- Setting up the workshop
- Making the mould
- Furnace heating
- Pouring into the mould
- Break-out operations
- Post casting processes

From Chapter 2, various aspects of workshop arrangements have been discussed and the safety aspects are fundamental in order that sufficient room is available for safe handling of the furnace and crucible during heating and pouring operations. As there are many arrangements possible, general principles, backed by common sense, will dictate a safe layout to ensure that the furnace can be monitored, controlled, and handled for loading and retrieval of the crucible, such as with the tongs and lifting tools shown in Chapter 2.

There should always be at least two, preferably three, experienced persons available during all heating and pouring operations, dressed suitably, as Personnel Protection Equipment (PPE):

- Foundry jacket and trousers
- Foundry safety boots, gaiters
- Foundry gauntlets
- Foundry apron
- Protective headgear, including visor

All PPE should be suitable for operations involving molten metal as per professional foundry-work.

THE WORKSHOP

- All metal to be clean and entirely dry, free from moisture, prior to furnace charging. At all times moisture shall be eliminated as contact with high temperature metal can lead to explosive reactions.
- The working space shall be moisture-free, and all floor space where molten metal could reach shall be protected with a layer of dry foundry sand to similarly avoid any danger of molten or hot metal contact with the floor, leading to fire or explosion risk.
- Fire extinguishers and fire blankets shall be of the appropriate type, condition and location, in order to contain any operational problems.
- Pre- and post-casting operations involving metal cutting, grinding and welding, shall always involve the appropriate PPE for activities, including welding repair as discussed in Chapter 6.
- An overview of the workshop should be undertaken by a competent person to ensure that all aspects, including material handling and ventilation, provide for a proper health and safety working environment.

Before starting operations, refer to the various precautions throughout the book and references in the Bibliography, such as Craske, 2012. It must be recognized that metal casting is a serious business that should only be undertaken with due care and consideration for the potential dangers involved, and only by persons with appropriate competence and experience, giving consideration to training.

Appendix II Useful Data

ELEMENTS LISTED

Periodic table no.	Symbol	Element
4	Be	beryllium
5	B	boron
6	C	carbon
11	Na	sodium
12	Mg	magnesium
13	Al	aluminium
14	Si	silicon
15	P	phosphorus
16	S	sulphur
17	Cl	chlorine
18	Ar	argon
19	K	potassium
20	Ca	calcium
22	Ti	titanium
23	V	vanadium
24	Cr	chromium
25	Mn	manganese
26	Fe	Iron
27	Co	cobalt
28	Ni	nickel
29	Cu	copper
30	Zn	zinc
40	Zr	zirconium
41	Nb	niobium
42	Mo	molybdenum
46	Pd	palladium
50	Sn	tin
51	Sb	antimony
73	Ta	tantalum
74	W	tungsten
78	Pt	platinum
79	Au	gold
80	Hg	mercury
82	Pb	lead

ABBREVIATIONS

AM   Additive Manufacturing, (eg. welding, powder metallurgy, 3-D printing)

AFS   American Foundry Society

CAD/CAM   Computer Aided Design/Manufacture

CI   Cast Iron

EPMMA   Expanded polymethylmethacrylate

EPS   Expanded polystyrene

FNB   Furan no-bake (sand pre-treatment)

ΔG   Free-energy change (thermo-dynamic energy)

GTAW/GMAW/OFW/SMAW (welding process – Gas Tungsten Arc; Gas Metal Arc; Oxy Fuel; Shielded Metal Arc)

HPDC   High Pressure Die Casting

LPPM   Low Pressure Permanent Mould (die casting)

NDT/DPI/MPI /RT /UT (non-destructive testing – Dye Penetrant; Magnetic Particle; Radiographic ; Ultrasonic)

NNS   Near Net Shape (product from forming or casting process)

PUNB   Phenol-Urethane no-bake (sand pre-treatment)

R_e Reynolds Number (measure of fluid flow)

RMS   Root Mean Square (statistical method used here for surface roughness analysis)

RT   Room temperature (20 deg.C/68 deg. F)

SG (CI)   Spheroidal Graphite/ductile cast iron

SM   Section Modulus (casting volume/casting area)

WM/FZ/HAZ/PM/BM Weld metal; fusion zone; heat affected zone; parent metal; base metal (weldments)

UNITS

Length:

Unit	equivalent
1 in (inch)	25.4 mm
1 m	1000 mm

Mass:
1 kg	2.205 lb
1 tonne	1000 kg
1 ton	2240 lb
(1 tonne ~ 0.98 ton)	
1 kgf	9.81 N; 2.205 lbf

Stress:
1 N/mm^2	1 MN/m^2; 145 lbf/in^2; 145 psi ; 0.145 ksi

Temperature:
0°C	32°F; 273°K
20°C	68°F
100°C	212°F

Density:
1 g/mm^3	0.03613 lbf/in^3

Scientific notation:
1	10^0
10	10^1
100	10^2
1000	10^3
etc.	

A NOTE ON UNITS

In the world of practical foundrywork, units in common usage can be SI (metric) or Imperial, often depending on geographical location; primarily the former for most countries apart from the USA, the latter being, however, of considerable importance in casting technology. But this is not necessarily universal in the USA, and especially the UK which persists in a characteristically idiosyncratic use of both systems, often simultaneously. However, despite this, things generally work better than might be expected, so it is useful to be familiar with both, as reflected in this book.

PRACTICAL CASTING AND PROCESS NOTES

Core Manufacture

An example of a practical mix is to take 750g of sea sand, with 30g of boiled linseed oil, sieved and mixed together three times, at RT. Produce required shape and bake in oven, allowing space for circulation, at 200°C for thirty minutes. Allow to cool slowly; this produces a good quality core, not too hard to prevent solidification shrinkage, but with sufficient strength to retain shape during cooling.

Furnace Lining Manufacture

Lining can be produced from commercially available 'Castable 1600', a refractory mix that can provide a furnace lining suitable for use to 1600°C, sufficient for many alloys, including cast iron. The refractory powder is mixed with water to a manageable consistency and the lining built up by plastering onto the vessel, by hand. Keep moist, for example by covering with damp rags to avoid too rapid setting, and dry over twenty-four hours, until it is ready for use.

Wax Burning

It is, perhaps, surprising that the burnout of the wax (as 'lost wax') requires considerably more effort than might be expected. The usual petroleum-based wax has ~120°C melting point (MP). However, it was found that a cycle involving steady heating to 700°C over a twelve-hour period was required to fully prepare the shell moulding by wax removal. It was found that the familiar 'candle wax' was a good alternative. This has an 80°C MP, is readily formed, of lower but adequate strength; and fully removed using a cycle of raising to 500°C in three hours, holding at temperature for one hour, making a four-hour cycle. The mould is retained pre-heated, ready for casting.

Appendix III Glossary

bi-films theory due to Campbell (see *Campbell, 2011*, Bibliography), showing the effect of entrapment and the behaviour of surface oxide films as fundamental to casting integrity.

bronze generic term for Cu-base alloy family, often used as shorthand for describing statues, but also applies as a range of commercially important alloys (*see* Chapter 5).

carbon vital element in composition of steels and cast iron, described in detail in Chapter 5.

casting solid product provided by solidification of molten material, normally after transfer into a shape defining vessel, (mould); may be metallic or non-metallic.

casting defects common casting faults, including porosity, voids, laps, tears, scabs, inclusions and segregation as described in Chapter 1.

cast iron the most familiar cast material, alloys principally feature Fe, C and Si (*see* Chapter 5).

chills metal blocks inserted into moulds, separated from the casting cavity, designed to cause a more rapid local cooling rate, normally in order to increase cooling rate and enhance metallurgical properties through reduced grain size.

cooling curves graphical description of alloy cooling rate, used in conjunction with phase diagrams to determine metallurgical structure and consequent mechanical properties.

de-gassing common method employed, prior to pouring into the mould, often of adding tablets to reduce trapped gas and reduce as-cast porosity.

dendrite micro-structural growth mechanism familiar in solidification of a cast metal, has important implications for subsequent properties of the casting (*see* Chapter 1).

destructive testing methods of determining mechanical properties of cast alloys, but at the expense of consuming the casting. Often done by casting spare material or special test-pieces.

dislocations micro-structural mechanism, operating on the atomic scale, which reconciles and explains the behaviour of all practical alloys which have lower than theoretical strength due to these inevitable crystallographic imperfections.

eutectic alloy composition as shown on equilibrium/phase diagram at point of lowest local melting point.

fettling operations involved with cleaning up raw castings, such as removal of runners, risers and surface rework, as in Chapter 6.

fluid flow movement of molten metal flowing from pouring vessel into the mould, prior to solidification.

foundry casting workplace.

furnace heating unit, normally with removeable cupola for non-industrial work, for melting the metal charge. More sophisticated units are very expensive to purchase and operate, used for increased volume and process capability.

gas laws Boyles and Charles, fundamental laws governing behaviour of gases at different temperatures and pressures.

gating method and arrangement for the system of passages down which the molten metal is rapidly directed into and through the mould, vital to a successful casting (*see* Chapters 4 and 7.

grain size fundamental building block of metal microstructure, generally seeking a small grain size for optimum mechanical properties, as in Chapter 1.

graphite form of carbon, occurring in cast iron as clusters or flakes, the morphology (shape) of which strongly influences mechanical properties, particularly ductility or its absence (*see* Chapter 5).

hardness Usually determined by standard tests by Vickers, Brinell or Rockwell indenting apparatus, provides a useful indication of the strength of a sample, without recourse to destructive testing. Care required in analysis of results of this apparently simple test. *See* Chapter 6 and Bibliography (*Tindell, 2012*).

heat treatment applied to castings, method for improving mechanical properties of the work, a post-casting process; can be low or medium-temperature for stress relieving; or metallurgical processing at higher temperature to harden, soften, change ductility or toughness, according to data derived from phase diagrams, cooling curves, and data (*see* Chapters 1 and 5).

inclusions extraneous particles or clusters deriving from the melting and pouring process, often deliberately manipulated to 'mop up' unwanted elements into harmless minor micro-structural islands, such as Mn-S inclusions in ferrous alloys. Unwelcome inclusions can be a critical source of weakness, important in high integrity castings such as i.c. engine crankshafts (*see* Chapter 1).

inoculation injection of carefully controlled compound, often in tablet form, at pre-determined time in melting/pouring cycle, to modify the casting process to provide specific benefits. Well-known method of producing Ductile (SG) cast iron, as-cast, instead of an un-treated Flake (brittle) cast iron (*see* Chapters 1 and 5).

investment casting also known as 'Lost Wax', highly versatile method, for precision, near net shape manufacture of many examples, as in Chapter 7. In use since antiquity, see 'Introduction'.

latent heat measure of the additional energy input or removed to facilitate changes in states of matter, eg. liquid to gas (*see* Chapter 1).

mould bespoke receptacle into which is poured the molten metal from ladle, through the gating system, into the mould cavity, in which solidification occurs, resulting in a cast product. The many types and systems of moulds and moulding are described in Chapter 3.

nucleation initiation point where the casting liquid metal begins the state change to solid, occurring at multiple discrete locations around the mould surface, depending on local conditions, including undercooling and surface effects.

NDT non-destructive testing, using surface and volumetric examination, typically employing radiography and ultrasonic methods, in order to search for and evaluate casting defects (*see* Chapter 6).

pattern solid shape modelled to form a mould cavity into which, usually after removal of the pattern, the casting fluid is poured. The pattern is often made from wood, but other modelling materials, or even a spare part to be replicated, can be employed (*see* Chapter 3).

phase diagrams also referred to as 'equilibrium diagrams', illustrate the phases throughout the composition and temperature range of an alloy.

piping central, linear region of casting defect, common in ingots with inadequate feeding that leads to segregation and voids producing a central weakness. *See* casting defects.

precipitation hardening atomic scale micro-structural growth of, typically, platelets that develop into barriers within the grain structure that inhibit the movement of dislocations, and thereby increase the alloy's strength. Most familiar in high strength Al alloys. *See* Chapter 1 and Bibliography (*Tindell, 2013*).

quench rapid cooling of product, from high temperature into water, oil, air or other medium. Normally associated with heat treatment of low alloy steels to increase strength, high alloy steels to arrest a ductile high temperature phase, or similar in certain Cu-base alloys. *See* Chapter 5.

sand the most common medium used for making moulds, but requires careful selection, treatment and testing when employed in casting. Discussed in detail in Chapter 3.

shrinkage shape change due to cooling from the liquid to final casting at room temperature. See Chapter 1.

slag agglomeration of impurities and oxide films that float on the molten liquid surface, requiring removal prior to pouring into the mould, otherwise entrapment in the cast is risked.

solidification process of transformation of state from liquid to solid after pouring into the mould.

surface tension 'skin' effect produced on the surface of liquids, the tenacity (strength) of which depends on the composition of the liquid, with a low surface tension providing good 'wettability' and mould-filling characteristics.

welding process of joining alloys through fusion of each part, normally with the addition of a welding consumable, creating a molten pool. This weld pool, consumable tip, and parent metal heated zone, are shielded from the environment by a chemical flux provided by the consumable, or an inert gas shield, depending on the process. Used extensively in post-casting operations, such as in rework of defect removal, or joining in a multi-piece casting. (*See* Chapter 6.)

Bibliography

ASM Metals Handbook, Vol. 15, *Casting*, ASM International, 1988

Ashby, M. and Jones, D., *Engineering Materials 2*, Elsevier, 2006

Aspin, B.T., *The Backyard Foundry*, Nexus Special Interests, Workshop Practice series, no. 25, 1975

Aspin, B.T., *Foundrywork for the Amateur*, MAP, Argos Books Ltd., 1975

Asthana, R., Kumar, A. and Dahotre, N., *Materials Science in Manufacturing*, Elsevier, 2006

Bailey, A. and Samuels, L., *Foundry Metallography*, Metallurgical Services, 1971

Beeley, P. and Smart, R, *Investment Casting*, The Institute of Metals, 1995

Black, J. and Kohser, R., *deGarmo's Materials and Processes in Manufacturing*, Wiley, 2008

Campbell, J., *Complete Casting Handbook*, Elsevier, 2011

Campbell, J., *Mini Casting Handbook*, Aspect Design, 2017

Charles, J.A., 'The Origins of Metallurgy . . .', pp1 – 12, Proc. Conf., Imperial College, London, 'Materials Science and Engineering, its Nucleation and Growth', The Institute of Metals, 2001

Copper Development Association (CDA), *Copper and Copper Alloy Castings*, Properties and Applications, TN42, 1991

Craske, S., *The Secrets of Bronze Casting*, The Crowood Press, 2012

Feinberg, W., Lost Wax Casting, '*Intermediate Technology Publications*', 1983

Higgins, R.A., *Engineering Metallurgy*, Part 1, English Universities Press Ltd., 1968

Hurst, S., *Metal Casting*, Practical Action Publishing, 1996

Meigh, H., *Cast and Wrought Aluminium Bronzes*, The Institute of Metals, 2000

Miodownik, M., *Stuff Matters*, Penguin Books, 2014

Open University, *Engineering Materials; 3, Liquid to Solid*, Open University, 1982

Open University, *Engineering Materials; 2, Phase Diagrams and Microstructure*, Open University, 1973

Porter, M., *Gas Burners for Forges, Furnaces and Kilns*, Skipjack Press, 2004

Semler, E. (Ed.), *Engineering Heritage*, Vol. 1 & 2, Institute of Mechanical Engineers, 1963

Spencer, N., *The Gayer-Anderson Cat*, The British Museum Press, 2007

Taylor, P.R., *Lost Wax Casting . . . review*, pp. 207 – 710, Metals and Materials, Nov. 1986

Tindell, H.A., *Engineering Materials*, The Crowood Press, 2012

Suppliers

CASTING SUPPLIES AND EQUIPMENT

Artisan Foundry Shop
Artisan Foundry, 7, Baileys lane, Hale Village, Liverpool, L24 5RG, UK
Tel. 0151 425 2376;
info@artisanfoundry.co.uk;
www.artisanfoundry.co.uk
Casting supplies; bespoke house-name and number castings; casting courses, including lost-wax and sand methods; and workshop hire.

Engineering and Foundry Supplies (Colne) Ltd.
Phillips Lane Works, Phillips Lane, Colne, Lancs. BB8 9PQ, UK
Tel. 01282 868411;
stephen@ef-supplies.co.uk;
www.ef-supplies.co.uk
Extensive foundry supplies and service for professional and amateur worker.

John Winter & Co. Ltd.
PO. Box 21, Washer Lane, Halifax, W.Yorks, HX2 7DP, UK
Tel. 0142 236 4213;
sales@johnwinter.co.uk;
www.johnwinter.co.uk
Large range of foundry supply.

Tiranti Ltd.
Alec Tiranti, Berkshire. 3, Pipers Court, Berkshire Drive, Thatcham, Berks, UK.
Tel. 0845 123 2100;
enquiries@tiranti.co.uk
Alec Tiranti, London. 27, Warrn St., Kings Cross, London, UK.
Tel. 020 7380 0808;
enquiries@tiranti.co.uk

Engineering and Model-making Suppliers

Blackgates Engineering
Tel. 01924 466000;
www.blackgates.co.uk

Brabbin & Rudd
Tel. 01204 521171;
www.brabbins-on-line.co.uk

Brian S. Pope
Tel. 0161 480 8322;
www.brianpope.com

Chester Tools
Tel. 01244 531631;
www.chestermachinetools.com

Chronos Tools
Tel. 01582 471900;
www.chronos.ltd.uk

Macc Models
Tel. 0161 408 2938;
www.maccmodels.co.uk

Machine Mart
Tel. 0844 8801250;
www.machinemart.co.uk

RDG Tools
Tel. 01422 885069;
www.rdgtools.co.uk

Temperature Measurement

Maplin
Tel. 0843 227 7315;
www.maplin.co.uk

Peak Sensors Ltd.
Tel. 01246 261999;
www.peaksensors.com

General

Augmented Agents Ltd.
Tel. 0161 477 3388 welding and small power tool suppliers

Bathgate Silica Sand Ltd.
Tel. 01270 76200;
wwwbathgatesilica.co.uk

BOC Welding
Tel. 0161 477 3388;
www.boconlineshop.com

Cast Metals Federation
Tel. 0121 601 6390;
www.castmetalsfederation.com

Copper Development Association
www.cda.org.uk

General Welding Supplies (NW) Ltd.
Tel. 0151 420 6900;
www.generalwelding.co.uk

Hobby Weld
www.hobbyweld.co.uk;
non-rental welding gas supply.

Institute of Cast Metal Engineers
Tel. 0121 601 6979;
www.icme.org.uk

Postscript

While this book has been primarily aimed at the 'enthusiastic amateur' – to be underestimated at one's peril, as some professionals may verify – nevertheless, the making of castings must be up there with the most testing of engineering disciplines that can reasonably be undertaken beyond the corporate world.

The essence has been an attempt to examine the 'state of the art', with indications of achievable targets, based on our own humble small-scale casting operations over the past couple of years. Yet it is not quite within our scope to take the next logical step – into high integrity, full-scale structural engineering projects. For this is an area where twenty-first century caution signals a pause – whilst in previous eras one might have continued headlong into the abyss.

But we can consider a means to the next level of castings, as the science is now available to enable those with resources of time, facilities and finance, to successfully melt and cast in some of the advanced alloys and processes mentioned here.

Indeed, the perfect casting is now a viable proposition (*see* Bibliography, Campbell, 2017) and the five-millennia quest for this holy grail of casting finally reachable even for the, sufficiently resourced, 'knowledgeable amateur'.

Index

3D printing 70
318 – Ti 6Al 4V 123
3-D printing 50

A
AFS – grain size, sand 63
Ag 12
ageing 102
Al 56 123
Al – 12 Si 17
Al – Cu 30
Al – Zn 121
Al alloy heat treatment 101
Al alloys, UK
LM0 103
LM12 103
LM13 103
LM16 103
LM2 103
LM20 103
LM21 103
LM22 103
LM24 103
LM25 54, 60, 103
LM26 103
LM28 103
LM29 103
LM30 103
LM31 103
LM4 103
LM5 103
LM6 103
LM9 103
Al alloys (USA)
201 95
222 95
355 95
356 95
360 95
390 95
512 95
520 95
535 95
712 95
850 95
852 95
Al oxides 33
Alaca Houk, Ankara 10
alloying elements; Ag, Na, Sr, Sn, Ti, Zn. 99
alloying elements; Al, Be, Bi, B, Cd, Cr, Cu, Fe, Pb, Mg, Mn, Hg, Ni, P, Si, 98
AM 49
Antioch process 67
Ar 24, 121
arsenical copper 11
As 9
ASTM 97
Au 12
austempered SG CI 118

B
bainitic matrix 118
bells 15
Benin bronzes 12
Bernoulli's Theorem 80
Bessemer Converter 13
bifilm 6, 13, 23, 25, 40, 85
Big Ben (London) 15, 86
binders – resin 59
Biringuccio, Vannoccio 16
bivalves 10
Blackheart CI 119
bottom-feed 60
Boyle's Law 24, 24
brazing/bronze welding 128
bronze 9, 12
Bronze Age 49
burners (gas) furnace) 44

C
C 13
CAD/CAM 49, 70
Carbon Equivalent, CE 114
cast iron, (CI) 12, 47, 112, 113
casting boxes 48
casting-on 11
cavities – shrinkage 77
cementite, (FE3C) 132
centrifugal casting 74
ceramic moulding 67
charcoal 10
Charioteer of Delphi 16
Chicago Stock Exchange 15
chills 56, 78
Chvorinov's Rule 28
CI repair 132
CI 24
CLA 75
Co 121
Co – base alloy 122
coke – solid fuel 41
collapsability 59
Colossus of Rhodes 17
compressive strength 64

cooling curves 27
copper 9
copper-base alloys 103
cores 92
Cosworth process 23, 73
counter-gravity filling 72, 102
creep 21, 121
creep test (10,000 hr) 69, 122
Crooks, Sir William 25
crucible 41, 47
Cu – 12Al 9
Cu – base alloys 40, 47, 56, 105, 109
Cu – base alloys, UK; HCC 1, CC 1-TF, SCB 3, DCB 3, DZ R1, DZ R2, HT B1, HTB3, Si brass 106
Cu – base alloys, UK; PB 1, CT 1, PB 2, PB 4, LB 4, LB 2, LB 1, LB 5, LG 1, LG 2, LG 4 AB 1, AB2, CM A1, CN 1, CN 2 107
Cu – base service – bearings, gears, other 111
Cu – base service – fresh water, sea water 110
Cu – Zn 12
Cu-base alloy 30
Cu-Pb 11

D
damping capacity/internal friction 114
defects – laps 33
defects – shuts 33
defects (casting) 20, 23
dendrtitic growth 31, 60
Denison, Edmund Beckett 86
density 21
deoxidisers, Ni, Cr, Cu, V, Ti, Zr 116
Derby, Abraham 14
design – riser 76
design rules, castings 92
destructive testing – tensile, bend, impact 136
Deville process 73
die casting HPDC/LPDC 73, 74
diffusion coating 139, 140

directional solidification 26, 75
dislocations 102
DPI 137
drag/cope 5
ductile iron (SG) cast iron 40, 117
ductile iron (SG) cast iron inoculants Ce, Mn, S, Mg, O 117

E
Eagle Brass Foundry 53
electrodes 134
electroplating 139
emerging processes 75
emissions (fume) 43
enamelling 139
epoxy resin pattern 66
equiaxed grains 32
equilibrium diagram Fe C 112
equilibrium diagrams 105
equilibrium diagrams; Cu Zn, Cu Sn, Cu Al 108
Eros (London) 17
evaporative pattern – lost foam 71

F
Fe 30
Fe – C 115
feeder 26, 78
fettling 124
fluid flow 20, 24
fluidity 116
FM process 60
foamed plaster mould 67
foaming agent 67
Ford Motor Co. 53
Free Energy (ΔG) 29, 128
free graphite flake 26
freezing range 26
furnace 41
fusion welding 128

G
gases 24

gating system 21, 25, 56, 78
geometry effects 77
Georgius Agricola 16
GMAW 130, 131
graphite morphology 114
gravity pouring 67
Great Bell of Beijing 15
Great Budda of Kamkura 11
Great Peter Bell, York Minster 87
grey CI 112
GTAW/TIG 17, 130, 131
guns 15
gypsum 66

H
H 24, 58, 100
Hall, Les 50
hardfacing 139, 140
hardness 126
HB 132
He 24
high alloy CI 119
high Ni alloys 67
high pressure die casting, HPDC 120
hot-dip coating 140
Huntsman cast steel 13

I
inclusions 33
Industrial Revolution (UK) 14
inoculation 30
investment casting/lost wax 69
Ironbridge, Shropshire 14

K
Kearns Machine Tool Co. 52
Kr 24
Kremlin Great Bell 15

L
lamallar flow 22
laps 137
latent heat 19

lathework 126
Law, Charles 24
Law of Continuity 80
Leonardo da Vinci 15
Liberty Bell (Philadelphia) 15, 85
liquid 100
lost wax process 9, 10, 11, 49

M

machinability 126
machine tool beds 115
machining castings 125
malleable CI 119
Maritz, Johan 16
martensite, CI 119
martensite, steels 102
matchplate moulding 67
Mears, George of Whitechapel Bell Foundry 87
Medieval 49
melting 41
metal pattern 66
Mg 30, 56, 121
micro-foundry 35, 47, 60
microstructure 20, 126
mild steel 13, 113
milling machine 126
mis-en-couleur 12
Mn 14, 115
modification (Al – Si alloys) 41
moisture control 41, 48, 58, 63
mono-crystal 75
mould 21, 40, 41, 49, 71
mould dilation 76
moulding – no-bake 57
moulding – sodium silicate-CO_2 57
MPI 137

N

N 24
Nahal Mishmar treasure 9
NDT 18, 40, 72, 137
Neolithic 9, 24

Ni 121, 123
Ni – base 56
nucleation 20, 29

O

O 123
OFW 131, 134
oven (heat treatment) 46
over-ageing 102
oxidation 100, 139

P

P 13, 115
painting 140
parting line – moulds 93
patination 139
pattern 40, 49
patternmaker's shrinkage 27
pattern-plate mould 55
permeability 60, 64, 67
phase change, sand 64
phase diagrams/equilibrium diagrams 32
pickled 12
piping 27
plasma 25
plasma arc 127
plaster moulding 65, 66
polymorphic 100
porcelain enamel 140
porosity 23, 27
power – mains/solar 47
precipitation hardening 101
productivity 56
purification (of melt) 79

R

radiography 72
Re – Reynolds no. 21
residual stress 91
rheocasting 74
Rhodes, Ivan (VOC) 54
risers 56, 78, 124

Rn 24
Rolls Royce, aero 53
Royal Brass Foundry 16
RT 138
runners 56, 124

S

S 13, 14, 115
sand – dry moulding 56
sand – grain size 63
sand – green 56
sand – silica, zircon, chromite, olivine 55, 60, 64, 65
sand casting 55
scabs 79, 137
sculptures 16
Section Modulus 91
segregation 31
semi-solid casting 74
shape control 33
Shaw process 68
shell moulding 58, 70
shrinkage 25
shrinkage – centreline 77
single crystal 69
SMAW 130, 140
Sn 9, 11
solar power 48
solidification 20, 25
solidification shrinkage 76
sprue 56, 80
squeeze casting 74
stainless steel 56
Statue of Liberty (New York) 17
steels 119
Stone Age 49
stone moulds 10
STP 19, 24
surface tension 21, 30

T

Taylor and Co., Loughborough 81
tears 137

tensile stress (casting, internal) 91
testing – destructive, in-process, sampling, NDT, microstructure 135
thixotropic 74
Ti 67, 121, 123
Ti alloys 122
Tumbaga 12
tungsten carbide, WC 119
turbine blade 69, 122
turbulant flow 22

U
under-cooling 27
UT 138

V
vacuum 24

vacuum moulding 59
Van der Waal forces 24
Velocette Owner's Club, VOC 54
viscosity index 21
voids – macro, micro 32

W
wax pattern 70
Weber No. (We no.) 79
weld – WM, FZ, HAZ, BM 128, 132, 133
weld solidification 127
welding consumables, electrodes, E Ni Fe Cl, E Ni Cl 133
welding 24, 127
Wertime Pyrotechnology 9
wetabilility 30
White CI 119

Whitechapel Bell Foundry 11, 80, 81
Whitehead Foundry 53
Wright and Platt Co. 52

X
Xe 24

Z
ZA 8, ZA 12, ZA 27 121
ZAMAK alloys 120
Zn 12, 120
Zn – base alloys 73
Zr 30

Other Metalworking Guides from Crowood

Brazing and Soldering

978 1 84797 836 3

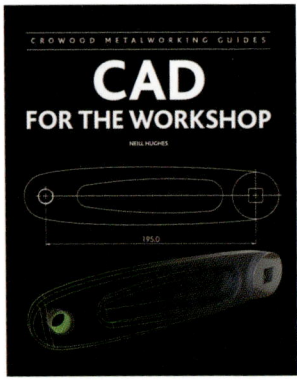

CAD for the Workshop

978 1 84797 566 9

CNC Milling in the Workshop

978 1 84797 512 6836 3

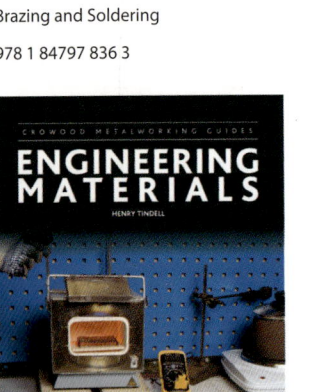

Engineering Materials

978 1 84797 679 6

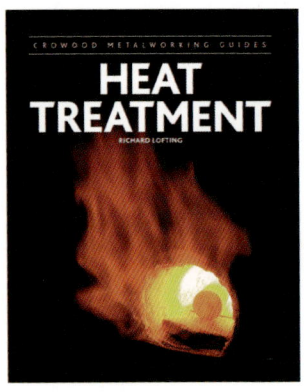

Heat Treatment

978 1 78500 441 4

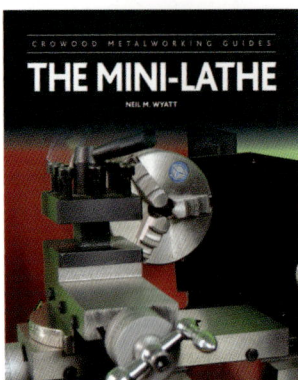

The Mini-Lathe

978 1 78500 128 4

Screwcutting

978 1 84797 999 5

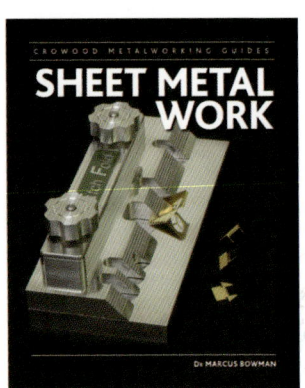

Sheet Metal Work

978 1 84797 778 6

Workholding for Machinists

978 1 78500 238 0